TALKS
ON
AGNI

by
Torkom Saraydarian

SARAYDARIAN INSTITUTE
P. O. Box 267
Sedona, AZ 86339

Dedicated with gratitude
to
The Agni Yoga Society

Library of Congress Catalog Card No. 86-72214

ISBN: 0-911794-56-5 (paperback)

WORKS BY TORKOM SARAYDARIAN

The Bhagavad Gita (translated from the original Sanskrit)
Challenge for Discipleship
Christ the Avatar of Sacrificial Love
Cosmos in Man
A Daily Discipline of Worship
Dialogue with Christ
The Fiery Carriage and Drugs
Five Great Mantrams of the New Age
The Flame of Beauty, Culture, Love, Joy
Hiawatha and the Great Peace
The Hidden Glory of the Inner Man
Hierarchy and the Plan
Irritation the Destructive Fire
I Was
The Legend of Shamballa
The Psyche and Psychism
The Questioning Traveler and Karma
The Science of Becoming Oneself
The Science of Meditation
The Symphony of the Zodiac
Synthesis
Torchbearers
Triangles of Fire
The Unusual Court
Woman Torch of the Future

CALL OR FAX TO ORDER:
SARAYDARIAN INSTITUTE
P. O. Box 267 · Sedona · AZ 86339
Phone 520-282-2655 ◆ Fax 520-282-0514

Torkom Saraydarian has given a series of lectures on Agni Yoga using the publications of the Agni Yoga Society, located in New York City. Some of these talks were public; others were for private classes. These talks have been compiled into one volume, for the interest of those who want to study the Agni Yoga Teaching.

In addition to giving classes on Agni Yoga, the author has also presented slides of the paintings of the great artist, Nicholas Roerich, explaining the vision and spirit behind them.

Agni Yoga books, as well as slides and reproductions of the paintings of Nicholas Roerich may be obtained by writing to the Agni Yoga Society, 319 West 107th Street, New York City, New York, 10025.

The author does not claim that his interpretation of verses taken from the Agni Yoga Teaching in any way exhausts the deeper meanings which one can discover through meditation and living a life in harmony with the Teaching.

TABLE OF CONTENTS

CHAPTER 1

THE SEVEN YOGAS

When we say yoga, fanatics scream and say, "He is talking about something different than our religion and traditions." But if they understand what yoga is, they will find that it is deeply religious and psychological and does not contradict any religion.

Yoga means unification, integration, concentration, alignment, becoming oneself, and at-one-ment. Yoga is a complete system for progressive achievements. Wherever there is unity, there is yoga.

The secret of yoga is that you can never understand it nor can you be a yogi until you experience or actualize the meaning of yoga. Yoga is actualization of the unity of the universe and Cosmos by reflecting that unity and synthesis through your thoughts, words, actions, and labor. A yogi is a person who lives in the consciousness of unity and synthesis.

The great Teachers of thousands of years ago knew and taught that the only solution to all problems is *unification*. Yoga has many deep meanings. For example, yoga means love. If a person is doing any labor with love, grace, and gratitude, he is a yogi. If a person is spreading peace, gratitude, and unity all over the world, he is a yogi. If he is doing his labor with all his heart, mind, and soul, he is a yogi. If he is not dividing people and creating conflict among them, he is a yogi. If he is organizing a group dedicated to the human welfare, he is a yogi. Yogis work for one humanity.

1

If a psychiatrist is creating unity within your system, within your emotions, thoughts, and activities, he is practicing yoga. If you are shaking hands with love, sincerity, and dedication, you are doing yoga. Yoga also means synthesis, or to adapt many different things in such a way that unity is created.

The great Teachers said that yoga must be taught all over the world and that everyone must learn about yoga and express yoga throughout his whole life, so that he eventually becomes a yogi. Unless you experience or actualize the philosophy and meaning of yoga, you cannot understand what yoga is. You can look at a delicious food and name all the ingredients, but you don't really know the food until you eat it, digest it, sense it, feel it, and assimilate it. This is the same with yoga.

In many religions, the goals of life are given as follows:

1. to please God.
2. to be perfect as He is.
3. to be like Him.
4. to inherit His kingdom.
5. to be transfigured.
6. to be immortal.
7. to be resurrected.

These are exactly the goals of yoga. Yoga starts from the fundamentals in order to achieve these goals. The school of yoga throughout history is divided into seven branches. The first branch of yoga taught man how to control his body, how to make the human being a total, coordinated unit. This first yoga was called *Hatha Yoga*. Hatha Yoga is composed of 49 main exercises called asanas. This yoga was created 18 million years ago. Through these exercises, man could align and adapt the electrical instrument within him — which is the mental body, mind, and brain — with the muscles, the nervous system, and the glands. These exercises were designed to coordinate the nervous system and the muscles with the volition.

When the Teachers saw that after two or three million years people had already achieved this coordi-

nation between the physical-etheric and mental vehicles, they ordered Hatha Yoga to be stopped. If we do
Hatha Yoga now, we are retrogressing and creating
problems in our nature. This is why many great Sages
tell us that Hatha Yoga is now dangerous for the
human body; but people still persist in it. Twenty or
thirty years later, they will see the effects of it. Hatha
Yoga was given for a specific purpose at a certain
period of time. Now that the goal has been achieved, it
should be left alone.[1]

The second yoga given was called *Laya Yoga.*
Laya Yoga was the science of the centers, the etheric
chakras. People have 77 chakras within their etheric
bodies. These chakras correspond to the nerve centers
and the glands; there are 77 glands plus nerve centers
and ganglia. These ganglia needed to be adapted to the
centers. The centers are the dynamo behind the glands
and ganglia.

Laya Yoga coordinated the human being and
opened the centers very safely through an exact
science of thinking about the centers, visualizing certain colors, and sounding certain notes. The Teachers
of Laya Yoga were great clairvoyant people. They
watched their students while they did Laya Yoga to see
what was happening to their etheric, emotional, and
mental bodies and their centers; to see how they were
coordinating, what petals[2] were opening and closing,
what dangers might be approaching, and what things
should be avoided.

Today *Kundalini Yoga,* which is one branch of
Laya Yoga, must be done under the supervision of
clairvoyant Teachers. But many people ignore this
warning and try to raise their kundalini fire themselves. In doing this, they severely burn their nervous
systems. Over the years I have seen maybe 200-300
people with damaged spines, organs, and other parts
of the body as a result of doing Kundalini Yoga. I
advised them to stop Kundalini Yoga.

Laya Yoga must also be put on the shelf for a while,
although it is still used in the Ashrams. If a disciple or
initiate has a pure physical body and emotional body,

he can practice Laya Yoga without creating any friction when the fire is released. Such disciples and initiates may use this yoga to put their centers in communication with higher centers of the universe.

For example, if a Third or Fourth Degree Initiate wants to coordinate his heart center and build a communication link with the Heart of the Sun, he might practice Laya Yoga to open the twelve petals of his heart to absorb the energy coming from the Heart of the Sun. This is a very advanced technique. You must be really purified to do it, so that when the center starts to radiate and receive the central energy of the solar system, you do not burn or damage your vehicles.

The third yoga created was called *Bhakti Yoga*. In Sanskrit, "bhakti" means worship. Bhakti Yoga raises your consciousness into higher levels of the emotional plane. Through your worship of a prophet, a Great One, or a great vision, you polarize, transform, and transfigure your emotional nature, so that you become unified with the image you are worshipping.

In Bhakti Yoga, you worship something that you want to be. Something that is higher than you are pulls you up from your lower consciousness and creates a higher consciousness, a higher level of beingness within you. This is why worship is so important. When you worship God, Christ, any angel, or anything that pulls you out of your misery or your present state, you are practicing Bhakti Yoga.

Bhakti Yoga raises you to the level or the vibration of that which you are worshipping. Worship means to be magnetized by the image toward which you are sending all your emotional and mental energies.

The fourth yoga was called *Karma Yoga*. Karma Yoga means to labor with grace, love, and gratitude and without expectation. Karma Yoga is described by the words of Christ when He said that whatever you do, you should do it with all your heart, mind, soul, and spirit.

How can we do our duties and uphold our responsibilities in the best way possible on this earth? It can be done through Karma Yoga.

The fifth yoga created was called *Jnana Yoga*. In Sanskrit "jnana" means wisdom. Through Jnana Yoga, you reap the wisdom of the ages, contemplate it, and then act, live, think, and speak in wisdom. Through Jnana Yoga, you always act in balanced intellect and balanced love, with a balanced outlook on life. When you start developing this kind of wise outlook on life, you are becoming a jnana yogi.

Jnana Yoga is a state of consciousness in which you, as a human soul, stand in the light of your Inner Presence whenever you think, talk, write, or labor in any field. This great Presence within you is sometimes called your Inner Guardian, or the Inner Source of Beauty, Goodness, and Truth.

In Jnana Yoga, you come to a stage where you can stand in the light of your Soul and say, "My Inner Master, now I am ready with my whole life to be Your disciple, to express all the beauty and virtues that You radiate to me." You are no longer the victim of your body, emotions, money, intoxication, marijuana, cigarettes. . . . You stand now in the light of your Soul. You are a disciple who is asking, "My Inner Lord, You are the Presence within me. Please give me Your wisdom so that I live in Your wisdom."

In order to practice this yoga, people must go through severe discipline, taking a hammer and chisel and shaping their physical, emotional, and mental nature. Jnana Yoga means to chisel your nature and slowly adapt it to the vision within you. This vision must slowly take shape; you must become something different. Jnana Yoga means to become more loving and understanding. Jnana Yoga means to be more watchful and awake. Jnana Yoga means to be more sacrificial and synthesizing.

The sixth yoga given was called *Raja Yoga*. Raja Yoga means to become the master of yourself. "Raja" means the king. Raja Yoga is kingly yoga, or yoga that makes you king of your petty urges, drives, appetites, and cravings. You become your own master. You become the master of your emotions, your sneaky jealousies, hypocrisies, deceptions, fears, anger, hatred,

and greed. All these things are now under the feet of
the raja.

A raja yogi says, "I am the king." The person
becomes the king of his own inner empire. It is actually
more difficult to be the king of your inner empire than
it is to be the king of a great nation. Many kings are the
slaves of their emotions. They are not really kings but
slaves.

If you become the king of your own inner empire,
then you are really *the* king. The first thing a raja yogi
conquers is his ego, the idea that the whole world is
revolving around the axis of himself. The second thing
a raja yogi conquers is his vanities. A vanity is something that you think you are or you have, when you
don't. The king sees himself exactly as he is. If a person does not see himself as he is, he is not a king of his
nature. A king really knows what he is.

Raja Yoga is the exercise or the discipline to be a
soul.

The seventh and newest yoga was publicized
starting in 1920. This yoga was called *Agni Yoga,* or
the yoga of synthesis. Agni Yoga means unification of
your physical, emotional, and mental nature and your
soul with the Fire of God that is within you and in the
universe.

You built a physical body, emotional body, and
mental body through Hatha Yoga, Bhakti Yoga, and
Jnana Yoga. Then through Raja Yoga you became a
soul. You are now a being, but a separate being. But if
you want to be a greater being, you must renounce
what you are. You must ascend to the ocean of God
— Fire. You must become a fiery energy.

The first sign of an Agni Yogi is that he radiates
enthusiasm in everything he does. Enthusiasm is the
fire of the Gods. In Agni Yoga, no impurity exists
within you when the fire is lit. You can no longer think
in terms of separatism, hatred, selfishness, jealousy,
and greed. If you try to awaken the fire while you still
have these impurities, they will burn you and create
suffering for you, in the form of many diseases. This is
why great Teachers warn us that if we want to start

Agni Yoga, we must be purified; we must purify our emotions, getting rid of our anxieties and dark emotions. People buy Agni Yoga books and read them and think they are Agni Yogis. This is a vanity. First wash your hands, wash your brain, and wash your heart. Unless your heart is totally purified and filled with beauty, goodness, and justice, you cannot be a candidate for Agni Yoga.

In order to prepare yourself to be an Agni Yogi, you must pass through many disciplines of purity — purity of thinking, purity of feeling, and purity of action. This is because fire purifies. When purification is done, the soul can unite with the ocean of fire.

The quality of fire, the quality of the Sun creates all flowers, birds, life. . . . When the Sun is withdrawn, there is no life. In the same way, when the Sun rises on your inner horizon and you become united with that Inner Sun, you purify and synthesize everything, and you become a fountain of creativity. Creativity brings out the best that is within you and makes you a fountain of love, beauty, and goodness. This is Agni Yoga.

Yoga is becomingness, the process of beingness. You become a yogi when you experience unity with your body, emotions, and mind. Higher yogis are those who achieve unity with their Inner Guardian. The highest yogis are those who become one with the fire — the Flame.

There was a prayer given for students of yoga:

Avira Virma Yeti.
O Self-revealing One, reveal Thyself in me.

In other words, "You Who are a concealed beauty within me; You Who are goodness and love within me; You Who are synthesis and creativity and light within me, reveal Yourself so that I be like You." [3]

1. See Chapter XIV, "Words of Caution," in *Cosmos in Man,* by H. (Torkom) Saraydarian.
2. See Chapter XII, "The Chalice and the Seeds," in *The Science of Becoming Oneself,* by H. (Torkom) Saraydarian.
3. For further information on the seven yogas, read Chapter 27, "Seven Techniques for Unfolding the Consciousness," in *The Science of Meditation,* by H. (Torkom) Saraydarian.

CHAPTER 2

BUILDING THE FUTURE

I rejoice to see how the lightning flashes of foresight regarding people's welfare sparkle amidst your thoughts. These thoughts have to be launched into space. If you could daily spare half an hour for the future! Verily, the bonfire of your thoughts would receive Our welcome.

Let the things of everyday life vanish, but let the country of the future be embodied in thought. And what cleanses the spirit more thoroughly than thoughts about the welfare of others? And what tempers the armor of steadfastness better than the wish to lead others to Light? And what weaves a better smile than a desire to see the very last child laughing? I urge you to think thus about the future, to place daily a pearl into the necklace of the Mother of the World. And so, concisely and simply think how to adorn the Hearth of the World.

There should be no comparison with the past, for a wrinkle of the past is usually a nest of errors. One can sail past alien shores; one has only to admire the world of light bestowed upon all that lives. Light is the best bridge between the visible and the Invisible.

When one can think about the future not by the evening fire but in the radiance of the sun, then the dew drops of prana illumine the thinking brow.[1]

The future is not in the domain of time. It is a process of becoming. The future is not an effect but a creative source, an inspiring, ever-progressing ideal which challenges us and enables us to come out of our usual patterns of life and strive toward a new life.

There are two ways of building the future:

1. Through your deeds you can create your future — because you sow the seeds and reap the fruits.

2. You can have a vision and create new and conscious actions by the power of your vision.

A real vision is a part of the Divine Plan which flashes out in the higher mental realms. Like a magnet, it attracts you and creates within you a spirit of striving and a dedication to actualize your vision in your life and in the life of society.

The future of a human being is not only the result of his actions, but also the result of his visions. People forecast the future of a nation by observing the actions people take in their lives, but the future of a person or a nation totally changes when that person or nation begins to have a vision.

Our actions can be inspired by our physical, emotional, and mental pleasures or interests; or our actions can be inspired by a great vision. One can easily forecast the outcome of actions that are inspired by physical, emotional, and mental pleasures and interests, but it is very difficult to make a correct forecast when the person is caught by a great vision. The real future is the future which is built by the inspiration of a vision.

"Futurists" forecast the future based on the way things are going in the present and the way they have gone in the past. Such forecasting is not accurate and is sometimes even totally wrong, because it does not take into consideration a factor which plays a crucial role in creating the future. That factor is the *future vision.* The future vision creates hope, enthusiasm, and new and conscious actions to actualize the vision.

Man lives because of a vision, which creates a new activity not only in his daily life but also in his glandular system and the electromagnetic system in his body. Thus a person who is diagnosed as having only six months to live may suddenly regain his health and outlive the physician who forecasted his premature death!

In the new age, the future will not be the result of the past and present, mechanically calculated and logically presented; but it will be the *cause* which will introduce changes in thinking, feeling, and acting. It is the future that will control the present and the past.

To give a very simple example: there was a young girl who was very careless about the way she kept her bedroom. Her mother tried many ways to make her keep her room clean but failed. One day after breakfast she told her daughter, "Today your teacher is going to visit us. He wants to see our home and have lunch with us."

A few minutes later, the girl was busy putting her room in order. Her mother called to her and she said, "I can't come now; I am busy cleaning. . . ."

This girl's mother gave her a "future," and the "future" changed the course of the girl's action. Similarly, if a great vision or future is given to humanity, the forecasts of the futurists will not come true. When a vision of a great possible achievement is presented to humanity, the course of its activity will be inspired by that vision, and a new life will be the result.

The causes created in the past still exist; they cannot be eliminated. But the greatest moments in the history of humanity are those in which a *cause in the future* controls humanity's action and counterbalances or destroys the power of the *past cause.*

It is possible to be born again in the vision of the future and not be enslaved by the causes one created in the past. This was the esoteric philosophy Christ taught to His disciples. He taught that man must live life from the viewpoint or the domain of the future; his future vision must be horsepower of his action. Man must live "as if" he were a son of the Almighty Beauty, Goodness, and Truth. He must know that he can even break the power of his past deeds, recreate himself, and live as the embodiment of his vision.

Real hope is a shining light directed to our hearts from the domain of our future. Esoterically, the real man is his future, not his past. The future is the symbol of an ever-progressing beauty. On the path to the future, one must strive to live the future by manifesting his Inner Divinity, step by step.

Can't we learn from the past? Most of our wisdom is derived by studying our past and seeing the results in the present. Archaeological studies, arts and crafts, and great wisdom left to us by great Masters teach us valuable lessons. Every nation has its traditions, religion, and culture of the past which still inspire us. How to leave the past and look to the future?

These questions may be partly answered by saying that a person of the future knows the values of the past, but does not use them as standards for the present and the future. The standards and achievements of the past must not prevent us from searching for new standards and striving for greater achievements. When a past achievement or standard blocks our vision and prevents us from seeing things in relation to the requirements of the present moment and in relation to the future vision, the past becomes a grave.

The past is the expression of the level we were on, or of the vision we had. The future can be the expression of our new level and new vision.

In all religions, traditions, and cultures, there are three elements:

a. an element which is transient and obsolete.

b. an element which meets the needs of that time only.

c. an element which is timeless.

The timeless element is the creation of those Great Ones Who were living 5000-10,000 years ahead of Their time and Their creativity became a path for the future. Buddha gave His message 2500 years ago;

Christ gave His message 2000 years ago; but still we need to grow toward Their vision — which is projected toward the future.

It is true that we gather wisdom from our past. But we also have painful experiences from the past which can cloud our lives and prevent us from adapting ourselves to the present and to the future. The past can be observed if we approach it without emotions, or if we exhaust the painful contents of the emotions and see things as they happened. In such cases, the future must not be used as an escape or as a standard for the present, but as a phase for growth.

The past can be useful only to those who live in the light of the future. The future is the inner call for perfection, for unfoldment in Beauty, Goodness, and Truth. The future is the Purpose of the Great Life. This purpose is the dynamic power behind our progress. The future is the magnet pulling us out of imperfection toward the Purpose of the Great Life.

We can reach conscious immortality and master ourselves when we base our lives on the future. The concept of the future does not let us live the life of a machine or become a result; it makes us be a *cause*.

Our past reveals itself with all its mysteries when we penetrate into the future. But we are stuck in the past — in our traditions, religion, politics; in our ways of communicating, working and living. Our progress is programmed by Great Ones, according to the Purpose of the Planetary Life. This Life has Its purpose. Each life form in the body of the Planetary Life must advance to a certain degree to enable the Planetary Life to advance on Its path. Any delay in any living form in Its body makes Its progress more difficult. This is why Great Ones come to the world and try to hasten the progress of humanity, by breaking them from past attachments and presenting them with a greater vision of the future.

According to the Teachings of Great Ones, average humanity must at least enter the stage of development which is called *Transfiguration* — in which the physical, emotional, and mental nature is purified so that one can see the vision of the purpose of the Planetary Life and live a life of purity, beauty, and harmlessness. Advanced humanity must at least enter the stage of achievement called the *Great Renunciation,* in which one offers to humanity whatever he has and is, as a service and a sacrifice.

If human beings do not hold this vision in their hearts and strive toward it, they are counted as failures. The easiest way to fail is to attach to past concepts, to past obsolete values, traditions and religions which can no longer help us in this stage of evolution.

To progress toward your vision, you must free yourself from all those physical, emotional, mental, religious, and traditional hindrances if they have nothing to offer you on the path of greater service and achievement. Not only must you free yourself from these hindrances, but you must also search for those teachings which meet your present and future needs and enable you to keep pace with the rhythm of the demand of the Plan of the Great Life. In evaluating a teaching, you may ask the following questions:

Does this teaching develop in me universality and all-inclusiveness?

Does this teaching lead me into actions which are harmless, compassionate, and giving?

Does this teaching increase my efficiency to serve and sacrifice for the highest Common Good?

Does this teaching develop in me intuitive understanding, peace, serenity and enthusiasm?

When these questions are considered and worked out, you may realistically transform your own life and approach the path toward the future.

The first step toward the future is questioning. Ask yourself:

1. What is the cause of my action, emotional reaction, or thought?

2. What will be the effect of such an action, emotional reaction, or thought?

Finding the real causes for your actions, emotional reactions, and thoughts helps you to release the future within you or to make it manifest. Finding the effect of your actions, emotional reactions and thoughts helps you to eliminate those actions, emotional reactions and thoughts which are preventing the future from manifesting itself in your life.

Let us remember that effects are potential causes, and causes are closely related to the future. All our actions related to the personality vehicles are actions related to the past. All our actions related to transpersonal ideas and values are actions related to the future. This is true not only for individuals, but also for groups and nations.

In trying to answer such questions, you are taking the first step in controlling yourself and heading toward the future. In using such a technique of watchfulness you may avoid two great enemies of mankind: mass hypnotism and mass obsession.

People everywhere are open to posthypnotic suggestion. We do things which we really do not want to do, but anyhow we do them. Questioning slowly eliminates such a mechanical way of living.

Many people are obsessed by psychic forces. They are open to influences coming from the astral and lower mental planes. These influences and forces reach them through drugs, alcohol, rock music and sexual abuse. Obsession is very contagious, and normal people can easily be infected by such lower psychic influences.[2] When one consciously examines the motives and effects of his thoughts, emotions, actions and words, he can make a breakthrough and reject urges and drives that are forcing him to do things that he otherwise would not do.

A person of the future rejects all unconscious actions. He does not want to be pushed and pulled by forces whose nature is doubtful. He is a self-determined person. Unconscious living does not lead to survival or to the future.

Those who cannot live in the future commit suicide. First they commit moral suicide by burying themselves in the past, then they commit physical suicide. Give the hope of the future to anyone, and you can increase in him the power to strive, to survive and to create. Take the future from a person, and he goes deeper and deeper into the past and eventually commits suicide.

In questioning your thoughts, emotions, actions and words, you will be led into the future because you will eliminate those causes which are binding you to a life which is run unconsciously, in which you are asleep, in which you (your real Self) are not active.

The future is a progressive dance in which you must keep yourself alert and ever-advancing so that you can be part of the rhythm of the dance. The future is an ever-growing synthesis in which more and more elements are brought into harmony with the rest. The future is an ever-expanding awareness of your Self, an ever-penetrating process into the core of your true Self.

On the path toward the future, you create alignment, integration and fusion not only within your own system, but also in your family, nation and humanity. On the path toward the future, you hear more and more clearly the call of synthesis, and your life gradually turns into a service for the whole. All your actions become directed toward creating synthesis in politics, education, communication, arts, sciences, religion and economics.

The state of consciousness in which you are a prisoner is called the past. Whenever you are stuck in your physical, emotional and mental hangups, you are living in the past. Whenever you are able to free yourself from your personality limitations and strive to expand your consciousness toward the Divinity within you, you are already on the path to the future.

Those who can live in the light of their Inner Divinity and pave the way toward the inner core of man and the universe always live in the future, even if they lived 5000 years ago. Great Ones, like Buddha and Christ, continue to evoke efforts from the hearts of people to be like Them; They stand as the ideal of the future.

One of the qualities of the future is *timelessness*. Our physical, emotional and mental bodies are controlled by time. Time belongs to the past. The future is timelessness, or *duration*. Our real essence in expression, the unfolding human soul, is the spirit in manifestation which lives in timelessness. From the point of view of timelessness, he observes the birth, growth, maturity, old age and decay of the body, emotional nature and mental nature. Time controls them, but he, in his essence, is the Timeless Observer.

Arts radiating the future always endure the attacks of time. All phenomena in the world are composed of time and timelessness. Time is the outer appearance; timelessness is the inner essence. Whenever the outer appearance releases a flash of inner essence, one experiences the future.

Those who are identified with their outer form and its relationships live in the past. Those who feel they are essence grow into the future. We must try to live in the consciousness of the future in our striving for self-actualization, trying to bring into manifestation the Beauty, Goodness and Truth imprisoned within us. Any effort to reach an awareness of being the Timeless Observer is an effort toward the future.

It is possible that at certain times an individual or a nation oriented toward future values falls into actions that reverse his entire course toward the past. For example, the drug movement reversed the lives of millions and led them to the past, breaking in them the power of striving, the sense of responsibility, and the ability to formulate goals and make sound decisions. The interesting point is that drugs promised them a future of pleasure, joy, and peace, but instead led them to crimes of various magnitudes.

Disco and rock music came on the wind of modernity, but they focused the attention of the youth on the centers below the diaphragm, stimulating them with sexual and other lower instincts. These movements reversed the path of a segment of an entire generation, who otherwise would have been sensitive to future values. Aspiration toward love is not enough if one does not have the power of discrimination to free himself from the traps of sex and carnal love.

Our advertising system utilizes the technique of

leading people into the past and trapping them there. Try to see how liquor, cigarettes and nightclubs are advertised. Try to see how banks, insurance and fashion are advertised. So many products are advertised by using the past — the pleasure-points and fear-points in people — to cement them to their bodies, possessions and matter. The human soul faces stupendous difficulties trying to find his way toward the values of the future in such a labyrinth of confusion.

The same trend can be seen in world politics, in which the clamor of those who are oriented to the past is much louder than the voices of those who have the vision of the future. Try to see how world politics are based on territories, great "national interests," armaments, hatred, racism, iron curtains. . . . All these are like a heavy chain on the neck of humanity. Politics oriented toward the future are based on freedom, unity, sharing, peace, right human relationships, human rights, education and the sense of responsibility for all living forms.

The pollution of the earth, water and air is the greatest effect of activities based on past values and past interests. Greed, hatred, exploitation, separativeness and superiority will create greater weapons than we had in the past, which will wipe out the life-wave on this planet if the future-oriented people do not take firm and intelligent action.

People were naive enough to believe that the industrialization of the planet was the answer for survival. Survival is the gift of a future-oriented life. The future is found in the values of spiritual striving toward perfection. Without such striving, industry will turn into our grave.

Technocracy should be regarded as a device of the dark ones. The dark ones have often led people on to mechanical solutions, thereby hoping to occupy the attention of humanity, only to divert it from spiritual growth. Yet the problems of life can be solved only by the expansion of consciousness. It can be seen how mechanical hypotheses easily ensnare the hopes of humanity. Such also was the Maya of the ancients, which could be interrupted by the slightest shock.[3]

The purpose of life is to lead you into the future, in which you are continuously and consciously creative. Like a flower, you must bloom and give many seeds; your creative life must bring much fruit.

. . . So long as humanity refuses to learn to look into the distance, it will be impossible to decrease human sufferings. . . .[4]

The future is your highest good, your highest level of blooming, your highest degree of symphony, your destiny of glorious achievement. Once you begin to look into the future, your thoughts, emotions, actions, words and motives will slowly be controlled by it. The future will start to manifest through you.

Human suffering is the result of those thoughts, emotions and actions which are not oriented toward the future of humanity, but toward one's own separative interests. There is only one future: that is the future of humanity as one kingdom. All our future must fit into that future like pieces in a jigsaw puzzle. Our individual future must add beauty and power to the future of the whole.

Due to the unusualness of conditions of the future, it will be impossible to proceed by the old ways.[5]

The unusualness of conditions is the result of the expanding consciousness. When it expands, it creates new vehicles of expression. There are also other factors which bring unusualness of conditions. For example, our solar system is entering a new sign of the Zodiac. The effect of the Zodiac on humanity is increasing every day because of the expanding consciousness of humanity. Christ is in the process of externalization. Hierarchy is coming closer to humanity. Disciples are increasing everywhere....Because of all these and other factors, we have unusual conditions in the world. On one hand, we have increasing light; on the other hand, we have those who are influenced by materialism, separatism and totalitarianism. These two powers are creating a tremendous tension in the world, which can be used as either an opportunity for greater achievements or greater destruction. At no other time in the history of humanity have these two powers confronted each other in such a critical tension as they are doing now.

Unusual conditions are also created because of many people who function on higher levels, such as the higher mental and intuitional levels. All these factors, as well as the expansion of consciousness and changing level of human beings, reflect in life conditions and create very unusual conditions for humanity. Those who neglect the challenge of the new conditions and live according to the old ways of life will eventually pay a heavy price for their negligence.

People adjust themselves to outer changes in order to be able to retain their old ways of feeling, thinking and acting; but they cannot really leave behind "old ways" unless they think in terms of the new ways. It is our motives, thoughts, feelings and actions that must change. We cannot change them by using an airplane instead of a horse, or by speaking through a telephone instead of sending a messenger on foot.

The future is not something static or fixed to some degree of achievement, or to an image which we want to be. The future is an ever-developing, unfolding process in which man enters into progressively greater beauties and glories. The future of an embryo is to be a child; the future of a child is to be a young person; the future of a young person is to be an adult; the future of an adult is to be a Christ-like person; the future of a Christ is to be a Planetary Logos; the future of a Planetary Logos is to be a Solar Logos ....This is the meaning of the term "future."

. . . it will be impossible to proceed by the old ways. All new ones must remember this. . . .[6]

In esoteric literature, the "new" means progressive steps to the future. The new is another unfolding petal; another level of communication, response or synthesis. The new is closer cooperation with the Plan and the Purpose of the Creator.

The future and the new lead to ever-growing enlightenment on greater and greater scales, in which we never try to crystallize ourselves with any image or standard. Striving is a steady moving forward toward our spiritual destination.

"Old ways" refer to old ways of acting, feeling and thinking. An old way is the way the physical body imposes itself on you with its habits, urges and drives. An old way is the way the emotional body imposes its glamors and negative attitudes on you. An old way is the way your mind imposes its illusions, separative thoughts, fear, anger and greed on you. An old way is trying to solve our problems through wars, lies and selfish politics.

An old way is accumulation of riches while thousands need bread. An old way is to suppress people's freedom and exploit them. No one will go far with these old ways and new ones must know this.

Who are the "new ones"? New ones are those who see the vision of the new age and are ready to proceed on the path of perfection. New ones are those who pledge themselves to the service of humanity. New ones are those who are ready to sacrifice all that they have to work out the Divine Plan on earth. From the start, they must be directed to the right path in order not to be sidetracked by matter, positions, vanity, greed and so on.

Old ways are the ways of the past in which you were living. Try not to fall again into the ways of the past, but face the future with new ways.

All Great Ones taught new ways. As an old-fashioned tool cannot be used to repair a modern machine, so our old ways of acting, feeling and thinking cannot solve our modern problems. Our problems are no longer local, but universal. We have pollution problems, radioactivity problems, overpopulation prob-

lems, crime problems and many other universal problems. We are really in an unusual situation. All these
conditions cannot be faced by old ways and means.

> *It is the worst thing when men do not know*
> *how to escape from the old rut. It is dreadful when*
> *people approach new conditions with their old*
> *habits. Just as it is impossible to open a present-*
> *day lock with a mediaeval key, likewise it is*
> *impossible for men with old habits to unlock the*
> *door of the future.*[7]

The old rut holds us away from the future. The old
rut means the old grooves in which the wheels of all
our actions run without progress. The old rut is our old
habits, old stereotyped thinking and acting and old
cliches of reaction.

There are five steps which may help the traveler
on the path to live in the light of the future:

1. *Persistence* is the use of the willpower in the
action of striving. One should persist in what he is
doing on the path of Goodness, Beauty and Truth.

2. *Patience* is the use of the will to control negative
forces. These forces are the forces of the personality,
inertia, glamor and maya.

3. *Focus* is willpower aligning and integrating all
physical, emotional and mental activities with the
vision projected by the Soul.

4. *Meditation.* In meditation, the willpower reor-
ients the mind toward the Soul and toward the Intuitional Plane to absorb ideas and formulate them into
thoughtforms.

5. *Service* is willpower appropriating the inner
resources to the outer need.

The future is an ever-progressing vision of our
perfection. We emphasize the future because like a
magnet, the future coordinates all our activities and
expressions and causes us to achieve a higher state of
consciousness and more creative expressions. It also
helps us to think before we act or speak and observe the
effects of our actions, words and thoughts. It makes us

study and use the Law of Cause and Effect.

If your goal is your future, your future becomes the cause of your present instead of your past being the cause. Thus in a sense, you liberate yourself from the actions that you put into motion as causes in the past. In thinking about the future, in which you will achieve greater beauty and mastery, you shift your consciousness from the personality to Soul consciousness, because the Soul stands for your future. Those who have no vision perish because they are stuck to their lower vehicles and to the past, which is full of complications and failures.

Standing in the future eliminates the repetition of your failure images and replaces all failure images with images of success. Success is a contact with the future; it is caused by the inspiration given by the future.

Once I asked my father why flowers grow and blossom. He said, "Because they look to the Sun. . . ." We can look to the Sun within us — the future vision of ourselves — and also grow.

No one can grow unless he sees a future beauty for himself.

Those who are caught in the past try to solve their problems by revenge, by damaging the property of the other person involved, or even by killing him. The new method is different: you raise the consciousness of the other person to such a height that he destroys the hindrances existing in his nature and becomes your co-worker.

The past is a state of consciousness in which you are occupied with that which does not allow you to unfold and grow. The present is the state of consciousness in which you are occupied with the immediate needs of your personality at the expense of the needs of your soul. The future is a state of consciousness in which you try to manifest the hidden Divinity within you.

Past failures must not affect you in such a way that you never try again to be successful or daring. Past failures may even teach you how to be successful in the future. Past pains should not prevent you from trying to make new agreements and new friendships. When the past prevents you from having a new future, a future you want, that past must be thrown out of your consciousness. New possibilities and future expansions are lost when you identify with past events and live in the past. To create animosity in the hearts of children against those who did wrong to their parents is a method through which hatred and crime are perpetuated.

> . . . *Seldom does the preoccupied one perceive the future.*[8]

A preoccupied one is a person who is busy with the past; with his personality, selfish interests; with his separative plans and actions. Such a person can never perceive the future because the future demands an ever-inclusive viewpoint and an ever-increasing self-renunciation. A preoccupied teacher is one who makes people obey him or worship him. A real Teacher of the future is one who makes people obey principles and laws and worship beauty and truth.

To work for the future means to work for the revelation of the Divinity in man.

> *It is wise to draw the line between past and future. It is impossible to calculate all that has been done — it is incommensurable. It is better to say: "Yesterday is past; let us learn how to meet a new dawn." We all grow, and our works are expanding with us. After twenty-seven years no one is a youth, and we all can then understand the achievement of Service. It is unworthy to rummage in yesterday's dust. Henceforth let us establish a new step. Let us begin to labor, surrounding ourselves with a thousand eyes. Let us acquire purity of thought and co-measurement of actions. Thus let us fill our days; let us become used to mobility and decisiveness. Likewise, let us not forget that there is nothing on Earth higher than the given Plan for the Common Good. Let us*

*manifest understanding of the Teachings of life.
As Moses brought forth human dignity, as
Buddha impelled toward the broadening of consciousness, as Christ taught the good of giving, so
now the New World is directed toward the far-off
worlds!...[9]*

1. Agni Yoga Society, *Leaves of Morya's Garden*, Volume II, pp. 181-182.
2. See Chapters 15, 32, and 40 in *The Psyche and Psychism*, by Torkom
   Saraydarian.
3. Agni Yoga Society, *Fiery World*, Volume I, para. 349.
4. Agni Yoga Society, *Infinity*, Volume II, para. 82.
5. *Ibid.*, para. 84.
6. *Ibid.*
7. *Ibid.*
8. Agni Yoga Society, *Leaves of Morya's Garden*, Volume I, para. 119.
9. Agni Yoga Society, *Community*, para. 81.

CHAPTER 3

THE FUTURE

The *future* refers to what we are going to be on the path of our Divine destiny. On this path we had a past, which is very remote and lost in the darkness of eternity. We also have the future, lost in the light of Infinity.

We have developed apparatuses through which we are able to see the great Cosmos and also the smallest things: atoms, protons, electrons, etc. There are other things that we did not see before, but we are just starting to see, such as human emotions, human radiations, and human thoughts. For example, if we could see the effect of a word going from someone's mouth into Space, it would be more amazing than anything in the world. Some clairvoyants say that every word we utter creates a geometrical figure; then it changes into a color. When it goes from the etheric level to the astral plane, it becomes a mathematical symbol. In the mental plane it turns into words again; in higher planes it plays the colors of music. A great Sage, speaking about speech, says that devas do not hear but they see the colors of your emotions and your thoughts.

There are many things waiting for us in the *future*. The future is a state of human awakening. Most of what we are doing here on earth is nothing else but sleeping under a big blanket, called the physical body. Very few people are awakened. Very few people can see.

26

> *. . . we prepare during earthly existence the*
> *future beautiful gardens. Thought in all its con-*
> *structiveness also creates our own future happi-*
> *ness. Thus we proceed by means of thought beyond*
> *the limits of Earth.*[1]

This verse means that we are preparing our future now, at this moment. With whatever we are doing at this moment in this life as physical, emotional and mental actions or responses, we are building our future.

Buddha once said something very beautiful: "All that we are is the result of what we have thought. All that we are is founded on our thoughts and formed by our thoughts." Man pays very little attention to his thoughts, but it is his thoughts that are building his future existence. For example, whatever we are now is the result of what we thought in previous lives. If you don't like this life and the way you are living, the way your body is, the way your emotions are, the way your mental equipment is built, do not blame anybody else because *you* built it in the past. Try to improve your present thoughts so that in the future you will have the best body, heart and mind.

It is very important that we control our future. In what way? By living in a way that will lead us to our future. For example, if you want to have a great mind in the future, you must work on your mind now. If you want to have a healthy mind, you must think healthy thoughts. If you want to have a beautiful physical body, you must perform only those actions, emotions and mental activities that are in harmony with each other, and this harmony will create a harmonious body in the future.

It is not a mystery now that our invisible electro-magnetic sphere or etheric body is the conditioning factor of our physical body and that this energy system around us is controlled by our thoughts. For example, suppose you have a golden radiation, with beautiful hues in it. Then suddenly a thought of fear, hatred, or jealousy comes in and boom — it makes your sphere all black. Your whole electrical system is short-circuited. All that we are and all that we are going to be is the result of our thoughts.

People are very careful about putting money in the bank. They say, "Twenty years later I will have 20,000 dollars." But they do not think about what bank they are putting their thoughts into and what kind of thoughts they are putting into it. There is a more important bank than the bank where we are putting our dollars. In that bank you are putting all your capital; you are building the capital of your future and it will create earthly joys and heavenly joys. If you deposit material money and do not pay attention to your future becomingness, then you are losing whatever you build here. Your unfoldment of the future is like a garden in which you are going to bloom.

In esoteric literature, man is symbolized by a flower. Man radiates fiery flowers in his aura. For example, we are told that, when a person is unfolding spiritually, his head center looks like a lotus; another golden flower appears near his shoulder blades; another on his throat; and another between the eyebrows. These etheric centers are like flowers. When a person is really developed, which means flourishing and blooming, he is like a beautiful blooming tree.

When you have 200 blooming trees, then you have a garden. This is what M. M. means when He says that we should prepare our future garden by pure thoughts. Thoughts build the future. If your thoughts are really low-quality, you are going to be a low-quality person. If your thoughts are very high-quality, then you are going to be a great creative genius because that is what you worked for. Whatever you give to Nature, Nature gives back to you, as your bank does — and always with greater interest.

Christ once said that if you plant a fig tree, don't expect cherries from that tree. If you plant a fig tree, you are going to harvest figs from it. If you plant a cherry tree, you will harvest cherries. If you plant creative, high-level, beautiful thoughts, you are going to reap a beautiful life and happiness.

When we talk about happiness and joy, we think that they are only feelings or emotions. They are not. Happiness means harmony; joy means greater harmony, symphonic harmony. Bliss means Divine harmony.

Harmony is created when your thoughts are pure, when your words are pure and when your emotions and actions are constructive and loving. When they are in conflict, you have chaos. Most of the time you create chaos in your own sphere. For example, you write a letter and say, "My dear friend, I really missed you. You are so beautiful; I really like you and want you to come back. We will go on trips," etc. Then when you finish the letter you say to yourself, "My goodness, I really don't like him, but one must write these things." Suppose you have a friend with you and he asks, "To whom are you writing that letter?" You answer, "To a stupid person. He thinks he is something, but you know. . . ."

What did you do? With the letter you created a beautiful symphony; with your remarks you distorted that symphony and created chaos. Now there is chaos in your aura. This is why hypocrisy is not good — because it creates chaos. Lies also create chaos.

If you are living a double or triple life with your expressions, you are really creating chaos around yourself. When this chaos penetrates your subtle bodies — your mental, emotional, etheric and physical centers — you find yourself in a very unhealthy condition. You may blame everything else and everyone else except yourself, but you are the only one to be blamed because you created that chaos.

All that we are is the result of what we have thought. From thought comes action.

Try to guard your thoughts. Immediately when you start to think of something ugly, try to stop thinking that way. With your negative thoughts, you create a stagnant pool and then sit in it and drink from it. Always check your thoughts and see if they are pure.

When Christ was asked who would enter the Kingdom of God, He said, "Bring that little child to

Me....If you will be like this child, you will enter the Kingdom of God." You must be pure like that innocent, happy, beautiful child; but you must also have intuitive guidance.

It is your good thought which is the ship that travels toward the stars of your future. Your thought conditions your future, not only on the Earth but beyond it. When we see the whole objective manifestation with all the galaxies, constellations and stars from the viewpoint of Infinity, it's like a little flower fallen into the ocean of Space.

Man is not limited to physical manifestation; he has different manifestations — emotional, mental, intuitional, atmic, monadic, divine and Cosmic. Thoughts are like arrows taking us toward the future. They form our rocket which pulls us away from the Earth.

In another place the Sage says that "the greatest antitoxin is a pure thought." He says that pure thought can cure many sicknesses.

An instantaneous emotion can be very mechanical. It comes like a current of force, hits your ears and eyes and creates associations. Immediately you start reacting. But your thought may be alert and say, "What is going on here?" Thought is your hammer; if you control it, it is your watchman.

In the *Bhagavad Gita,* Arjuna says to Krishna, "My Lord, to control the mind is as difficult as to control the wind." Krishna answers, "Yes, it is difficult, but by effort it is possible." You must tell yourself, "Because others did it, I can do it." This is how we are challenged to surpass ourselves.

Human nature will always conquer. Watch how a little child paints a picture of a man. He makes the eyes like a fish, the nose like a cucumber, the ears like potatoes. . . . His efforts are rough now, but eventually he can become a painter if he works at it. You are more than matter, more than emotions, more than mind, so you can be the master of these three things. How? By practice. Even your dog can learn to sit and jump and do tricks. Your body is no worse than a dog's; your body can learn too.

When I was working as a high school principal, one day I asked one of my students if he had worked on his lesson. He answered, "Yes."

"How long?"

He said, "Half an hour."

"How many hours did you spend in bed?"

"To be truthful," he said, "twenty-two hours."

He was a comical boy.

This is what we do: we work for half an hour and the rest of the time we waste. How much have we grown in these past billion years? We are still dying; we still have pain; our teeth still bother us. How much have we grown? One inch in ten billion years. Why? Because in that ten billion years we worked on ourselves for only ten hours. Those ten hours are our life, not the ten billion years.

We must face ourselves. We may see the effects of our deeds, but we do not learn from them. The most important factor in the process of improving ourselves is to see our motives and change them. People often see the effects of their bad deeds; they even enjoy seeing them. But when they begin to see the thoughts behind their actions and the motives behind their thoughts, they may change the level of their consciousness. As their consciousness expands, they correct their motives.

A motive is a motivating force within the mind. Sometimes a motive is a fear, a glamor, or a blind urge based on past suffering or obsessions. Seeing our motive can reveal to us the cause of our activities and clear them up.

It is after such a cleansing process that we can contact the real motivating urges within us. These are the energies of the Soul, which are ready to radiate and create. This is done by an esoteric method of observation, in which the observer gradually withdraws himself into higher levels and touches the motivating forces within himself. Once he contacts them and replaces them with real motives, he meets himself. The Self is the highest motivating power in man.

. . . One can foresee how in the course of time

an astrochemical basis for many manifestations
will be found. And each record of them will be of
great service in the future.[2]

At the time when you were born, for example, what kind of chemistry was affecting your nervous system, your etheric body and your mental body? Astrochemistry is the combination of energies and forces that are pouring down into our solar system and our planet and conditioning the manifestation of cultures and civilizations. All that we are and all that we do is the effect of our responses to these forces and energies. Later we will know how to utilize these energies to further our evolution toward greater dimensions.

At the exact time when a baby is born, he is in the most impressionable state. Energies and forces coming from constellations, planets and even comets leave a great impression on the electromagnetic field of his body and this can have a decisive effect on his life. The mixture of these energies and forces creates the astrochemistry to which the Teacher is referring.

Of course, we must know that energies are impersonal. It is the level and depth of our responses that condition the effect of energies. Also, the different combinations of energies and forces create different types of mechanisms or forms through which the consciousness functions. As the elements combined with different elements or in different quantities produce different chemicals, so it is with the combination of energies and forces. This is the foundation of the science of astrology, if it is taken as the science of energies.

It is very important to note that you can control astrochemistry by changing your being and your responses. This is why an average horoscope chart prepared by an average astrologer does not work for an Initiate.

Dreams about the future are widespread. Pro-
phecies are disseminated by the thousands and
people in various countries are becoming accus-

tomed to definite dates. . . .³

Here the future refers to your chronological future. It is the time which is waiting for you; it is the outcome of your actions. We are told that the Inner Dweller contacts the personality and often warns him or prepares him for future events. It takes a very subtle perception to see the difference between a warning and one's destiny.

. . . One can so build one's life that each day will, as it were, be the end. But one can so illumine one's life that each hour will be a beginning. Thus one can rebuild one's earthly existence beneath one's very eyes. Only in this way will the questions of the future and the understanding of fiery perfectment become perceptible. . . .⁴

Can you do this? Try sometimes to say to yourself, "Let me do my work and put every paper in its place today because tonight I may die." If you do this, you will see that you are doing things more precisely and more beautifully.

Each hour can be a beginning.

Fiery perfecting means we are building our higher nature with great inspiration, with great beauties, with great visions and revelations and with great sacrifices. We are building our future by working consciously every minute as if this were the end of our life. We must say, "Let me do my best in this one hour because maybe in the next hour I will not be here." And this is a possibility.

Let us be future-oriented without forgetting that we are still on earth.

---

1. Agni Yoga Society, *Fiery World*, Volume I, para. 241.
2. *Ibid.*, para. 282.
3. *Ibid.*, para. 303.
4. *Ibid.*, para. 308.

CHAPTER 4

FIRE AND THE FUTURE

Agni means fire, and yoga means union. Agni Yoga means union through, by, or in fire. The fire we are referring to is the true Core of man. Man is essentially a Spark from a Cosmic Flame.

In occult literature, fire is divided into three parts:
a. fire by friction
b. solar fire
c. electrical fire

Fire by friction is the electricity we use, or atmospheric electricity, which renders us great service as an agent of communication.

Solar fire is mental fire, or fire from the Sun, which causes enlightenment, expansion of consciousness and transmutation. It is like a bridge between the personality and the spiritual man. Our Solar Angels are sometimes called Fiery Meditators.

Electrical fire comes from the Central Spiritual Sun and is related to our Essence. This is Agni in its Solar manifestation.

We are told that fire by friction originates in the sphere of the Sun, which is the nourisher and sustainer of life in the solar system. Solar fire originates in the Heart of the Sun and is related to love and to the conscious realms of human beings. For the average person, solar fire is his consciousness. In the advanced disciple, it is love-wisdom. Electrical fire originates in the Central Spiritual Sun and is related to our Essence, the Self, the Spark within the form of man and to Infinity. It is the source of all creative urges.

From the point of view of Christian and other religious literature, the Central Spiritual Sun is the Father, the Source "from Whom all things proceed and to Whom all things return." The Heart of the Sun is "the word made flesh," the Christ. On human levels, it is the Solar Angel in man, Who is the bridge, a way by which achievement is possible. The visible Sun is the light of the Holy Spirit, the substance, or the personality. All of these are fire and in the Scriptures we are told that our God is a burning fire.

Agni Yoga refers to this fire. Through this fire a person must travel the path of transformation, the path of transmutation and the path of transfiguration. In other words, a person is going to be fiery. When he becomes purified, he will be a fiery being. And because no impurity exists in fire, the more fiery he becomes, the purer he will be.

How, then, does sickness come into being? Any place in your aura where the fire is extinguished is an entryway for fiery elementals which cause trouble. Microbes are fiery elementals of a low order.

Man, who is the Central Fire, the Monad, is going to become himself by passing through a fiery transformation. Then the physical body will be purified to the highest degree and man will be electrical. This is our goal. Then the body will not say any more, "I am weak; I am tired; I am getting old." All of these expressions do not refer to reality. When you are really your Self, you will be a Master, a fiery Angel, the fiery Self.

There are foods that are fiery and foods that are not. If we put into our stomach foods that are not equal to the degree of fire in our sphere, we cause trouble in our system. For example, alcohol is fiery, but it is destructive fire. Smoking is fire, but it is also destructive fire.

What do we mean by "destructive"? There are two courses in the universe: involution and evolution. We are now just passing through materialism and going toward spiritualism. If we stay on the involutionary

path, we will cause a terrible conflict in our nature and
we will become a battlefield between two forces, destructive and constructive. These two forces will battle
on the field of our physical, emotional and mental
planes. This is how we invite suffering into our vehicles.
     There are fiery emotions in our emotional body.
There are fiery thoughts in our mental body. Thoughts
are fiery forms or flames. Science now measures mental waves; they are electrical. Our whole body is electricity. It is charged by electricity. We ourselves within
the body are the source of the electricity which infuses
all the atoms.
     And what do we do? We work against our own
transformation, bringing destructive fire into our physical, emotional and mental vehicles. Then we say, "I
don't feel good." Why don't we feel good? Because we
took that smoky thought into our mind; we took a
burning fire into our emotional nature — hatred, for
example. Hatred is fire. Jealousy is fire. Whenever we
are jealous, we can create stomach ulcers because the
secretions of the glands are fiery and they eat the walls
of the stomach.
     This is why in esotericism we are told that all of
Creation emanated from an invisible Sun: fire, unapproachable fire, the burning fire that the Scriptures
say is our God, from Whom all things proceed.
     Christ once said to one of His disciples, "If you
really want to reach a higher state of consciousness,
you must be baptized, not only by water but by fire."
Agni Yoga is the means of transformation, gradual
sublimation and transfiguration by fire and in fire, to
become a fiery being. Once you become fiery, you burn
out all ugly thoughts and emotions.
     Agni Yoga is a method by which we purify our
entire physical, emotional, mental and spiritual system through fire and then stand in the fire. There is an
old verse that says something like, "You are like iron
soiled by the earth. You must be burned in the fire in
order to be purified."
     How can we be purified? Meditation is nothing
else but a fiery purification process. Certain trials are

part of the process of fiery purification. Abstinence, endurance, willpower — all of these are fire.

When you extinguish a flame with water, do you know what you are actually doing? Water is liquid fire; hydrogen is fire; oxygen is fire. You are putting out a fire with another fire. This is why a great Sage says, "You are going to overcome the fire of world-hatred by the fire of love, by the fire of silence and bliss." We control lower fire with higher fires.

What is the future Agni Yoga talks about? It is the spiritual future, not the chronological future. The term "future" does not mean tomorrow, next year, next month. Instead, it refers to your future *becoming*.

When you take a little acorn in your hand, you are looking at a big oak tree; you are looking at the future of the acorn. Agni Yoga talks about the state of achievement in which the seed has unfolded and is blooming to its perfection.

Whatever has happened in the past and whatever is happening in the present is of no real value in reference to the future — which is *you*.

> *In the ancient pharmacopoeias and in various ancestral medical records you are struck by the number of allusions to mixtures for bringing the organism into a transcendental state. You feel that this is not a form of necromancy or witchcraft, but a special way of seeking one's future. Hence, it is clear that our remote ancestors were far more solicitous and thoughtful of the future than our contemporary scholars. For us, the future is relegated either to the confines of hellfire or to the province of an electrical manifestation. The powerful life-creating potency of Fire is unrealized; the effulgent, radiant manifestations are not comprehended and the very Hierarchy of Light itself is regarded as either a phantom or a bugbear. There are many who wish to evade the future, preferring to call themselves dust. Yet even the learned shudder at the question as to whether they wish to pass through Fire. . . .[1]*

In many traditions, we often hear about herbs,

liquids, stones and flowers which bestow immortality on man. In fairy tales, wise men appear and give a mixture of herbs and flowers to a person and he becomes immortal. Down through the ages, hundreds have tried to find a formula that will cure all diseases. M.M. calls this kind of research "a special way of seeking one's future."

What is one's future? One's future is immortality. Immortality exists; man has always tried to find ways and means to be immortal. No matter how many times a person dies, eventually he is going to conquer death and the body.

Unless a person has a vision of his real future, he is tied to the earth. A criminal is a person who is a slave of the past, of the body and of his urges and drives, beyond which nothing exists for him. He is blinded by his own physical existence.

What are we learning in our schools and universities? With all due respect for the knowledge imparted in these institutions, knowledge of the *future* is lacking. We are being prepared in our schools to make money and to enjoy life. We enter life and the race of competition in fear, in hatred, in jealousy; and all we have learned is for the survival of our physical bodies, or how to make money and make ourselves happy, even at the expense of hurting others. The time will come when our universities will teach the science of the soul, the science of immortality, the science of contact with the Higher Worlds; they will teach the future.

Once I was talking with a screenwriter who wrote mostly criminal stories. "Why do you make these crazy movies? Create something beautiful that we can show to children," I said to him.

"But that doesn't make money," he said.

We had a big argument and he pretended to be convinced that I was right; but when I saw his new movie, it was still all crime.

We read that crime has increased 100 percent. This means that our taxes are going up. Our taxes are going up because we are not preventing criminal activities. When M.M. talks about fiery baptism, He is talking about the purification of life.

Suppose you are in a boat with other people and the boat is sailing on the sea. Then somebody lights a fire in the boat. Do you just sit and watch? Do you say, "Let him play"? You don't — because you are in the same boat with him.

Throughout the centuries we have changed in many ways. Our hairstyles have changed; our clothes have changed. We now have refrigerators, radios, television... but we still hate; we still kill.

You tell a man who smokes marijuana, "Don't smoke." And he says, "I can't stop," and he continues to smoke. He can't help himself because he is not using electrical fire to put out the lower fire of desire. If you do not resign or detach from lower values, you cannot find higher values.

I had ten or fifteen friends when I came out of the monastery. We didn't know what to do, so we said, "Let's drink!" Every weekend we bought ten or fifteen bottles of good wine and we drank and drank and drank. The next day, all of us were sick, but the next week we would drink again. Then one day I read a poem by Paul Verlaine. He said you must always be drunk — but drunk with beauty, ideas, visions, creativity.

Now when I write an article, I am drunk. When I play music, I am drunk. When I speak, I am drunk. There is a higher intoxication, which is called *ecstasy*. Ecstasy is a process of fusion with higher energies — when your consciousness is expanded into higher mental levels and comes in contact with intuition, freedom and beauty.

The Agni Yogi is one who is in a continuous process of fusion with higher spheres, from which pour down the joy and bliss of one's own Essence. So often instead of contacting such levels, we satisfy ourselves with earthly pleasures, which if carried too far, eventually turn into the causes of our suffering.

The concept of Shambhala is actually linked inseparably with fiery manifestations. Without the application of purified Fire it is impossible

*to approach the higher concepts. Throughout
the entire world people are divided into those
who are conscious of Shambhala as the Highest Measure and those who deny the future....*[2]

We are told that Shamballa is the Father's Home,
the Stronghold, the head center of the planet, where
the Will of God is known. It is formed by great streams
of energy, in the whirlpool of which great Initiates
function. It is the Highest Measure because it leads the
evolution of all kingdoms in Nature.

All Nature aspires toward Shamballa. This is the
Center of highest achievement on this planet, which
inspires vision, bestows revelations and extends the
call for conscious evolution. This Center is, in a way,
the last home of a human being on this planet. It is *his
future*. All conscious evolution is directed toward that
Center, toward that Achievement.

Mankind is divided into two groups of people:
those who deny Shamballa as the possiblity of ultimate achievement and those who are conscious of
Shamballa as the guiding star to their Selves, age after
age.

Once when I was giving a lecture a young boy
asked, "Why are the Great Ones called Masters?" I
said, "A Master is your future. Eventually you will be
so beautiful, so graceful, so powerful, so righteous and
so victorious that people will look upon you as their
ideal, as their dream, as their future. When you become
such a person, would it be wrong if people who are in
your present stage of consciousness called you a
Master?"

Shamballa is the future.[3] It stands for the great
revelations to come, for great achievements of human
beings to come. Those who function in Shamballa
were once men and women like you and I, but throughout many centuries, They mastered life. This is our
glorious future, too.

Those who do not believe in Shamballa deny their
own future. Once Christ said, "In the future, you will
do greater things than I did." This is a great affirma-

tion of the future of the human being. Our future achievement will be so great that eventually we will become petals in the head center of the planet.

> . . . People must become accustomed to the fact that the perfecting of conditions of existence must be accelerated, but this must not resemble convulsions. On the contrary, people should not be satisfied with outworn customs; they should learn to rejoice at the new. Joy about the new is already wings to the future.[4]

". . . the perfecting of conditions of existence. . . ." The first step in this is self-improvement, improvement of our physical, emotional and mental forms, actions, reactions and responses. It is very interesting to note that man has a natural inclination to improve himself and his environment.

Most of our struggle is to improve conditions on earth. We know that selfishness, greed and hatred complicate conditions on earth and even distort or disturb the natural harmony between man and the universe. But in spite of this, there is a general aspiration toward improving the conditions of the earth. This aspiration and striving toward improvement are the result of inner pressure. The spirit of man unfolds and demands proper conditions in which to express itself, as the sap in the tree wants to rise in order to help produce flowers and fruit.

Think of how much our communication system has been improved throughout the ages; every day we have new inventions and better ways to live. All of these things are improvements, but they are improvements of *outer* forms. The conditions of existence can really be improved when man improves his nature, his morality, his thinking, his motivations, his communication with higher sources, his intuition and his will-power. Improving outer conditions without first improving our inner conditions leads us eventually to self-extermination.

"*Joy about the new. . . .*" The new is the next stage

of our awareness, the next stage of our creativity, the next stage of purification. The new is the next step toward the ideal, toward the prototype. The new is an ever-expanding step toward inclusiveness and synthesis. This is the future to which M.M. is referring.

> *Even a savage can fly in an airplane, but let us not think that formerly it was any better. I have shown you the records of the Thirty Years' War in order that you may understand how, even in comparatively advanced countries, coarseness and ignorance have ruled. Records of refined Rome, Egypt and Babylon could be cited, at which the heart would shudder. Hence, all who look to the future should continue to knock for admission....*[5]

To "knock" means to use your willpower to strive, to work harder, to improve, to surpass your many limitations and to step on your past so that you may be admitted into the future. To knock means to use all of your abilities, talents and genius in a focused striving so that you unfold and bloom. We may be proud of our cars, airplanes, radios, televisions and refrigerators, but they do not necessarily mean that we are improving inwardly.

I remember one day when our Teacher showed us a sprouted pea. On one of the leaves around the seed there was a clump of earth. "You see," he said, "this tiny little seed strived underground and at last broke through the earth covering it. As a sign of victory, it still carries the earth on its shoulders. This is what striving is. We may learn from the pea." This is the knock which achieved the response of admission.

The real Teaching is fiery striving. With striving, you can do almost anything to improve your condition and unfold your Inner Beauty. You must never cool down in your fiery striving; on the contrary, year after year, you must become more fiery and a better warrior for the future.

> *... What has been said about peacemakers is the more correct, since because of them there*

arises a proper attitude toward the future. . . .[6]

Christ once said that the peacemakers will be called the children of God. Peacemaking is first of all an outer activity through which men, families and nations establish better relationships in order to improve their lives and not waste their energy, money or lives in hatred and war. It is after peace agreements that national and international life blooms.

Many greedy people in the world believe that war makes jobs and money because it mobilizes all labor toward a goal. This notion is disproven by highly educated people who think about the welfare of humanity. From now on, war will create destruction, mass annihilation, diseases that cannot be controlled and mass starvation. Such conditions will not be profitable for anyone. Armament factories and other war-related concerns that directly benefit from war will not have healthy people to enjoy the income, even if they manage to escape the massive destruction.

The new motto of the future is peace, not war. Any war is a threat to all mankind. On the other hand, peace will let us have everything, including the money, energy and time which is otherwise thrown into the destructive fire. With such abundance, we can make greater breakthroughs into the secrets of Nature and alleviate the present danger to our health caused by our ignorance and greed.

Children of God are the men and women who stand for one humanity and for total peace and who make their voices heard everywhere in all activities of life. Children of God are the children of light and the children of the future, who are revealed by that increasing light.

Those who work for light and for peace are those who save our lives, our culture and even our money. War, crime and various kinds of abuses are the signs that we do not yet have peace within us. Peace starts within us. I do not mean that when we think about peace that peace will come. It is not that easy. Peace will come as a result of inner integration, alignment and at-one-ment with our Inner Guide and with our innermost Essence, which is our true Future. Thus, peace leads to the Future.

---

1. Agni Yoga Society, *Fiery World,* Volume I, para. 40.
2. *Ibid.,* para. 41.
3. Read *The Legend of Shamballa,* by Torkom Saraydarian.
4. Agni Yoga Society, *Fiery World,* Volume I, para. 47.
5. *Ibid.,* para. 141.
6. *Ibid.,* para. 144.

CHAPTER 5

CO-WORKERS

In the Agni Yoga Teaching a great emphasis is laid upon co-workers. A co-worker is a person who works to improve life as a whole and in all its aspects. He tries to improve human relations, the economic situation of life, education, politics, arts and sciences. Whenever a person is working hard with complete dedication to improve life, we say that he is a co-worker.

Co-workers are people who have the same vision and who strive toward the fulfillment or actualization of that vision. Co-workers have three important tasks to do:

1. Co-workers must establish right relations with the vision and be receptive to the impressions and implications of the vision. If they have a vision and they dedicate themselves to it, they slowly build in their consciousness the necessary requirements which make them real co-workers. Physically, emotionally, mentally and in all their relationships, co-workers must live in such a way that they create one harmonious whole with their vision.

If you have a vision but you cannot comprehend it; if mentally you are deficient, if your education is not complete, then you cannot actualize that vision in life.

2. Co-workers must establish right relations with other co-workers, bypassing personality differences. They must cooperate with their co-workers in such a way that they do not create personality reactions. A

45

real co-worker is a person who bypasses his own personality reactions, as well as the personality reactions
of other people. For example, if a real co-worker is
working in a committee and someone else is nervous,
angry or irritated, he bypasses it and concentrates
everyone's minds on the work or the task to be done.

Many great plans and visions fail because the
people who are trying to create, actualize or manifest
the vision start fighting with each other. Their jealousy, anger and fears come to the surface and the
whole work suffers. When you see a person in meetings
or in a job who is involved with his personality reactions, know that his vision or plan is going to fail.

3. Co-workers must develop the needed techniques
and apparatus within themselves to act harmoniously
with the vision and with other co-workers. A co-worker
must create integrity within himself. He must be physically, emotionally, mentally and spiritually dedicated
to his job. If a person's emotions are fighting against
his mind, if his thoughts are fighting against his body,
or if his body is so lazy or distorted that it is rejecting
the labor and cooperation, he cannot be a co-worker.

In the Agni Yoga literature there are many references to co-workers:

> . . . The future is so beautiful and so broad. Let
> your names be written down among the names of
> the great co-workers of evolution. . . .[1]

The future is your unfoldment, your blooming
throughout ages until eternity. You are like a little seed
now, but that seed is going to become a beautiful bush
or tree. Then it will give flowers and fruits. No matter
through what the world passes — wars, revolutions,
crimes — man is going to improve. The world can be
destroyed, but you can still improve. Every experience
and event that happens on the path of your life leaves
traces in your mind. Eventually you can realize why
these events happen, how you can avoid such events,
and what you must do to develop yourself. The future is
your blooming and your future and your unfoldment

are always beautiful.

A co-worker is a person who always thinks he is going to be beautiful in the future. Unless you realize or think that you are going to be beautiful — more educated, more transformed, more intelligent, more healthy, more creative — you cannot be a co-worker. You must be progressive in your soul.

Some people become depressed because of their shortcomings, their vices and the things they do wrong. It is good to feel that you did something wrong, but you must not become stuck in that feeling. You must say to yourself, "My destination is a glorious future. I am going to overcome every kind of hindrance and fulfill my destiny." If you do this you are a co-worker and you are trying with millions of other people in many fields of human endeavor to carry the wheel of evolution toward perfection.

Some people think that the Teaching is only related to religion. This is not true. The Teaching is related to politics, to communication, to art, to science, to religion and to finance. Whenever people try to improve life in any field, they are co-workers.

"*Let your names be written down among the names of the great co-workers of evolution.*" Before you die, you must be able to say, "I did something great for humanity." If you did one thing for one person, if you uplifted someone and made him realize the vision of life, then your name is recorded in the computer of the Hierarchy as a co-worker. You must strive to put your name on that list of the co-workers of evolution. Evolution is the process of steady unfoldment and improvement of life.

> *. . . We summon those co-workers who know the difficulties. We call to those who will not turn back. We summon those who know that joy is a special wisdom. . . .*[2]

The Great Ones tell us that people are needed who know the difficulties of life and how to labor in life. If you are working for humanity, you must sometimes

work 24 hours daily. One of the great qualities of a
co-worker is that he does not consider time in his labor.
A co-worker does not work for time. When the job must
be done he does it whether he is sick or depressed,
whether his wife left or his girlfriend or boyfriend
didn't call, whether the soup is ready or not. A co-
worker works and finishes the job.

The great Sage, M.M., says that the greatest
method to shorten time is dedicated labor. In dedicated
labor, you don't have measurement of time. You may
work ten hours and when the work is finished, you
think that you only worked for one hour.

If you start laboring, you will see that the greatest
wisdom in labor is joy. Joy makes your muscles work.
Joy makes you stand above the personality reactions.
Joy makes your mind extremely sensitive to the
impressions and inspirations that are coming from the
vision that you have in your mind. If you don't have
joy in your labor, you pull others down and create
irritation in them. Irritation creates tremendous repul-
sion.

A co-worker is a magnetic person. The field in
which the co-worker labors is a magnetic field. Unless
it is magnetic, it is a disturbing factor in humanity. A
co-worker is not a disturbing factor; a co-worker
creates a magnetic field around himself. That magnetic field comes into being when he does his labor
with great joy.

> . . . look for co-workers there where they think
> about new life.[3]

A co-worker is a person who appreciates the past
but looks to the future. Do you want a life that is more
organized, more beautiful? If so, you must create a new
life. New life is the new actions and reactions of the
heart and your relationships with others. New life is
the transformation of your life — of your emotions,
your thinking, your ideas and your visions. Only
those who think in terms of new life can be co-workers.

> *How to choose coworkers? Only by their irre-*
> *placeability. It is correct to value a man when his*
> *place cannot be abolished. . . .*[4]

A co-worker cannot be replaced because he is always progressive, unfolding and going toward the future. He is continuously adapting himself to the requirements of the new conditions.

> *There are two kinds of people — the first prefer*
> *to exploit the labor of others, while the second like*
> *to attain by themselves. Pay attention to the*
> *second, among them you find investigators and*
> *coworkers . . . .*[5]

Who can be a co-worker? The one who depends on his own hard work, physically, emotionally, mentally and spiritually. He works hard to advance himself and can say at the end of any job, "I did this with my own sweat and tears."

If a person is working in any field and he is not investigating or searching — which means, he is not expanding and deepening — he will stay on the surface and he will become useless. Only the person who is searching and trying to penetrate more deeply into ideas, into the thought world and into inspirations and creativity can be a co-worker. A co-worker does not sit at home and say, "The trees will one day ripen and I will go and open my mouth and the fruit will drop into it."

> *. . . One must keenly distinguish the motives*
> *of coworkers. . . .*[6]

A great Sage says that the Hierarchy selects its co-workers on the basis of their motives, not because of what they did or what they are. Your motives are the first indicator of what your essence really is. A man may donate 50,000 dollars to an organization, but his intention is not to help but create some trouble. You must find the motive behind people's actions. You must find the motive behind others' work and even behind their service.

> ... A true musician does not think about each
> finger's calling forth a sound; only a pupil consid-
> ers which fingers are convenient to use. The true
> coworker does not think about the intended appli-
> cation of the qualities of labor. The music of the
> spheres is blended with the song of progress of
> labor. . . .[7]

A co-worker is so expert and so dedicated that he doesn't need rules and regulations to do things; he knows instinctively how to do them. Just as a musician playing the piano does not think about which finger he will use on which key, a co-worker is so dedicated and integrated that he doesn't think about his labor; he just performs it. The labor pours out of his heart.

> ... Each one who is glad not to work is no
> coworker of yours. You may ask whether the ser-
> vices of the newcomer are recognized by ungrateful
> humanity. Each complainer is no coworker of
> yours. You may ask whether he himself is respon-
> sible for the past or others are. Your coworker will
> not impose responsibility for his past on others....[8]

M.M. says if someone wants to come and be a co-worker, first give him really hard work in order to see his true face. If he escapes from the job in half an hour or two hours and never comes back again, he is not a co-worker.

As the co-worker does not measure time, he also does not measure any labor given to him to do. You can load and load and load him; and as you load him he becomes more balanced and stable so that he handles the increasing load on his shoulders. A person who cannot be a co-worker panics under the slightest pressure.

Co-workers never complain. The great Sage says that complaining creates an element in the air that is very disintegrative to the electromagnetic body. If you see people around you complaining, know that they are not going to be co-workers for many lives.

Sometimes a complaint hides itself under different masquerades. A complaint may manifest as gossip, malice, slander, hatefulness, jealousy. . . but at the bottom the complaint is there.

If you give someone a job and he doesn't do it well and then blames it on the typewriter, on his broom, on his brush, etc., he is not a co-worker. A true co-worker says, "I was wrong. I didn't prepare myself. I didn't have the necessary skill; let me develop it." If a person can see himself as he is, he can be a co-worker. If he is not able to see exactly what he is and he continuously covers himself, he cannot be a co-worker.

> . . . consider that even the most clumsy co-worker can offer his stone for the structure. . . .[9]

If your motive is pure and your heart is in the right place, you can do something for the world.

> . . . it is necessary to educate the co-workers through labor and by the affirmation that each co-worker is a part of the whole. . . .[10]

Sometimes when a person is elevated into a better position, he thinks he is the king of the whole situation and others are his subordinates; he thinks he is the one who must make all the decisions about what is to be done. This is a very ugly situation. As a co-worker improves, he loses himself and his self-interest in the interest of others. He tries to make them so beautiful and up-to-date that they even surpass him.

If you don't have this spirit, you cannot be a co-worker. You must always be thinking how you can make somebody else better than you, because you can graduate from the level where you are only when you put somebody else in your place. This kind of action demonstrates greatness of spirit. With this kind of behavior, you improve much faster because you don't worship yourself, but the labor.

It is so unfortunate that in churches, groups and other organizations people worship only themselves and forget about the work. If the work is not glorifying them, then the work has no value for them. It is the work that must be glorified and man must fade in the symphony of the labor. Each separate note and measure in the symphony does not stand up and say, "I am the symphony." Each note and measure adapts itself in such a way that the whole symphony is complete. This is the same with the co-worker and any labor.

. . . one must feel himself to be a true co-worker.[11]

People think you must be scientists, lawyers, doctors and that's all. These are merely tools in your pocket. Your life-destination is to be a co-worker. A co-worker is one who works with the Creator. He takes part in His plan and in His purpose. A co-worker does not worry about his business, about his family, or about his nation; but he thinks about the Creator and what the Creator wants him to do. He says, "I am ready now; let's do it, Lord. If you can put me in any place to do something, I am ready for it." He says, for example, "Lord, I am a scientist. I tried to make my mind really scientific. Do you have any vacancy where I can fit and do something?"

...Verily, our co-workers must expand the consciousness.[12]

A little consciousness sees one inch. A broadened consciousness can see one mile . . . but that field of vision must become ten million miles! Your vision and your consciousness must expand so that you do not stay in any place too long. You must be promoted because promotion is the economy of Nature. This is a very advanced idea.

The disciple who has responded to the call of the Teaching and is aflame with all fires of devotion is verily the coworker of the Cosmic forces....[13]

Devotion does not simply mean to go to church and light a candle. Devotion means to forget your own interest in the interest of the greater whole.

Life progresses by gradual development. When you are developing, life tests you on every level, even though you may not always recognize it. For example, when you decide to be peaceful all day, immediately someone calls and makes you really upset. You did not pass the test. Every time you decide to improve something, the test comes. This is what the economy of Nature means. Nature cannot promote you unless It knows that you are not going to misuse Its energies.

M.M. says that co-workers must pass through certain stages before they become real co-workers:

> *The degrees of attainment are: alarmed; inquiring; knocking; hearkening; reminiscing; transmitting; sword carrier; puissant; lamp of the desert; lion of the desert; coworker of the creative principles; creator.*
>
> *Each degree is sub-divided thrice; the order must be passed gradually. He who strives attains swiftly, but the deserter casts himself down.*[14]

The "alarmed" stage means that suddenly you come to the realization that life is painful, that life is suffering, that life is separatism, that life has many problems, that many people exploit life. To be alarmed is a good sign.

The next stage is to "inquire" about what life is for, to search, to find answers.

"Knocking" is an aspiration or desire to find out what things really are. How are you going to knock? By sitting and thinking, meditating, and creating; by trying to make yourself a virtuous human being; by trying to know your own value. Then you must try to live the experience which you found by knocking and entering.

In "hearkening," you listen to the things you hear, to the things that are told to you. Hearkening means that you are very serious about living a life of beauty, simplicity, and harmlessness.

In the stage of "lamp of the desert," desert refers to the desert of life. Desert consciousness is the ability to understand that you should not be attached to anything. This is similar to the experience you may have in a desert when all you see is sand and sky and you feel that *you* don't exist in the vastness of the sand and sky.

To be a lamp means to have a purpose, a goal in life. You shine like a beacon on the dark stormy sea so that other ships can see the light and direct their own course. When you become a lamp in the desert, everything blooms; everything in life takes on significance and meaning. Life was a desert for you before because you were not seeing the beauty of it. As a lamp, you can see all the beauty of life, even the beauty of suffering and pain — because they are messengers of wisdom leading you into greater understanding and cooperation.

The "lion of the desert" has power, energy and influence. He is a protector and an example of steadiness, endurance and energy. He is a lion because he embodies great principles.

Real power and fearlessness do not come to you when you enslave or exploit people; when you depend on your sneakiness, fanaticism and separatism to control them. You achieve fearlessness only when you become the manifestation of a principle.

From this verse, we see that the stage of being a "co-worker" is a very advanced stage. To be a co-worker, you must prove that you can stand on your own feet without expecting help from anyone. You must be able to live in the desert — isolated, insulated and alone, but you must also be a lion — one who speaks, writes and lives the principles for which he stands.

> *Least of all do people understand success.*
> *Usually, when the success of a task commissioned*
> *by the Hierarchy and imbued with the help of the*
> *Hierarchy, is attributed by the spirit steeped in*
> *selfhood to its own merit, the success turns into a*
> *heartache of the spirit. When a co-worker requires*
> *adoration of himself for fulfillment of the task*

given him, he closes by this very act the records of the space. The records of life passing on in all earthly glory reveal so many beggars in spirit! A co-worker who presents to the community the idea that the Hierarchy will act in accordance with the affirmation of the successful co-worker introduces truly a belittlement of the Hierarch. How difficult it is to introduce among the co-workers the true concept of success! Indeed, only humility of the spirit and the feeling of gratitude are appropriate. Who gave all possibilities? Who has given the direction? Who has manifested all good? Only the Hierarch, only the Leader, only the Forces of Light. Successful co-worker, examine thy armor; on each link is inscribed — Hierarchy. Not I, myself, nor mine, but Thine, O Lord!... [15]

The foundation of the success of any person, organization, or nation is cooperation. A healthy body is a body in which all the parts cooperate with each other. A successful group is composed of people who cooperate with each other. Even an atom cannot progress in life if it does not find other atoms with which to cooperate.

Life is the result of cooperation. When the field of your cooperation increases, your success increases too. Cooperation means to have a vision and to organize all your physical, emotional, mental and spiritual efforts to actualize that vision without letting your personality interfere. Cooperation means to focus your energies, your forces, your thoughts and your emotions to make beauty work; to create more beauty; to create more goodness; to create more truth. It is the vision that pulls you up into cooperation.

1. Agni Yoga Society, *Letters of Helena Roerich*, Volume I, page 28.
2. Agni Yoga Society, *Community*, para. 156.
3. Agni Yoga Society, *Brotherhood*, para. 583.
4. Agni Yoga Society, *Agni Yoga*, para. 331.
5. Agni Yoga Society, *Aum*, para. 587.
6. Agni Yoga Society, *Agni Yoga*, para. 132.

7. Agni Yoga Society, *Community,* para. 153.
8. *Ibid.,* para. 220.
9. Agni Yoga Society, *Agni Yoga,* para. 310.
10. Agni Yoga Society, *Fiery World,* Volume III, para. 35.
11. Agni Yoga Society, *Aum,* para. 510.
12. Agni Yoga Society, *Infinity,* Volume II, para. 399.
13. Agni Yoga Society, *Agni Yoga,* para. 649.
14. *Ibid.,* para. 107.
15. Agni Yoga Society, *Fiery World,* Volume III, para. 52.

CHAPTER 6

THE FIRE OF AGNI YOGA

The Sun that we see is the densest point of the true Spiritual Sun which ensouls the entire solar system, penetrating into each form and each atom. All that exists in the solar system is parts of the body of the Central Spiritual Sun, as all our organs and parts of the body form one unified mechanism.

We have the visible Sun, which is the focus of the energy flow. We have the Heart of the Sun, which provides energy, not only for the outer manifestation through the visible Sun, but also for all subtle formations on higher planes.

The visible Sun provides activity and motion in the physical, emotional and mental planes. The Heart of the Sun provides the sensitivity which makes possible all communication, transmutation, metabolism, photokinesis and expansion of relationship. The Central Spiritual Sun provides and evokes the willpower, which creates harmony, symphony, synthesis and the urge for perfection.

The visible Sun controls the personality of the advanced person. The Heart of the Sun is the Soul nature in Solar manifestation. The Central Spiritual Sun is the Self in advanced units within the solar system. Thus all is the manifestation of the threefold Sun, a unity in trinity.

Any change and any motion in the Sun are instantaneously registered in the hearts of all forms, whether the form is conscious or unconscious. As the differen-

57

tiated or individualized units advance on the path of their evolution and initiation, they gradually register more and more of the influence of the Sun and grow toward the Sun. As they register the pulsation of the Heart of the Sun, they become aspirants and disciples who act as condensers and transmitters of heart energy or Solar wisdom to the lower units. As they register the inspiration of the Central Spiritual Sun, they become advanced Initiates who cooperate with the Sun, the Source.

Once a person is sensitive to the Central Spiritual Sun, he lives, moves and has his being in the Will of that Great Life. Such a person is a direct outpost of Divine light, love and power. In Eastern phraseology, he is called an *Agni Yogi,* a person unified in fire. This fire, which is the essence of man, can be used:

to heal
to radiate light
to radiate love
to radiate power

All this can be accomplished by a technique of yoga called *Agni Yoga.* Yoga means:

1. harmony with the highest principles
2. concentration
3. unity
4. expression of essence
5. fusion
6. purification
7. synthesis

Agni Yoga means to bring your Inner Essence into expression, to bring your Inner Fire of spiritual electricity into expression through these seven qualities.

1. *Living a life in harmony with the highest principles* or standards within you. The expressions of the highest principles are simplicity, synthesis, beauty, truth and sacrifice. As you express these virtues, you harmonize your life with the symphony of the inner radiation of the essential Fire. As your life is harmonized, the Fire flows through your actions, emotions, thoughts and speech.

2. *Concentration* means to have a goal and totally

dedicate yourself to that goal, no matter what. By concentrating yourself on a spiritual goal, you bring yourself into alignment with the Inner Fire and form a channel of expression for it.

3. *Unity* means to act, to feel, and to think as if you are one with the Existence, without any line of separation. All life must be dedicated to unity in all departments of human endeavor. Only through a unified consciousness can the Fire manifest without the danger of destruction.

4. *Expression of essence* means to live a life of purity on all levels, a life of synthesis on all levels, a life of illumination on all levels, and a life of revelation on all levels. It means to strive to manifest these four qualities of your essence through all your efforts. As you express these qualities, the Inner Fire fuses with your vehicles, synthesizes them into a whole, and galvanizes them into the light. Then you pass through an experience of transfiguration, which is the result of the release of Fire.

5. *Fusion* means to submit your personal, separative, ignorant will to the will of your Inner Essence. Any time you feel you are doing something wrong, do not do it, because it will prevent you from fusing yourself with your true Self. Any deviation from your true Self is an act which leads you into isolation and weakness. In fusion, you let the spiritual power flow through all that you do on all levels.

6. *Purification* means to remove all obstacles in your threefold personality that hinder the flow of electrical fire — such as glamor, inertia, illusions, and impurity of thought, emotion, or action. Through purification you unify yourself; you unify your personality with the Fire. You know that no welding can be done without first cleaning the metal. No transmutation is possible without purification through Fire.

7. *Synthesis.* To synthesize means to create harmony and unity; to bring different elements into harmony through their real essence; to make yourself a living part of Creation; to know that nothing is separate from the Whole; to know that all that exists is one

unit; to see unity in all diversities.

An Agni Yogi is a person who unifies himself with the whole, with the essence of all. Because he is truly unified with Fire, he radiates Fire: will, purpose, energy, joy, and bliss. An Agni Yogi is a living fountain of beauty and creativity. Because of such people, life progresses and beauty is manifested.

Agni Yoga is divided into three stages.

1. The first stage is the stage of "becoming yourself," in which you try to contact your own Inner Self, gradually changing your level of consciousness from the physical, to the emotional, to the mental level; then to the Intuitional, Atmic, and Monadic Planes, until you make contact with your Innermost Self. When you contact the Self, you become the Self.

2. The second stage is union with the Self in every human being. The union with the Selves in others is possible only after you unite within yourself and become your Self. In this stage, you become a totally sacrificial and compassionate person; you live in such a way that there is no difference between you and others.

3. The third stage is unity with the Self of the universe. This Self is latent in every form in the universe, from the mineral and vegetable kingdoms to the solar systems, galaxies, and zodiacs. This is the stage where Cosmic consciousness starts.

This is the path, and we are told that every sincere student and dedicated worker must travel it. It is a very hard path, and its whole unfoldment is nothing else but *yogism*.

Yogism is unity with the Spirit within your Self, unity with the Spirit within other Selves, and unity with the Spirit of Cosmos. All development and all knowingness is a process of at-one-ment, integration, alignment, and fusion with the Divinity within you, within others, and within the universe.

In Agni Yoga or the Yoga of Fire, the fiery Spark travels to the Source of Fire in cyclic, gradual identification with manifested Fires. How to release the Fire in man and in the planet? People have many methods to heal, to teach, to uplift, to organize and to lead; but all these methods may eventually lead to failure. There are things that integrate and heal the physical body, the emotional body and the mind, but they do not have lasting effects until the Central Fire is found and its energy — psychic energy — is released.

How can the *Agni* or Central Fire be released and integrate and align the personality, the Soul and the Spirit? The first step is to release the fire of destruction and clean all that cannot resist the fire. You must use the destructive fire to clean:

habits
glamors
illusions
laziness
uncontrolled speech
negative emotions
thoughts based on hatred, lies, untruth or ego

Then you must live a sacrificial life. A sacrificial life is a life that is dedicated to the welfare of nations and all humanity.

The second step is construction, thinking in terms of wholeness and unity. The third step is transfiguration of your physical, emotional and mental nature; your life, your city, your country and the world. As human beings create unity and harmony, the greater centers will unite and the world will turn into a symphony. This is the object of Agni Yoga.

Agni Yoga has high standards, which we call virtues and spiritual achievements. Agni Yoga is not yoga through which you accumulate knowledge, but a yoga through which you live according to standards and to your vision of achievements.

To evaluate anything in the world, you must have standards and needs. A standard is not a need; a standard is a value which you agree with. A need is a requirement, a necessity in any part of your being. When you have a need, you must discriminate and evaluate things that can meet your need. You evaluate things according to their qualities and behind this evaluation must exist your standard.

We say, "These books are good because they deal
with the subject in which I am interested. These other
books do not appeal to me because they do not deal
with the subject in which I am interested." There is
also another attitude in which we have books on the
same subject and some of them meet our standards
while others do not. We appreciate only those books
which meet our standards. Our standards are conditioned by our beliefs, our traditions, our education and
even by our glamors and illusions.

Standards are also found on different levels. We
have our personal standards; we have national standards, global standards, or spiritual standards. At first
we use our personal standards, but as we progress on
the path of our evolution, we use the standards of
greater and greater wholes. This is what makes a person great. Personal standards are limited in their
scope of vision, but standards of greater wholes require
greater unfoldment and greater understanding.

In each person, there is a real standard and a false
standard. Real standards are the result of our experience, discrimination, analysis, research, compassion,
and broad, selfless viewpoints. False standards are
based on prejudice, superstitions, selfishness, separativeness, ignorance and negative emotions. It is the
conflict between these two standards that creates
great tension within ourselves and in society.

A person may also have true standards but live by
the false standards of others and thus create eventual
self-defeat. Appreciation is an act of recognition of
values which not only meet your true standards but
evoke a higher value from you.

Real standards slowly emerge as we progress on
the path of becoming our true Selves. On the personality level, most of our standards are related to our personality, to our physical, emotional and mental nature.
Even if we have higher standards, on this level they
are used by the lower standards. On the transpersonal
level, the true standards appear and we try to apply
them in all our relationships and expressions. But it is
on the spiritual levels, within the field of the Spiritual

Triad, that for the first time we realize that the real standard is the human Spark, the Self — Who is the measure of all things.

The type of the ray of the Self does not have any effect on the standard, but it has an effect on the way the Self expresses Himself. But no matter through what ray the Self expresses Himself, in all His expressions the standard remains pure.[1]

Initiation is a process of coming closer to the deeper standards in the human being. Initiation is a process of leaving false standards behind and fusing your consciousness with true standards. After the Third Initiation, you gradually turn toward becoming the standard itself.

This is why an initiate is an independent, free, self-determined, and self-actualized person. He acts according to what he is in his highest nature. His standards are not distorted reflections of higher standards, but extensions of the light of the same standards dimmed according to the capacity of the level. He evaluates and appreciates what other people do on their own level. He does not impose his standards on others because higher standards cannot be unconsciously applied on lower levels. He uses the method of inspiration and challenges people to strive, to be creative, and to gradually change their level. An initiate knows how to inspire people toward higher standards, by presenting standards that can be applied on their own level.

It is very interesting that things are tested in fire to prove their worth. There are three fires on three levels: personality fire, transpersonal fire, and spiritual fire. Each lower fire leads to the higher one, once it is directed to higher values.

Man uses these three fires as his standards on three levels. Initiations are a process in which the contacted fire burns the false standards and establishes a true standard of values.

On the highest level, the electrical or spiritual fire burns not only all false values but the mechanism of the false self. The spiritual fire acts as a magnet for the consciousness. As the consciousness is drawn toward the spiritual fire, the person passes through a severe experience of detachment. The light on higher planes reveals greater values, in whose beauty the former values fade away.

Personality values are subordinated to Soul values when the consciousness is drawn up or lifted up to the Soul levels. In the same manner, Soul values are subordinated to Triadal values when man's awareness begins to function there. As the human consciousness is raised from plane to plane by the magnetic power of electric fire, the individual passes through experiences of detachment, not only from individual values, but from national, global, and solar values. Thus he focuses on higher and higher planes, detaching himself from the values of the lower planes.

Yoga is the process of unification. The real essence of man is scattered in various planes and caught in many glamors, illusions, posthypnotic suggestions, and false "I"s. The scattered Self must recollect Himself, focus Himself, and attain continuity in His wholeness.

In ancient times we were told: "Man, know thyself." In the new age we are told: "Man, be thyself." This is the real yoga.

---

1. See Chapter VI, "The Rays and the Human Soul," in *Cosmos in Man*, by T. Saraydarian.

CHAPTER 7

AGNI YOGA AND LIFE

Those seeking to be Agni Yogis should take periodic retreats away from all outside influences. These influences include television, friends, family and routine work. A retreat should be a time of seclusion so that an inner tension may be achieved.

The purpose of a retreat is to intensify the spiritual focus upon the personality. The Soul intensifies Its focus upon the personality so that the personality becomes flooded with the Soul's purpose, plan and intention.

One of the techniques of the dark forces is to prevent you from being alone with yourself. Many people are influenced by such attacks. They hurry from one place to another, from one person to another, keeping company with others or killing time with certain amusements. Such people are afraid of being alone. They feel lonely and depressed if by chance they find themselves alone. Some people even try to ignore their self in order to escape the judgment of the Self.

Those who want to be Agni Yogis must cultivate the spirit of loneliness. They must feel happy, joyful, and more creative during the times when they are alone because in lonely moments one has a greater chance to meet his Self, to utilize his time creatively, to contemplate his future and to see himself as he is. One can also meet himself in a great danger or in a great ecstasy; but why wait for such moments when one can easily and naturally meet his Self by exercising daily a period of total retreat?

At the beginning, it is not easy to use such a time creatively and immediately have contact with one's true Self. But by striving, during retreat one eventually rejects the daydreaming tendency of the mind, the pleasure-seeking imagination of the emotions and the laziness of the body. Each retreat must be used as a time of healthy introspection, creativity and planning for new changes. Loneliness conceives future heroes and great talents.

A time of retreat is required to create a channel between the Higher Self and the personality. Eventually, this channel carries the flow of future visions and creative spiritual forces to the life of the personality.

In order to build this channel between your higher visions and your personality, a regular period of retreat is required. This may be a half-hour daily, a half or whole day weekly, one weekend a month, one week a year, or any other amount of time which is possible to be set aside for reflective meditation. In this manner, you build the channel through which you will flood the physical, emotional and mental nature with spiritual intention and energy. A focus of incoming energies will fuse, master, beautify and transform the personality into a blossoming of creative endeavor for the Hierarchy.

What is the Hierarchy? Many teachings mention the Hierarchy and It is simply:

the Christ and His disciples.

the Christ and the Invisible or Victorious Church.

the Christ and the Masters.

The term "Masters" means those disciples who have mastered or conquered life.

During the time of your retreat, try to keep the theme of the retreat in your mind. Let's say that you have gone to the mountains for three days and you are going to study the Agni Yoga literature about becoming a fiery server. Whatever you do, keep the thought of "fiery service" in your mind. You may be physically walking or swimming, but mentally try to think about fiery service. If you keep this thought in your mind, new vision and insight will come.

Then try to bring the energies of your Soul into your daily, practical life. Before you go to sleep at night make a resume'of the highlights of the lessons or readings which you concentrated upon during the day and with these thoughts in your mind, go to sleep.

When you awaken in the morning, write down in your spiritual diary any experiences you had along this line while you were asleep. Did you feel that you had been in an Ashram? Was anyone talking to you about fiery service or other related matters? Were you explaining something to another person, or did you dream that you were giving a great lecture? Whatever it is, be sure to make a note of it.

By taking a retreat and seriously focusing our attention on a topic of study, we come closer to the Source of inspiration. This is how true progress is made upon the Path. The Source of inspiration can give us vision and direction for future accomplishments.

Agni Yoga is the ability to find your Innermost Self and impose His rhythm on the personality life. In Agni Yoga every cell in your constitution becomes fused with the purpose and frequency of the Self. Each of the other yogas works on just one of the bodies, but Agni Yoga makes you the conductor of the whole symphony. You become coordinated and fused in such a way that you act as a total being from a core of Divine Intent.

We say that Agni Yoga is the yoga of the future because the future is the manifestation of the Self. The physical, emotional and mental bodies are the past realization. The future is the realization and awareness of the Self. This will entail the mastery of the Self over the physical, emotional and mental bodies. The future is yogism, which is actualized after a firm decision to exercise the authority of the Self over the vehicles of expression.

Agni Yoga means to look at all life from the viewpoint of the future. The future will be imposed upon the present and the past, which means that it will be imposed upon the personality.

The real Self is the future. This future is going to project itself upon the physical, emotional and mental bodies so that the personality becomes one with the future vision.

In the life of the Agni Yogi, there is no indecision or wavering between choices. The Agni Yogi never makes up his mind to do one thing and then reconsiders because "on the other hand. . . ." He saves himself much time, energy, agony and trouble because his yes is *yes* and his no is really *no*. This is the real implication of Self-mastery.

The lower bodies are mechanical: when a rhythm is exerted upon them, they gradually synchronize with each other. Before the Self can exert His rhythm upon the lower bodies, you must go through many phases of purification, in order to use the bodies for your higher visions and dreams. There are elementals which control the physical, emotional and mental bodies. These elementals want to have a master who tells them what to do. They are craving for a willpower to obey. When they see that there is no willpower, they become like dogs with no master and do anything they want. But when you show them that there is a strong willpower, they say, "Yes, sir," and they do whatever you tell them to do.

Your elementals want to obey you because they already agreed to do it. That is why they came and formed your body. Instinctively they know that their only salvation is to obey you. How are they going to survive if they do not obey you? They will obey you just like faithful and loving servants if you impose your will upon them.

I knew a dog trainer who said that he trained dog owners and not dogs. When I asked him to explain, he called a nice dog over to us. He said, "Lie down," in a sweet voice. The dog just sat there panting. Then he told the dog to lie down in a confused tone. The dog went and started to play with a ball because that was what he wanted to do. Then the master became very stern and said in a commanding voice, "Come here and lie down!" The dog ran to the trainer and lay down immediately. When the master meant what he said, the dog obeyed.

It is the same with the elementals: when you mean what you say, the body, emotions or mind will do what you say. If you mean it only twenty percent, they will obey only twenty percent. The elemental will say, "He is playing with me, so I will play with him." When you give halfway orders, you get halfway responses.

Let's say that you want to quit smoking. You take your cigarette and make a big production out of stamping it out, but in your heart you still really love that cigarette. You will never quit smoking because you do not really want to quit. When you really mean what you decide, your physical entity will not oppose you. There will be no opposition to your will and you will become a nonsmoker. This is Agni Yoga because it comes from the Self. The elemental knows that its salvation is to obey the Self.

Every great decision is followed by immediate change because there is no opposition to it. But when you are half-attached and half-Self, none of your decisions will be effective because you are divided within yourself. This is why M.M. tells us to stay away from flickering lights or lukewarm people. Lukewarm people are those who are mixed: they are part Self and part physical, emotional or mental bodies. They are not in control of themselves and they cannot be effective influences in the world, because they don't have faith in themselves and the little faith they have is mixed with the desires of the various elementals.

Sometimes it happens that the body is in opposition to the will of the elemental, but this happens only in the case of sickness. The elemental never gets sick, but the body does. There is a problem in the body because something is out of order and is not following the plan for the body. Sickness is abnormal and results in degeneration.

We say that humanity as a body is sick right now because it is not following the Divine Plan. If humanity were healed, it would function as a beautiful symphony, expressing love through sharing and right relations.

Some people are awakening to a greater reality: they are discovering that their bodies are like garments which can be taken off. They are realizing that they can consciously withdraw from the body and have continuity of consciousness. This awareness leads to the understanding that we are not the bodies.

This disidentification with matter will kill the six monsters which threaten the survival of the human family: fear, hatred, jealousy, anger, revenge and greed. If a group of people can come to this awareness, they will be like Masters to humanity and will be able to lead their brothers into right living and sane thinking.

How will Agni Yoga help to accomplish this? Agni Yoga leads to the Self and the Self is the Fire within each atom, cell and person. Agni Yoga teaches us how to release this Fire and join with the Self of the universe. The Self, the awareness unit, must release Himself from the physical, emotional and mental atoms so that He becomes a unified field of fire. Here again we can see that real yoga moves from the higher to the lower bodies.

Let's say that you are a highly advanced person, a real Self. Everything that you do and say will be united with the Fire of the universe and will awaken the Fire within others. When the Fire is awakened in others, they become one with you and with all those who are releasing their Divinity. There is no separation; they are part of the unbroken circle.

This applies to individuals, to groups, to humanity and to Cosmos. There are higher beings who are trying to release the Fire in us so that we may graduate into a higher spiral of evolution. Someone in the galaxy is trying to help us and we are trying to help the kingdoms below us. We are all like cogs in a big machine: each has its function and the health of the whole is related to the health of the parts. All of Cosmos is related. The Fire of Cosmos is the same in all.

In the Agni Yoga Teaching, we read:

Maitreya wishes to hasten all. Maitreya wishes that all should be successfully accomplished. Maitreya wishes you joy. Maitreya wishes to grant to humanity the gift of the fiery experience of Agni Yoga. Maitreya wishes to transmute life on Earth, in the radiance of the Mother of the World. Yes, yes, yes! The beauty of life is limitless!
An Arhat sees with the eyes of the heart. An Arhat sees with the eyes of the heart the beauty of reality. An Arhat sees with the eyes of the heart, and the essence of the future calls Us. Verily is that creativeness affirmed by Us.[1]

"Maitreya wishes to hasten all." According to the esoteric Teaching, our planet is late on the path of its evolution. It is necessary to hasten our steps on the path, if we want to eventually be graduated from the school of the planetary experience instead of falling into the labyrinth of a life of pain and suffering.

"Maitreya wishes that all should be successfully accomplished." The accomplishment of the seed latent in every individual will be to become a flower and fruit. In every person there is a plan, put there at the moment of individualization and this gradually must manifest in its totality. This is the responsibility given to each person and this responsibility must be successfully accomplished.

As a builder watches all the workers accomplishing their individual plans for the whole building, so Maitreya watches everyone so that they hasten in their jobs and bring them into culmination and the whole building reaches completion.

"Maitreya wishes you joy" because He knows that when one hastens his steps on the path of his spiritual evolution and brings into completion the duties and responsibilities entrusted to him, he transcends pain and suffering and lives in joy. Joy is a state of being-ness in which the human soul builds an uninterrupted communication with the harmony of the Higher Worlds and radiates beauty and peace toward the world.

"Maitreya wishes to grant to humanity the gift of the fiery experience of Agni Yoga." In the Himalayas or in India, Christ is called Maitreya. It is Christ Who released the Teaching of the Fiery Union, or the Teaching of unity through spiritual fire. It is this unifying, uplifting, transforming fire that will bring human beings together and inspire them for cooperation and synthesis.

The Agni Yoga Teaching has been given since 1922 and at the present it is translated into more than ten languages. In their present form, the Agni Yoga books are a treasury of wisdom which has no parallel in the esoteric literature of the world. This gift must be read, assimilated and lived so that, equipped with fire, we meet the needs of the coming age of Maitreya, the Age of Christ.

"Maitreya wishes to transform life on Earth, in the radiance of the Mother of the World." The feminine principle must be put into action in order to balance the affairs of the world. The feminine principle is love-wisdom, compassion, care for Nature, care for every human being. The feminine principle is the mother principle. If world affairs are handled with the feelings of a mother, the children of the world will be safer and guided and life will not be the same. A mother will not encourage her children to annihilate each other. She will want them to cooperate, live together and enjoy life.

"Yes, yes, yes. The beauty of life is limitless." The Agni Yoga Teaching sees limitless beauty everywhere, on earth and in space. It is this beauty that must challenge us to strive toward perfection. Agni Yoga stands for beauty. It says:

> Repeat Beauty again and again, even with tears, until you reach your destiny.[2]

Agni Yoga believes that it is through beauty that one can go beyond his limitations.

"An Arhat sees with the eyes of the heart." An Arhat is one who lives in intuitional awareness. He

sees things in a holistic light, in inclusive understanding and compassion. He sees things from the standpoint of One Life. He sees "the beauty of reality," not through logic, reason or mind, but through the heart. He feels and senses reality; he lives in reality. He lives the beauty of reality as a part of the beauty of Cosmos.

"...*and the essence of the future calls Us. Verily is that creativity affirmed by Us.*" The call of the essence of the future is the cause of all creativity going on in the Cosmos. The central *Cause,* which in religion is called the Father or the Purpose or the Will, is calling its Sparks back from the world of unreality to the world of Reality. Affirmation of the Cosmic creativeness is the progressive steps of the Sparks striving toward the future. The future is the highest achievement, the end of which cannot be perceived by mortal beings.

The Cosmic Heart is the central organ in the galaxy, Which controls the life currents of all life forms existing within the galaxy. Just as your heart pumps energy and blood to every cell in your body, the Cosmic Heart sustains the energy system in Its body. If there is a living organism, it must have a heart or the equivalent of a heart. The system must receive its energy from someplace. We call this center, the heart. All hearts are linked together throughout the galaxy.

Agni Yoga sometimes calls the Cosmic Heart, the Cosmic Magnet. It pulls hearts which are sympathetic to It into the stream of Its beneficent love. When we join with the Cosmic Heart, we release the Spark imprisoned and enslaved in the physical, emotional and mental bodies.

In *The Secret Doctrine,* we read that the intention of an atom is to be a man and the intention of a man is to be a god. How does this happen?

Once upon a time you were a little Spark in an atom. You worked and struggled with matter until you were released. Throughout ages you have been releasing the Spark within you into greater and greater flames. You are going to go from flame to flame, until you become the Self that you have been striving to actualize.

It is interesting to think about man's relation with fire. When the fire in matter was released or discovered, it brought a great change in our lives. Then we found electricity and through electricity a new civilization came into being. Now we are using laser beams. We are harnessing the fire of the Sun; and very soon we will discover the most powerful fire latent in the heart of every man. This is the fire which is used by Great Ones as a means of creativity, construction, destruction, healing and purification; as a means of Self-actualization and at-one-ment with spatial fires.

Agni Yoga is the Teaching of how to discover and utilize this fire which is the essence of man. Once this fire is released, man will never misuse other fires and fire will unify and synthesize all.

The Great Teacher of Agni Yoga emphasizes the need for equilibrium and balance. Equilibrium and balance are sometimes considered as states of inertia; whereas the true meaning of equilibrium is a steady balance in ever-progressive states of beingness and in ever-changing conditions.

Progress always begins by breaking the equilibrium gained upon a certain level of achievement. In this transitory state, balance is lost until the new level is achieved and equilibrium between the new conditions and the advancing human soul is established.

Equilibrium and balance are achieved through the instrumentality of the Fire of the heart. Balance is related to the conditions of the mechanism which carries the Fire, the Self. Equilibrium is related to the relationship between the Fire of the heart and the Fires of Space.

As the bodies keep their balance in advancing conditions, the fire reaches new levels of equilibrium with the Fires of Space. Equilibrium is that state of the Fire of the heart in which it can surf upon the Fires of Space without losing its direction.

Equilibrium is achieved when the vehicles of fire have enough balance to allow the Fire of the heart to communicate with the Fires of Space without losing its equilibrium. Equilibrium is established when the intake of Spatial Fire is equal to the creative activity of the Inner Fire.

Thus creativity is a process of maintaining equilibrium and in the meantime advancing the equilibrium on still higher levels by allowing the Inner Fire to absorb and assimilate more of the Fires of Space. This is why the ancients considered creativity a fiery labor.

Equilibrium must be achieved in our thinking, words, and actions. Higher equilibrium cannot be achieved until there is balance in our daily life. This is very close to what Christ meant when He said that whoever is faithful in small things will be faithful in greater things also. If you lie ten times daily, your mouth will never be able to contain the truth. If you are responsible in the smallest details of your job, you will be responsible in the large areas also. If you can be trusted with the smallest of secrets, then you can be trusted to hold your mouth with top-secret information.

M.M. says to train and test people. If they do small tasks with their whole heart and without complaining, they can be entrusted with greater responsibilities. But don't give them greater jobs until you have tested the quality of their hearts.

When I was in the army during World War II, two men were sent to our office and I was told to promote one of them to sergeant. The commander asked me to do it, and I chose one of them. The commander was really surprised at my selection, since the one I chose was not as impressive-looking as the other.

He asked me how I had made my decision. I told him to look at the shoes of both of the men. The impressive one had some dirt on his shoes, and one of the laces was untied. He was not faithful to the image of being a soldier in small things, so I did not expect him to be faithful in greater things. As it turned out, he was a very bad soldier, and we would have been in real trouble if we had given him any authority.

We can apply this method to other things also. For example, if someone opens his mouth and says something very ugly or nasty, record it. There is a leakage somewhere in his aura and energy is escaping. Even though he may later apologize and say that he loves you, there is a leakage there and he is not in control. You don't know when he will betray his love again. Being sorry doesn't mean that he is healed.

A friend of mine used this method in trying to select a secretary. He put an ad in the paper and about twenty girls responded. Each one had dressed really nicely and seemed to be qualified. But he did something sneaky by putting a little hairpin on the carpet. Only one of the applicants bothered to pick it up. She was the one he hired.

Thus the existence of balance and equilibrium can be observed in any situation, on any level. Try to create equilibrium by balancing your life and activities with your spiritual goals and intentions.

There are stages in our development and evolution which are called:

> animal stage
> animal-human stage
> human stage
> Man-God stage

Each stage is a stage of relative equilibrium between highest and lowest. Speaking about the fourth stage, the Teaching explains the deeper meanings of equilibrium and balance:

> *Much has been spoken about the Man-God, aspiring towards deification. Many are the memorable records, citing the Images striving towards higher worlds. But how dimly are they formulated in the human consciousness! Man-God is to man only One who departed to other worlds! But We Brothers of Humanity seek and proclaim Man-God upon Earth. We revere all Images, but none more than the great Image of Man-God who bears in his heart the full "chalice," ready for flight but bearing his full "chalice" on Earth. Renouncing his destiny, he strains his Fiery Being. In the fulfillment of his destiny man confirms the Cosmic Magnet. Man-God is a Fiery Creator. Man-God is*

the Carrier of the Fiery Sign of the New Race.
Man-God is flaming with all Fires. So inscribe in
the records about Man-God: Arhat, Agni Yogi,
Tara — so shall We inscribe.[3]

It is the destiny of man to release himself into
higher and higher realms of Creation, but the Man-
God renounced the process so that He could stay with
humanity. He wanted to help us by being the link
between the visible and invisible worlds. From the
standpoint of evolution, if we didn't have a Christ, a
Krishna, or a Buddha, we would be in chaotic darkness.

The Man-God stands as a link between the higher
and the lower, so that we may be brought into the path
of balance and equilibrium.

In the creativeness of an Arhat the heart
manifests that striving which is attested by the
Cosmic Magnet through the education of the striv-
ing combinations. The existing creative tension of
the striving heart of an Arhat is so aflame with the
fire of space! To bring about the manifestation of
the progress of evolution, to afford affirmed truth
and knowledge and to link humanity with the cur-
rents of evolution — this stimulus inspires each
move of an Arhat. This tension sets into motion all
feelings and subtle energies.
Thus acts the manifested Friend of humanity.
These spatial strivings are Our foundations of
cooperation. Similarly sustained are the centers of
the fiery Agni Yogi as a Friend of Humanity. Yes,
yes, yes! Thus We serve the progress of humanity.[4]

Striving is a steady expansion of beingness which
leads to identification with the Self.

In the book, *Hierarchy,* we are given the following
practical advice. It is good to emphasize the everyday
advice that we are given, since through it we can transform our lives:

One yogi won the reputation of being a great

wit, because he would unnoticeably rearrange var-
ious objects in the house. And when asked why, he
answered, "I am observing whether you have
become blind." Verily there are few who notice the
changes in their surroundings. But the first sign of
an "eagle-eye" is to notice the minutest changes,
since on them depends the vibration of the whole.[5]

These changes refer not only to the changes of the
location of objects, but also to changes in thinking,
feeling and acting. Those who are progressing on the
path of perfection must develop seeing eyes.

Observe how people change in the way they speak,
in the way they write, in the way they walk and in the
way they relate. These changes have reasons and
causes behind them. With outer changes try to notice
any change in your own body — the way you talk, the
way you write, the way you feel and think — and try to
find the causes and reasons for these changes.

When you see changes in others, you also see
changes within yourself. The whole idea of this verse
is to emphasize the importance of the seeing eyes and
of clear observation. For example, let's say that you
are driving your car and a noise develops which you do
not notice. The noise may be something which will
make you lose control of the steering wheel and have
an accident when you are going seventy miles per
hour. But if you notice the noise, you will be able to do
something about it to insure your safety.

If you notice the changes in others, you will be able
to calculate more accurately the potentials they have
and in what direction they are heading. Notice people's
expressions in different situations and you will know
the contents of their hearts. This is vitally important
for a leader of the future. You will really become a
leader of the heart.

Being an "eagle-eye" applies to politics also. Try not
to see everything from the viewpoint of personal interests. Withdraw from the personal level and watch
events from a detached point of view. Notice slight
changes in the financial picture, in international relations and in national concerns. Is there a change of

policy? What changing attitudes does it reflect? Who is responsible for the changes? Do these changes benefit the majority or just a small interest group?

This kind of observation is so important for a leader because when an organized group of people plans to destroy a nation, they begin with very slight changes and slowly introduce more. For example, slowly they raise the prices and soon you see that there are labor strikes all over the nation.

Notice the moves the government makes. Notice how it changes when the president, governor, or mayor changes. You will see that it is really different than before. You will be able to forecast the future better when you notice the present changes. The root of these changes is in the consciousness. By observing the changes you will not be stuck with them because you will detect the motivation behind them.

If people had observed the causes of pollution 100 years ago, the world would now be a better place to live. We must also try to observe signs that cause changes in our own behavior. For example, if humanity had been smart 200 years ago, we would have known that the Seventh Ray energy was coming into the planet. This energy stimulates sexual energy because it goes to the sacral center. Look at the changes in the world in the past 200 years and you will see the evidence of this energy.

The most important thing is to observe change. To look with an eagle-eye means to see the smallest details. An eagle can see the movement of a small field mouse for two or three miles. Like a rocket, he can swoop down and catch that little mouse. If you apply this type of attention to your business life, you will see how much improved your relations will be. One little thing that you notice in someone else's attitude, manner of expression, or appearance can be the thread that saves your life.

Agni Yoga is related to the entire life. Life as a whole must go through a process of transformation if we want to proceed toward our Cosmic destination.

1. Agni Yoga Society, *Hierarchy,* para. 8.
2. Agni Yoga Society, *Leaves of Morya's Garden,* Volume I, para. 252.
3. Agni Yoga Society, *Hierarchy,* para. 14.
4. *Ibid.,* para. 22.
5. *Ibid.,* para. 47.

CHAPTER 8

AGNI YOGA AND THE
REGENERATION OF THE WORLD

*The purification of religions predicates a new
direct relation with the spiritual world. Christ,
Buddha, and their closest coworkers did not use
magic formulae but acted and created in full
blending with the spirit. Therefore, in the new
evolution the former artificial methods must be
abandoned. Remember cause and effect. The mechanics of yogism are no longer suitable for the
regeneration of the world. . . .*[1]

When religions are purified from those elements
which hinder their beauty and effectiveness, then they
will form a bridge of direct contact with the spiritual
world. The purpose of religion is to create those means
through which man transcends himself and establishes communication with higher values, with greater
concepts, and with the Source of the spiritual life. The
words of Buddha and Christ are the direct Teaching of
how to establish such a contact and through this contact transform our lives and the lives of those with
whom we come in contact.

Agni Yoga is a direct approach to the spiritual
world without "the mechanics of yogism [which] are
no longer suitable for the regeneration of the world."
One of the main goals of religion is the regeneration of
the world. This can be possible if people build direct
contact with the spiritual world and renew and trans-

81

form their lives and the life of the world. This will not be possible if religions with "artificial methods" are accepted. It is not appropriate to indicate all these artificial methods, which are abundant in almost all religions. The followers of religions and their leaders must reach the state of consciousness where they see the need for the purification of religion and for making it a direct communication system with the Higher Worlds in man and in the universe.

There should be cyclic conferences in all religions to periodically eliminate all those elements which prevent closer fusion in humanity and closer communication with the spiritual values and transcendental states of consciousness. Thus religions will build a path of continuous elevation toward higher values and synthesis.

"Artificial methods" refer to asanas and to various physical yogic practices, which are both dangerous and outmoded. "Artificial methods" do not refer to those ceremonies and rituals which connect the human and angelic worlds. Every time there is a manifestation of creativity, there is a ritual. Every movement in the lower strata is actually a reflection of activities, movements, rhythms, colors and music orchestrated on higher levels. Creativity means to find the right combination for the translation of higher phenomena onto the lower planes of existence.

"Direct relation with the spiritual world" is not found in chanting, in Hatha Yoga, or in any common ritual. Direct relation with anything is found through the amount of energy you put into establishing and maintaining contact with it. Whatever you sow, you will reap; where there is a cause, there will be an effect. This is a scientific process which demonstrates that you manifest whatever you put your energy into.

You cannot buy the spiritual life, nor can you buy the Teaching. You must live the highest principles and study the Teaching, seeking a greater depth of understanding. In this manner, you will form electrical lines within yourself and build a bridge to Higher Worlds. You progress by the Law of Cause and Effect. When you serve and sacrifice in true humility, you will grow in awareness, creativity, and light.

The keyword in the above verse is "regeneration" —"for the regeneration of the world." This refers to the regeneration of religions, governments, financial systems, legal practices, and the spiritual approach. M.M. is speaking of the regeneration of the methods by which human beings approach life and participate in it. For this reason, humanity must approach things from a new viewpoint. Superstition must be replaced with scientific fact; prejudice, hatred and separative thinking must be replaced with the principles of love and right human relations. Greed must be replaced with the beauty of sharing and cooperation.

The regeneration of religion is the key to the regeneration of the world. When people put meaning into their lives through sound spiritual striving, the affairs of human beings will change. The present method of paying a quarter to light a candle and beg for forgiveness after transgressing against the rights of others is leading us around and around on the same donkey trail.

When churches really demonstrate the example of the lives of their originators and encourage their members on the path of perfection, we will see the regeneration of the world through the regeneration of religion. Children will be raised in a true spirit of respecting the essential Divinity in all manifestation. Children will know the value of life and deeply feel the wonder of God's creation. They will feel the responsibility to protect what is worthy and smite that which is evil and against the good of the whole.

When M.M. speaks about the "mechanics of yogism" as "no longer suitable for the regeneration of the world," He does not include Agni Yoga in this statement. Agni Yoga is the process of total unity, of becoming oneself, of becoming fire. As a little Spark of God, each of us seeks union with fire, and Agni Yoga is the term that we use to name this process of becoming fiery.

In the Bible, we are told that God is a burning fire.

When you are becoming your Self, you are actualizing the God-fire, the Divinity within you. When you become God-fire, everything that is unworthy, separative and personal is burned away. When the process of purification by fire is complete, you are an Agni Yogi, a *unified one*. You are one with the whole Creation.

M.M. speaks of co-workers of Christ and Buddha. These are Agni Yogis who have passed the Third Initiation and are serving for the regeneration of life.

The life of an Agni Yogi is the life of labor for the Plan of God. An Agni Yogi is a co-worker of God. None of his plans are personal, but he is a person of great plans. The Agni Yogi is a person of tremendous vision who is constantly working and adjusting his plan to the surrounding conditions, so that the great Plan for which he labors is manifested. His life is a reflection of the great Plan; his life is a piece in God's puzzle.

As you advance on the spiral of evolution, you become united with your Self and with the essential Divinity in all manifestation, but you do not lose your individuality. You manifest the Self in you, but you still maintain your own private existence.

> . . . *Having Infinity before one, yet not losing an hour and valuing the use of each minute — is Yogism. . . .*[2]

Here a very subtle beauty about the creative principle is revealed. The present and Infinity are one reality; they are joined in the mind of the Creator. Yogism is unity with this principle. The activity and value of the present are determined by its worth in Infinity. The Agni Yogi works for that which is timeless.

Working for Infinity is the hardest thing for the average person. He wants his rewards now so that he may consume them for his pleasures, because he is tied to the moment and cannot see beyond today. He is not a conscious builder of Cosmos, and he is not a co-worker of Great Ones, Who seek to manifest the Divine Plan and Purpose. (When we speak about the Plan, we refer to the vision of Christ. He expressed a part of this vision in His Teaching; the rest He formulated in His soul but did not pass to His disciples at the time He was with them.)

On the other hand, the Agni Yogi is awed by the Infinite. He is inflamed by the vision of perfection, which waits only for the actualization of its full potential. Knowing this, the Agni Yogi does not waste one second. Every second for him is an opportunity for expansion and expression.

The average person is overwhelmed by the Infinite because he feels his own limitations and that he will never be able to overcome them. He gives up, and he satiates his present appetites.

The Agni Yogi, being identified with his Divinity, does not become tied to the limitations of the present. He simply sees them as steps on the path to perfection. He does not become discouraged by the challenge of the vision because his heart responds to the call of glory. For him, limitations are not defeating obstacles; they are merely rough places in the marble which must be smoothed before the sculpture is complete.

When I was nine years old, my father taught me a very good method of overcoming discouragement. One beautiful spring day he said, "We are going for a hike."

"Daddy, where are we going?" I asked in excitement.

"To the top of the mountain," he said.

From the bottom I thought that it would be an easy mountain to master, so I started running up the path. But halfway up my feet were sore, my legs hurt, and I was very thirsty. "This mountain is too big," I said. "Let's go back."

My father said, "We can rest for a minute. Look back. See how far we have come in this short time. We are not in the valley any more." We had walked about six miles and fairly far up the side of the mountain.

Suddenly I drew a deep breath and gained more courage from what I had already accomplished. I thought that if I could do that in one morning, then I could go the rest of the way in just a few hours.

My accomplishment gave me the strength to continue. I was so happy when we got to the top of the mountain. It was a real victory for me and I often remember that morning when I was ready to quit walking. If the same happens to you, just sit for a minute and quietly look back to where you were when you began. You will see real progress and it will give you the courage to continue.

An Agni Yogi does not waste one second because he is firm in his faith of future achievement. Even if everything around him is falling apart, he believes in his heart that all will be well. He knows that the power of one Agni Yogi can save the world. He can see the construction after the destruction. He knows the destiny of manifestation is greater life, so he does not become defeated by temporary setbacks.

The greatest disciples are those who do not abandon the battlefield. They are people who do not give up because of momentary failure, wrong decisions, or other people's criticism and gossip. They rise up from their defeats like phoenixes — recharged and ready for another day on the path of Eternity. Great disciples face any and all dangers with the Fire of Enthusiasm. They are prepared to sacrifice everything, even their lives, for the victory of Beauty, Goodness and Truth.

This is the life of the disciple. He fights the darkness because he knows that it will destroy him if it is not dispelled.

Some people say that they have all eternity to work out their salvation and they use this as an excuse to wallow in pleasures now. They feel that the future will take care of the mess they are creating now. They don't realize that they will have to clean their own mess in the future. They don't care about air pollution now and they don't consider that they may not have air to breathe tomorrow. They never consider the adaptations that the body has to make in order to live in bad air. Such people do not understand the damage they are doing to their permanent atoms, which will bring them much pain and suffering in the future.

The disciple does not use the limitlessness of Infinity as an excuse to dance while the building is burning.

The disciple does not care about those things which are tied to the finite. He knows that desire is tied to the finite. If you give a man a thousand dollars, he will soon want a million. The disciple sees attachments to the finite world as a rejection of his Divinity, and he lives only for the Divine Manifestation. He does not betray his own Divinity by identification with limitations.

The disciple may be made the king of this planet, but he will not lose himself in his greatness. He will look to the heavens and wonder at the beauty of the stars. He will not die in the grave of this limited world because he seeks to explore his Infinite Self in the mystery of the Infinite. He sees himself as an expanding point of light in an ocean of light. He gives birth to himself with each new penetration into the Cosmic Space which surrounds him. He goes deeper and deeper into Space and unifies with it. The disciple becomes immortal through his quest for reality, the limitless Beauty which *is*.

The Bhagavad Gita says that God pervaded Space with a fragment of Himself. Can you imagine that all existence is just a fragment of one great Being? This is Infinity.

> . . . *Pupils should rejoice at every message.*
> *Contemplate the spiritual guidance of One Teacher.*
> *Thy spirit presses onward —*
> *At the Gates I shall await thee.*
> *My Breath shall warm thy hands, and I shall guide thee along the mountain path to the Temple.*
> *Love Me and thy power will be multiplied and thy strength doubled.*
> *Thy spirit transports thy body beyond the earth.*
> *Thou must rejoice in the ascension through pure teachings.*[3]

"... *Pupils should rejoice at every message.*" There are messages in every event, if we hear them or see them. Once we hear or see the message, we feel that we are *guided*. This gives us a deep joy. There are also other messages that come from Space, from your own Master, or from your Soul. We must "rejoice at every message" because it connects us with Higher Worlds.

"*Contemplate the spiritual guidance of One Teacher. Thy spirit presses onward.*" Contemplation is a process of unification with guidance and with the One Teacher. The One Teacher is the source of all light and wisdom.

"*At the Gates I shall await thee.*" Gates are those openings within the planes of our consciousness which are entered every time we take an initiation or expand our consciousness and become aware of a higher reality. The Teacher will meet you on every step of your achievement, to encourage you, to charge you, and to give you a new vision. As you ascend, you will feel the cold of higher states of awareness, as if you are climbing a mountain. This cold is the cold of renunciation, loneliness, and awareness of all that is going on in the world. But His "Breath shall warm thy hands," so that you receive inspiration and power to dare and strive toward the Temple — which can be the vision of your achievement or the stronghold where the Great One guides the destiny of humanity.

"*Love Me and thy power will be multiplied and thy strength doubled.*" In loving the Teacher, you follow His path; you serve His purpose; you receive energy because love unites you with Him.

"*Thy spirit transports thy body beyond the earth.*" As our spirit is elevated and purified, our whole nature goes through a process of transfiguration and becomes sensitive to impressions coming from higher sources. Eventually the material body is spiritualized.

The pure Teaching is the Teaching of unity with the highest, and as you elevate yourself you will find greater resources of joy.

When you are on the path of continuous progress, you must have devotion and love. It is impossible to ascend without these qualities. They are the fire which keeps your being aspiring onward and upward to greater achievement and unity.

Love in this context is the response to the magnetic pull of the One Self. You love Infinity, and you strive to become one with the Infinite Self.

Devotion needs detachment. Devotion encourages you to strive for the object of your love while you drop all those activities, interests, and habits which separate you from achieving oneness with your Beloved. Devotion focuses you in the fire of your love.

> *Love thy Spiritual Teacher.*
> *Thy destiny is to bring the inextinguishable Light*
> *to ardent hearts. . . .*[4]

Your Teacher is a bridge between you and Higher Ones. You must likewise be a bridge between your Teacher and lower ones, until the bridge is completed between the two extremes. You must take your place on the ladder of Infinity and try to advance a level by elevating those under you. You will progress through your service.

When you love your Spiritual Teacher, you see His vision and respond to it to the best of your ability. You seek to serve Him in His effort to actualize His vision, and you are very careful not to create any obstacles on His path. You seek to make your path an extension of His. The most important thing is not to become discouraged when you compare yourself with Him. Don't lose your Divinity by identification with your failures and weak points. Move forward with the faith that you will overcome all troubles and make your life a true value in the scheme of existence.

Remember that "thy destiny is to bring the inextinguishable Light to ardent hearts." You receive this Light from the wisdom of your Teacher's words, and it cannot be put out. It is inextinguishable, and it is your duty to put it in the hearts of others. One by one, you must find others who are devoted to Beauty, Goodness, and Truth and inflame their hearts with the vision of perfection which leads to unity with the Eternal Light.

Look upon yourself as a tree which is going to become a forest. You begin with just yourself and drop seeds into the surrounding ground. In 100 years there will be 50 strong trees by your side. In 500 years there will be a whole forest surrounding you. Just as each tree carries the genetic structure imprinted in it, each heart you reach will carry the light that you share with it. In this way, you increase the light in the world. This is how a great victory for light will be won.

> *A happy and blessed Guide is given to each one.*
> *Know to give thyself with all thy strength to Him alone;*
> *Else will the door be opened and the currents crossed.*
> *Invoke the blessed Guide not by question but by affirmation.*
> *If I shall send a message through your Guide, the current will be direct.*
> *Hearken not to those who approach during your apathy.*
> *The window open to the darkness brings the voices of the night.*
> *But the call of love will bring the answer from the Beloved.*
> *Love Those Who have chosen thee.*
> *Realize the ties which bind thee to thy Guide and naught unworthy will approach thee.*
> *Love! Discern! Strike evil! My Blessings be with thee.*[5]

When M.M. speaks about the Guide, He speaks about a responsibility and not an office. Your guide is the one who takes the responsibility for your spiritual direction. A guide is not necessarily a person who holds a position with degrees and recognition for status earned. You may have a human being as your guide, or you may be guided by your Solar Angel. When you advance a little more, your Master guides you. . . . We all have guides, but they are in relation to our level. Similarly, we all have the potential to be a guide in our own right.

To understand the first four lines of this verse, let's look for a real-life situation as an explanation. Affirmation is intuitive agreement, intuitive verification. If the Inner Guide tells you to go into a dark room and wait for a stranger, don't question him. Just say, "Yes, sir," and know that you will be protected. Don't worry about yourself; just do as you are told and everything will work out in the long run.

"Realize the ties which bind thee to thy Guide." The ties are real, and it means that your every movement affects Him, and His movements influence you. If you realize this, "naught unworthy will approach thee."

"Love." Increase your love, and really love with all your heart. Do not be a goody-goody person, but *"discern."* See things *as they are,* and do not compromise when something is evil. "Strike it," with all your might, without fear, because — "My Blessings will be with thee."

---

1. Agni Yoga Society, *Leaves of Morya's Garden,* Volume II, pp. 47-48.
2. Agni Yoga Society, *Hierarchy,* para. 187.
3. Agni Yoga Society, *Leaves of Morya's Garden,* Volume I, para. 76.
4. *Ibid.,* para. 82.
5. *Ibid.,* para. 89.

CHAPTER 9

GLORIFIED LIFE

As we come into the new age, the Teaching becomes more concise, direct and synthesized. The presentations are becoming shorter because they deal with the most essential. In the new age, we don't have time to waste on secondary matters. We must go to the essence and understand it. Also, our intellects are keener than those of our ancestors, so we can understand with less explanation and examples.

When you read the books of the sixteenth, seventeenth and eighteenth centuries, you will see that the authors wrote 200 pages to say what we might say today in one sentence. New-age writing is going to be really meaningful. There will not be a page with one unnecessary word on it. Only that which is needed to explain the most essential will be written. Authors will have great respect for their readers, so they will not waste their readers' time. If you take away one sentence from a chapter, the chapter will lose its meaning. Compare this kind of writing with earlier writings in which you can delete whole sections and chapters without any effect on the meaning. The new-age Teaching is extremely focused, direct and condensed.

In my youth, I went from brotherhood to brotherhood in search of truth. I traveled to many places and studied with many beautiful Teachers. I read thousands of books, but I never found anything that could surpass the Agni Yoga Teaching. It presents the most essential in such a beautiful way — concisely and directly.

You can write a whole book on one sentence from the writings. In one paragraph there are enough seeds to sprout four or five books. You can discuss one paragraph for a year and still not finish it.

M.M. was thinking of the progress of humanity when He gave His Teaching in such a condensed way.

In your efforts to understand the Agni Yoga Teaching, you collect and coordinate your mental and spiritual powers. The discipline which you put them under makes them labor together in a harmonious way. Your mind will feel like it has been given lots of good nutrients to keep it active and healthy all day. These thoughts are the best food for our mental bodies.

Let's look at some of the Wisdom which M.M. has given us.

. . . *Strive for the life glorified.* . . .[1]

Sit down and think of all your possessions and all your expressions, and decide if they are glorified. If not, how can you put them on the path to glory? Look at yourself physically, emotionally, and mentally. Look at your job, friends, home, education, and life-goals. Are there elements in them which are against the highest or the best that you are capable of? Slowly you must try to eliminate your ugly emotions and ugly thoughts. You must find yourself refusing to go places which will not bring out the best in you, and slowly low-level friends must drop away. You must not want to do anything which lessens your nobility.

The glory in you that will start to shine out is your Divinity. The genius and talent that will radiate from you is the light of the Inner Sun within you that you are manifesting. As others feel the warmth of this radiation, they will notice your grandeur, the Cosmic beauty that you are expressing.

The whole sentence reads, "Strive for the life glorified and for the realization of purity." You can see efforts to purify the environment and the food we eat in today's society. People are becoming angry at the state of pollution that greed has brought us to. Emotional purity is being demonstrated in people's urge to love and spread goodwill throughout the world. Mental purity means not to be in glamor or illusion.

On a personal level, try to be really pure in everything that you do — especially in your speech. Ugly words contaminate your aura and attract additional ugly thoughts and emotions. In all things and at all times, strive for the realization of purity. This is the first great step toward achieving a glorified life.

Some people do not realize that smoking marijuana and taking other drugs bring a great pollution to the body. These substances do not allow your mechanism to work according to the natural laws and energies of the planet. Using them is like putting mud in your gas tank instead of gasoline.

We cannot stress enough the importance of keeping pure relations with others. Watch whom you associate with and what you do with them. If you mix too much with them, you share in their karma. You even pick up their etheric, emotional, and mental microbes and house them in your aura. People don't realize it, but even a kiss with the wrong person can be very harmful. A kiss can contaminate you and bring obsession into your body. A kiss with the wrong person can inject a tremendous amount of pollution into your body, which spreads into your organs and throughout your body. You will see the results when you are no longer physically healthy, emotionally stable, and mentally sharp.

. . . Put aside all prejudices — think freely. . . .[2]

M.M. tells us here to put preconditioned beliefs aside so that we do not limit our minds. There is no light where prejudice dwells; there is only dark murkiness where microbes live in slime. Hatred, fear, anger, jealousy, and greed are the names of these microbes in your system. When you have a prejudice, you block the vision of a united humanity from your own sight. This is a very sad and ugly thing.

At first, it is as difficult to put these prejudices

aside as it is to cut off your own arm. This is because you are identified with the false beliefs and you do not want to let them go. This is why so much crime is committed by prejudiced people. They will do anything to make their prejudices survive and then tell themselves that their crimes were justified because they were defending the truth.

You must stop prejudice by clear thinking, which means that you will not be limited by your former level. You should always try to assume new viewpoints and understand all sides of an issue. Try to have greater horizons, and your judgments will be wiser than before.

"Think freely." A young girl came to see me one day because she was very excited about a paper she had just finished. I took it and read it. It was typed and footnoted very nicely, but after reading it I gave it back to her and asked if she could think of something original about the topic.

"What do you mean?"

"Well, everything you say here is from a book, your teacher, or the newspaper. Don't you have anything to say about it yourself? Try to be really free in your thinking instead of copying what others have to say. Try another approach that people may not have looked at yet. Bring a new level and dimension to your paper with deeper thinking."

Three months went by, and she came to see me again. This time her paper was really beautiful. She had broken her former limitations by clear thinking. Instead of just looking "inside the box," she had looked at the top, sides, and bottom, too. She had really surpassed herself.

This is an example of putting the Teaching into living practice. This girl worked really hard for three months, and through her striving she achieved a new degree of freedom. She broke out of her limitations just like a baby chick breaks out of its shell when it is ready to be born.

People think that the Teaching is devotion and that repeating mantrams all day long is spirituality. The

Teaching is nothing else but continuous striving to break your limitations. This is done by observation and hard work. The Teaching is useless for us if we do not find and break our limitations.

The Teaching always challenges us to go beyond ourselves. In surpassing our limitations, we increase our ability to serve others in deeper and more meaningful ways. A person cannot perform a service or action which is beyond his present level. This is why the Teaching encourages us to go beyond ourselves. We must always be looking to our next breakthrough so that we may pass into new spheres of understanding.

If you read the stories of Great Ones, you will see that They were able to conquer nations and lead humanity because They were able to first of all conquer themselves. They broke Their own personal limitations, and in that exact degree, They were able to be useful to humanity. If you are acting from the confines of your own limitations, you also limit those whom you seek to help. All of your efforts to help others will mold them and imprison them with your limitations.

> . . . Be not downcast but full of hope.
> Flee not from life, but walk the path of salvation. . . .[3]

When a person has hope, he has proof that Reality exists within himself. He has the hope that one day he is going to be really beautiful in actuality. He has this hope because the beauty already exists within him — it simply needs to be brought to the surface.[4]

Hope is the reflection of the Reality that exists within. When you say, "I hope I am going to graduate . . . . I hope I am going to be victorious," the victory is already within you, but it has not manifested yet. Real hope is the evidence that whatever you hope for is already in existence.

What does not exist within man? All of Cosmos, all of Divinity exists within man. The source of all creativity is within man, so hope will never fail you. Your hope is actually a path upon which you build a way to bring the Reality into manifestation. Your hope becomes an invitation to your Hidden Glory, encouraging It to come out. Your hope ties you with your innermost Center of Divinity.

One day when I was twelve, a nurse who loved me very much asked my mother for permission to take me to a meeting. My mother let me go. There I was given a book which I read over and over again. I loved it so much. In that book, the nurse had underlined a sentence. At first I thought the book had been used, but she was quick to explain that she had done it for emphasis. She wanted me to really think about the idea given there. It was, "If a man did something, you can do it also."

What a challenge this gave to my young mind, and what hope also. It gave me a great inspiration to think that I could do as well as Michelangelo and Beethoven. Maybe I could even do better than they did. Who knows? What thrilled me was that I had the rest of my life before me and that I could do great things in the days granted to me. What a marvelous source of inspiration and hope those few words have been to me throughout my life.

"*Flee not from life.*" Life here means responsibilities. Whatever condition we find ourselves in, it is our responsibility to stay there and work it out. We must face the situation and try to improve it or overcome it. If you run away from your situation, the problems and conditions will follow you, and they will come to you again later, with a heavy tax. You cannot escape from your karma and your responsibilities.

Sometimes people come and tell you that you are beautiful and you should not have to live in the environment you are in. They urge you to pack your bags and leave; they urge you to go to a new city where you can take it easy. Most of these urgings are wrong. Throw them out and face up to your duties, obligations, and responsibilities.

By not fleeing from life, you walk the path of salvation. Salvation means mastery of life. You master your limitations, weaknesses, mechanical reactions, and all unconscious influences. Most of us live an unconscious life. We speak, act, and feel mechanically, and nothing is really under our control. When you begin to master your unconscious living, you are on the path of salvation. You are saving yourself by making yourself Divine. You are releasing yourself from the confines of matter.

It is a wonderful thing to take some of these verses and learn them by heart. When I was in the Middle East, I visited a man who was said to have memorized the entire *Koran.* I didn't believe it, so I went and asked him to recite it for me. "Do you have a few hours?" he asked .... He really knew all of it! What a great mental power that man had.

If you learn some of these verses, in times of trouble and complication one or two sentences will come to your mind. In many adverse situations, memorized wisdom will come to your help if you have faith in and love for that wisdom.

Sometimes when troubles come your way, you say a prayer asking for courage or strength. When we pray, we hope that an answer will come. My father once told me that all Space is like a big ear: everything you say is heard by Space. None of your words are ever lost.

If your prayer comes from your solar plexus, it has little power. But if it comes from your heart, mind, and intuition, your prayer has a mighty power behind it. When it comes from your soul and higher levels, the color, music, and beauty of your prayer will be exceptional. The devas and angels will see that there is someone who needs help.

Many times unspoken prayer is very diffused. Try to focus your mind, so that you can speak clearly and distinctly on the mental plane. Try to practice telepathic communication with a friend. When you build telepathic communication, the words you speak mentally become like sounds in your friend's ears. You can literally hear each other's voices. This is the way to build and develop yourself for higher communications.

Prayer is not the same thing as hope. Hope is the reflection of something that already exists within you.

Hope is a magnet which pulls you together and thrusts you toward the culmination of the manifestation. You wouldn't have hope if things didn't already exist within you.

Hope opens the path toward realization. Hope enables you to strive toward realization and achievement of your destiny. What is your destiny? — Divinity. Hope puts you on the path toward your Divine Self.

Faith is directly related to hope in this verse. Faith exists because the reality which is in you reflects in the mirror of your mind. You see it and believe in it totally. It is so beautiful to you that the present state doesn't matter to you. You have seen the reality of the future, and you will strive with all your might to actualize it. This is why some people can devote whole lifetimes to a cause with such joy and vigor. They have faith; they have seen the destiny for which they strive. They love it because it is Divine, and they are identified with the Divine in all. Through their efforts, they work to unite with the Divine in themselves and in others. They see their labor as beauty, while others see it as drudgery.

> *My Friends! Happiness lies in serving the salvation of Humanity . . . .*[5]

Happiness does not lie in parties with your friends, in the passing pleasures of the moment, or in the satisfaction of your sexual drive. There is something much greater beyond our physical, emotional, and mental needs, drives, and urges. Are you working beyond these mundane aspects of life? Is there a dream or a fire in your heart that makes you want to do something for humanity?

One day a very bright young man from East Los Angeles came to see me. He had just won a scholarship to the U.C.L.A. Medical School. He was very excited about his future as a doctor. He said, "When I get my degree, I am going to heal the really needy and not charge them one penny for it. I want to serve people with all my heart and spirit."

I was really impressed with his intentions. One

day a couple of years later, he invited me to a birthday party that was being given for him. I asked him how his studies were going. To my surprise, he said that he had quit school and bought a big rubbish truck because he could make so much money with it. I told him that he was living for money and nothing else. He also said that his father went to Las Vegas every week and gambled for him so that he made even more money.

Striving must not be stopped by material satisfaction.

Notice that M.M. says that happiness lies in serving *humanity* — not your race, religion, or tradition. I used to wonder why my Teachers always instructed us in terms of humanity and not in terms of religion or nationality. One day I asked one of my Teachers about it. He held out his hand before me. "You cannot serve this hand without serving the whole body," he said. "You must serve as if you are serving all people in the world."

> ...The fire of fearlessness will brighten thy hearth.
> We send the light to those who smile at darkness.
> Thy spirit is already in ascent, and the flaming
> heart will not be blighted by cold.[6]

The darkness mentioned here is the darkness of fear, animosity, jealousy, hatred, ignorance, slavery, and totalitarianism. When you smile, you take heart and light comes to you. The light that is sent is the result of contact. When you smile at darkness, you are sent light or the power to disperse the darkness.

> "Love each other — beware of disunion. . . ."[7]

This is such an important factor in our progress. How can we serve the body if we are constantly wounding it with gossip and cutting it with lies? Criticism and pride also create disunion, which corrupts us mentally, emotionally, and physically. They make our energy reserves stagnant pools from which we cannot draw health and vigor. Think about others as you do yourself. This is the meaning of union.

Ugly things that we do to one another have a very strong power over our subconscious minds, and they become posthypnotic suggestions. If your mother or girlfriend dealt with you in an ugly way, it is very likely that you will deal with others in a similar manner. Sometimes the wound that has been inflicted will not surface right away. It may take years or even lifetimes. Sometimes these wounds take centuries to heal.

Notice how many times you promise yourself that you are going to be really high-level in all of your dealings; then when somebody steps on your tail, you bite him with your gossip and criticism. This must be stopped if you are ever going to release yourself from the wheel of life. You must learn your lessons and then go on. The tests are the exams to see if you can pass to the next higher level. Every time you gossip or criticize someone, you fail and you must start the course again. And each time you fail, the course gets harder, so that you will really pay attention and learn the next time.

"*Beware of disunion.*" This is a warning to us, and it is also an injunction to have group consciousness. Even if someone harms you, forgive him and go on. Do not divide yourself and the group with low-level emotions and thoughts. Just continue on your way and try to preserve the integrity of the group.

> *Strengthen the consciousness of Our Presence in thy life. . . .*[8]

People who are able to do this feel the presence of the Great Ones in their lives. When they are faced with a decision, they consider how it would stand up in the eyes of Christ. When they are thinking negative thoughts, they stop and think, "What if Christ is listening to me now?"

People who feel the presence of the Hierarchy in their lives are very watchful of their physical, emotional, and mental activities and expressions. Soon they begin to feel the presence of God in everything, everywhere. They begin to relate to others differently and function with more dignity and responsibility. They take a major step forward on the road to becoming conscious in their evolution.

If you feel the presence of the Great Ones near you, you will live in light and in beauty, with a well of courage to draw from. Sometimes you will come up against a situation and you will feel a strong presence near you, or you will be overcome by a great emotion or a new determination.

. . . Turn thy mind toward the joy of creation . . . .[9]

Only after you have entered the human kingdom can you appreciate the beauty of life and the joy of creation. Go outside and participate in the grandeur of God's handiwork. Wash your spirit with the light of the Sun and invigorate your body with the fragrance of the flowers and trees. Renew yourself in the beauty of spring grass and the joy of watching birds in flight. Send beautiful thoughts to the Creator.

A pure thought ever ascends.
At the feet of Christ it blossoms, radiant. . . .[10]

When you look at a blooming flower and feel great gratitude, imagine that you are in the presence of Christ. You will help to form His garden, which is composed of pure thoughts. A Great One says that pure thoughts create flower formations and that a thousand devas come and dance around them.

In your gratitude, send something beautiful to the Great Ones — send Them a flower. What a marvelous way to participate in the beauty of Creation. You can become a gardener in God's field.

---

1. Agni Yoga Society, *Leaves of Morya's Garden,* Volume I, para. 1.
2. *Ibid.*
3. *Ibid.*

4. Read Chapter 56 in *Challenge for Discipleship,* by Torkom Saraydarian.
5. Agni Yoga Society, *Leaves of Morya's Garden,* Volume I, para. 4.
6. *Ibid.,* para. 6.
7. *Ibid.,* para. 10.
8. *Ibid.,* para. 15.
9. *Ibid.,* para. 19.
10. *Ibid.,* para. 21.

CHAPTER 10

THE TEACHER

The aim of the Agni Yoga Teaching is to show
humanity how to achieve fiery union with the Fire of
Cosmos. The first requirement for this is purity. The
aspirant must purify himself of physical, emotional,
and mental obstacles which prevent him from climbing the mountain of Infinity.

Sometimes we are lazy, and our inertia keeps us
from starting the long climb upwards. We are content
to sit at the bottom of the mountain and make excuses
about how life is keeping us tied to our present position. "I would have gone to college, but they didn't give
me a scholarship...." "I would have gotten that job,
but they gave it to someone else because he always
flatters the boss. . . ." You need hard work and sacrifice to achieve anything. Look at anyone who really
achieved, and you will see that he is a person of sacrifice who knows the value of heavy labor.

Many people are carrying heavy emotional boul-
ders which weigh them down so much that they cannot continue on the path upward. The aspirant can see
the vision, but he cannot let go of his attachments. "I
would meditate and study my lessons, but my husband
doesn't like me talking about that 'funny' stuff...." "I
would observe full moon meditations, but I can't go
without my cigarettes and beer for three days. . . ." "I
would visit old people in the hospital, but they don't
always appreciate my giving up an afternoon for
them...." Is this what you are going to tell Christ

when He comes and asks you why you didn't try to talk with Him daily or at least visit Him when He was old and sick?

Many of us have other big rocks which block our path. These are separative ideas on the mental plane which prevent us from seeing the beauty of unity which is at the summit of the mountain that we are climbing toward perfection. "I don't want to be seen with him because he is a member of a different religion...." "My nation is the best and we should have the best of everything. I don't care if others don't have enough. Let them go find their own...."

M.M. gave us the Agni Yoga Teaching to encourage us and enlighten us on our path. He tried to show us the methods of overcoming our little self so that our real Self can manifest through our life.

The essence of M.M.'s Teaching is condensed in twelve virtues. By making these virtues a part of our character, we will clean our field of the six ugly weeds that destroy our beauty. These weeds are jealousy, greed, anger, hatred, fear and revenge. The twelve virtues are the names of the twelve petals of the Inner Lotus. They are:

1. striving
2. courage
3. daring
4. discrimination
5. solemnity
6. harmlessness
7. service
8. compassion
9. patience
10. fearlessness
11. gratitude
12. responsibility[1]

It is much more important for us to actualize these virtues than it is for us to accumulate a great deal of knowledge in our minds. Sometimes we think that it is easy to attain these virtues, but this is not true. The highest value of a person is measured by his expression of these virtues. The highest sublimation and initiation that a person may achieve is based upon mastery of these virtues.

These twelve virtues are the foundation upon which we must "adorn the temple of the Spirit." The Spirit dwells in these twelve virtues, so they form the temple. As a result of the manifestation of these twelve virtues, we have great visions, ideas, revelations and beauty. All of these adorn the temple. They are the jewels that sparkle in the light of the virtues.

Wherever there is beauty, there is the Spirit and we must worship it. Wherever there are truth and courage, there is the Spirit and we must worship it. We must worship the Spirit wherever we find it radiating its glory in goodness, beauty, truth and joy.

In the Piscean era, adornment meant praise, flattery and being happy. But in the Aquarian era, adornment will mean fusion and complete at-one-ment with the twelve virtues of the temple.

In order to adorn your temple, you must be detached from the lower personality. Adornment is happy, blissful detachment from the limitations of matter. Attachments are sores which fester and make your temple a sick and weak structure upon which you base your life. Virtues are rays of sunshine which bring health, warmth and growth. So be virtuous; be beautiful.

Very often in the Teaching, M.M. reminds us of the need for careful vigilance over our vehicles.

Slumber and such dusty manifestations should be avoided. The manifestation of the Shield should be treasured.[2]

Slumber is satisfaction, inertia and laziness. Slumber is an attitude which makes you say, "Tomorrow I will do it. Let me sleep a little more today. I don't care if it doesn't get done." Dust accumulates where there is no action.

A man's shield is *sattva*. It is his radioactivity, his highest vibration, his level of awakeness and his degree of responsibility. If you have these qualities, you will not slumber and you will never become dusty.

In esoteric literature, to slumber also means to be attached to the wishes of the lower personality. The mind says, "I don't want to study today. I will call my girlfriend and go to a party. I can study in the morning before the test." The emotions say, "I could do all these jobs for him, but he wasn't nice to me today. I think I'll tell him that I have a headache and need the afternoon off." The body says, "I know that exercise is good for me. Tomorrow I will take a long walk, but right now I think I'll have another piece of cake."

All of our miseries are directly related to attachments and unfulfilled expectations. This puts the Self in a state of slumber because He cannot manifest through all the turmoil of the lower personality.

Why do I sense the mountain spirit? The Teacher is sending His shield.
The Teacher wants to see you erecting a mountain.
The Teacher wants to see how nothing will affect you negatively.
The Teacher wants to see how courageously you can proceed.
The Teacher will point out when a grave danger is to be encountered.
The Teacher advises you to be ready for daring labor.
The Teacher will help you to conquer an evil hand.
The Teacher repeats not purposelessly the long-familiar thoughts.
The Teacher looks ahead.
The Teacher ordains to keep your spirit invincible.
The Teacher wishes to dispel fear.
The Teacher wants to make your judgment well-tempered.
The Teacher restrains you from grievances.
The Teacher advises to plan bold projects as before.
The Teacher is concerned about your health.
The Teacher wants you to travel.
The Teacher has warned enough.[3]

The Teacher is a person who sincerely lives in the light of the Teaching. His life is an expression of the

Teaching. A true Teacher tries to instill virtues in his students. If he does not challenge and test you ceaselessly, he is not a true Teacher. Escape from anyone who does not lead you to daring acts. Avoid those who are satisfied with less than your best. Walk away from those who encourage you to remain where you are. A true Teacher shows you how to strive and surpass yourself, through his own striving and through his constant reminders to you to check yourself.

A true Teacher is concerned with your spiritual development and not with your personality concerns. He gives you difficult tasks which make you stretch your talents to their furthest point of tensity. You become either really focused in the light of the Teaching, or you become one of the many who were attracted to the light but found it too hot near the flame. The latter fall back to a comfortable place and watch while others are transformed into beauties through fusion with the light.

A true Teacher is not concerned about pleasing your lower personality. It is interesting that many of our contemporary ministers have become the slaves of their congregations. They feel that they must keep certain members' personalities pleased so that large contributions will keep coming in for the church budget. A Teacher who lives the Teaching doesn't care about your personality nor does he care about your money. He cares only for your spirit. He "bugs" you because he wants to see you flower into an expression of Beauty, Goodness and Truth.

In order to test and develop the strength of his students' characters, the Teacher will create turmoil in his students' lives. He teaches the path of detachment, which leads a person to the mountain where courageous deeds result in the attainment of infinite perfection and wisdom. He creates in you a thirst for unity with the Divine, which can only be quenched by detachment from low-level physical, emotional and mental concerns.

The Teacher helps you to realize your points of vanity and transform them into flawless virtues.

These become the real muscles by which you pull yourself up to the point of release from all limitations.

When the Teacher is pleased with you, start to doubt him. A real Teacher cannot be bribed or flattered by anyone because these are acts against the Spirit.

Many times the lower personality of the student rebels against the Teacher; but the real Self responds because He knows that the Teacher is working for His manifestation. While the lower personality says, "This is too hard," the Self says, "Burden me more."

"Why do I sense the mountain spirit? The Teacher is sending His shield." When you climb to the heights of spiritual achievements, you sense the spirit guiding you toward the summit. You hear the words of the Great One: "Be courageous for I conquered the world." The inspiration of your Teacher is your shield against every kind of attack from inner and outer enemies, who try to discourage you and turn your steps back toward the shallow places of the earth.

"The Teacher wants to see you erecting a mountain." Thus the student of wisdom is challenged to do great things for humanity. Instead of digging holes and creating causes of pain and suffering, the student of wisdom must build institutions of beauty and light, in which people are devoted to the summit of their visions.

"The Teacher wants to see how nothing will affect you negatively." This means that you should try not to be upset by material or worldy things: "My boyfriend didn't call. . . ." "She yelled at me when I was trying to help her. . . ." "Everyone has seen this dress before and I can't afford a new one. I will be so embarrassed at the party. . . ." Is this going to be your level of consciousness all day long? M.M. wants us to learn how to be above these silly emotional concerns. The little bugs and flies shouldn't affect you in a negative way. If you are affected by them, you are attached to your own little shell. Sometimes you prevent yourself from making friendships because everything disturbs you. Try to forget the silly little things that really don't make any difference, and learn how to work with great joy.

This is a very important point because a disciple has no time to be bothered by little things that don't matter. A disciple who is really doing the will of his Master cannot be distracted by petty concerns. Learn to stand above these things. Be superior to the little distractions. Try to replace the negativity of distraction with the joy of labor.

We must make one point clear here: the Teacher does not tell you to hate material concerns. He does not tell you to be aloof and cold to everyone, but that you need to develop a spiritual detachment from little things so that they do not bother you. Spiritual detachment is very compassionate and loving.

When you are concerned with little things, it is a sign that you are attached to your lower personality. This means that you are changeable. As the little things change, you change; so you are not in control. But when you strive and labor to achieve spiritual stability, the little things do not affect you. You become steady in the flame and you stand above your emotions. You are in control of them, not the other way around.

"The Teacher wants to see how courageously you can proceed." The Teacher does not accept weakness. He wants you to be courageous because he knows that it is the energy of courage that transmits the power of the spirit. Fear does not let your intuition work. Courage works under the inspiration of the intuition, which uses the mind creatively. Many difficulties are put on the path of great labor. One of the tasks of the disciple is to remove them from the path, proceeding courageously.

"The Teacher will point out when a grave danger is to be encountered." The Teacher lets you deal with obstacles and barriers because in trying to overcome them, you develop and strengthen your spiritual muscles. But when a grave danger lies in front of you, the Teacher warns you and prepares you spiritually to handle it courageously and intelligently, or to bypass it through your wisdom.

Often dangers are premeditated plans of the dark

forces, which are related to you. In such cases, the Teacher can interfere and warn you and even help you to overcome the danger. Thus if you completely dedicate yourself for the service of humanity, the Teacher warns you when he sees a grave danger approaching. With the warning, he also gives you courage and then watches to see if you are fearless and daring.

The path of initiation is a very difficult path. You must work very hard to become the master of your physical, emotional and mental bodies. You must control yourself at all times and in all situations. The first and most important control that you must learn is the control of your personality at the time of dangers.

"The Teacher advises you to be ready for daring labor." Daring is expressed in endurance and fearlessness. A daring person is not trapped in his personality concerns. People may scold, insult and even curse you. They may be friends, family, or strangers. But just as Christ taught us in the Sermon on the Mount of Olives, you must learn to bless them. Do not hate, fear, or resent them. These reactions all come from your own expectations. Learn to detach from your expectations and bless those who oppose you. You are a disciple and you have a Divine heritage to manifest. You are above the common pettiness of daily strife.

The disciple must learn endurance. During the long night's vigil, you cannot take your blanket and run. You must have the courage to remain faithful to your responsibilities. No matter how grave the danger, you must have the steadfastness to endure. This is the life of a disciple.

Endurance is the quality by which a disciple meets all obstacles and limitations and proves that he can outlast opposition because his inner fires are stronger. He can see beyond the limited present to the future, which holds the completed picture. Just as a baby chick must break out of its shell in order to grow into a big rooster, a disciple must expand, grow and crack all limitations. Endurance is the quality which makes the disciple stronger than the opposing forces. Endurance builds virtues in him so that he becomes a real value to humanity and to the life of the planet.

Endurance eventually dissolves your karmic debts. If you don't learn to outlast your problems, they will come back to you in another life. It is better to finish with them now so that you may proceed on your path of evolution.

Many people give up when they meet a little difficulty. They try to escape to a place where everything runs smoothly for them. But all they end up doing is escaping from one place to another and never really accomplishing anything.

When I left the monastery, my first job was as a blacksmith at a railway station. I was hungry and without money and I really needed the job. I didn't know anything about blacksmithing, but I was willing to learn.

The first day at the job, the boss gave me a big hammer and told me to hit the anvil. I was shocked by the noise. I really hated the noise and I started to complain to the boss.

"Do you like to have food?" he asked me.

"Yes, I do."

"Well, either plug your ears, or learn how to go hungry."

I found some earplugs right away.

Then I had to learn many new things that I was not used to. During the first week of the job, my muscles were so sore. But I endured. I built my muscles, and I even learned eventually to enjoy the sound of the hammer hitting the anvil. There were several men hammering on different objects at the same time, so I created a song out of the noises in my mind. After a while, I even liked the rhythm they were creating.

You must stand in your spiritual beingness and conquer your personality. Endurance means not to lose your striving; once you stop striving, your defeat is close at hand.

Try to put joy in your endurance. For example, Christ said that when you are fasting, you should not walk around with a long face trying to get others to pity you; you should be joyful. Be smiling and cheerful so that no one knows that you are fasting. Learn how not to be a show-off. You will enjoy yourself much more by being joyful than by being a show-off.

You can see that this is not a Teaching which leads to an easy life. M.M. does not tell you to be lazy and escape your problems. If you say you do not have problems, it is because you do not realize your problems. To feel that you have no problems is the sign that you are the biggest problem.

"The Teacher will help you to conquer an evil hand." The disciple is not one who sits down and watches corruption and crime going on. He wants to help people in any possible way to stop corruption, crime and many social ills which are organized by evil hands. The Teacher makes the disciple aware of these things and then advises him how to improve his technique of fighting, in order to eliminate corruption and crime wherever and whenever possible.

"The Teacher repeats not purposelessly the long-familiar thoughts." Sometimes the student may resent the Teacher's repetition of a truth, but the Teacher has good reason to repeat it. He needs to create a point of focus within the student, so that he will exert more concentration and effort in a certain area.

Sometimes the Teacher needs to repeat himself to a student because of a change in the student's consciousness. For example, as you expand your perspective, your awareness increases. You understand more, and you unfold another layer of truth in your mind. As you progress, it is good to have certain truths repeated so that you take a new look at them. You will find many new things that you were never able to see before. They were always there, but you did not realize them. This is like looking at a high mountain on a cloudy day: you can only see the bottom of the mountain, but when the wind blows the clouds away, you can see all the way to the top of the mountain; and you see that it is a beautiful, sunny day.

"The Teacher looks ahead." The Teacher does not waste his time with your failures in the past, but looks ahead for your future successes and victories. He

inspires you with a vision. He encourages you to proceed toward a glorious future. He makes you see your next step on the path, your next project, your next service, your next labor to serve humanity.

"The Teacher ordains to keep your spirit invincible." It is easy to be discouraged in front of the accumulated dangers of the world and in the presence of increasing problems; but the disciple cannot allow himself to be depressed or broken-hearted, or to fall into the hands of his negative emotions. The Teacher inspires and uplifts the disciple if he has committed himself to increase goodness and beauty in the world. An invincible spirit is one who, in spite of conditions, carries the flag of beauty, goodness, righteousness, joy and freedom to the summit of the mountain.

"The Teacher wishes to dispel fear." Fear is one of the main barriers on the path of service. It paralyzes your work and your future plans. There are fears which we carry with us from our past, fears planted in us by our environment, parents, or teachers; fears accumulated in Space. All these fears individually or collectively attack us and try to stop our work of light, love and beauty; but the Teacher sends his ray and his courage at special times and helps us to overcome them. One of the responsibilities of the disciple is to dispel fear as much as possible.

"The Teacher wants to make your judgment well-tempered." A disciple does not judge people in general; if he has to judge, he is very careful and slow in his judgment so that he does not act against the principles of justice and righteousness. Generally, the right judgment is made after studying the situation from as many viewpoints as possible. A well-tempered judgment is a right judgment.

"The Teacher restrains you from grievances." Grievances are caused when you submit yourself to negative emotional waves. You are grieved because your friend forgot your birthday. You are grieved because someone dented the back of your car. You are grieved because the price of steak went up another ten cents per pound.

Emotional attachments and small failures and disappointments tie you to your emotional reactions. When this happens, you cannot use your mind properly. If you cannot use your mind properly, you cannot progress because you repeat your mistakes like a wheel stuck in the mud: the harder you try to get out of the ditch, the deeper your wheel grinds in the mud. The more attached you are, the heavier your emotions become and you cannot free yourself from them.

You must learn how to recognize your emotional attachments for what they are and leave them. Learn how to stop discussing your emotional problems because talking about them can create more heartache for you. Forget them and rise above them. Think of other, more positive ways to spend your time. Instead of calling a friend and complaining about your wife, visit a sick person in the hospital or read an inspirational book or walk in a nice garden. Learn how to be above your problems and not one with them.

Once a Chinese man was presented with a jar of muddy water. He was asked how the muddy water could be cleaned. He said, "Leave it there. The mud will sink to the bottom." You must learn how to separate yourself from your emotional concerns and rise above them. Think greater thoughts.

When you talk about your emotional problems, you entangle yourself in a web which you cannot break out of. You may have started out with a little jealousy, but then you weave a little fear with it and add lots of hatred. Then you find yourself caught in a web of emotions and you can hardly tell one from another. You cannot get out of the web because all these negative emotions are mixed together. They bind you so that your freedom is limited. They take your power and put chains on your potential.

The Teacher reminds you that you are crying for transient things. He wants you to build solemnity and discernment in your nature so that you can gather all of your forces together and be a powerful worker for the light. He doesn't want to see your energies dissipated because of physical, emotional and mental annoyances. Learn how to rise above them. Think greater thoughts.

Gurdjieff used to say, "The moon is eating you." By this he meant that the physical, emotional and mental bodies were eating the spirit. The spirit can become like meat in a dog's mouth when it is controlled by the personality — it gets eaten and soon becomes part of the dog.

"*The Teacher advises to plan bold projects as before.*" After you have completed one project, start another and then another and then another. The Teacher does not want you to sleep. Bold projects are daring projects. They evoke striving in you. In the urge to fulfill these projects, you raise not only the level of your consciousness but the level of your being too.

"*The Teacher is concerned about your health.*" This is why the Teacher M. gave so many hints and pieces of advice about how to keep our bodies healthy and strong, in order to carry on our service for humanity. For example, He suggests to us to have beautiful thoughts, to develop the spirit of gratitude and joy, to eat vegetables and grain only twice daily and to sleep well and not waste our energy. Only a healthy person can continuously carry on the responsibilities given to him by his Teacher in a world of hindrances and problems.

"*The Teacher wants you to travel.*" This is an interesting statement. Every disciple carries a highly charged aura and wisdom. The Teacher wants his disciples to go to many places to share their radiation and wisdom, to spread regeneration and also to come under the influence of various nationalities and learn and increase their treasury of experiences. Every real Teacher is connected with his disciples with threads of light and compassion. As the Teacher influences his disciples through his wisdom, the disciples also influence him through their thoughts and actions. This is why it is so important that disciples cultivate virtues and develop sensitivity to the directions of their Teacher.

1. Read Chapters 92-107 in *The Psyche and Psychism,* by T. Saraydarian.
2. Agni Yoga Society, *Leaves of Morya's Garden,* Volume II, page 108.
3. *Ibid.,* page 115.

CHAPTER 11

EXPANSION OF CONSCIOUSNESS

The expansion of consciousness is the goal of Our striving, and when Our co-workers carry this vessel a full cooperation is affirmed. Thus Our Brothers create, expanding the consciousness. The great experiment of Agni Yoga will bestow upon humanity the expansion of consciousness and the greater understanding of the two worlds.[1]

The Agni Yoga Teaching stirs your Inner Fire and awakens your virtues, dreams, and visions. It is designed to draw out the best that is in you so that it may be used for the service of humanity and the fulfillment of the Plan. The Agni Yoga Teaching ignites the fire within you, the Self which is trying to manifest.

The Agni Yoga Teaching is the Teaching of the Inner Fire, the manifesting Spark. Through your Inner Fire, you slowly sublimate, transform, and transfigure your personality and pave the way for the fuller expression of your Inner Divinity.

Once your Divinity starts to express Itself through your physical, emotional, mental, and spiritual life, you become like the flaming bush that Moses saw in the wilderness. This means that all of your actions, feelings, and thoughts radiate fire. They blaze forth with the innermost vision of Infinity, the everlasting path of development and perfection.

Those who are on the path of perfection must expand their consciousness. Without expansion of consciousness, one cannot develop, unfold, or become

118

a part of the symphony of the universe. To become a part of the Cosmic Symphony, one needs to refine and expand his consciousness so that he is able to see Cosmic synthesis which underlies all Creation.

There are numerous methods for expanding your consciousness. Let's take four of them. These four methods will provide you with a firm foundation upon which to build a bridge to the Higher Worlds.

1. The first method of expansion of consciousness is to view everything that is related to you from the viewpoint of the future. By viewing your past experiences, thoughts, feelings, and impressions from the viewpoint of your future goal, you release yourself into greater light. You do not become stuck in the limitations of the past, but you strive toward the beingness of the future.

Living in the past means that you cannot develop and unfold beyond your past level of limited achievement. Your past failures repeat themselves in the present, so that in the future you will not be free of their limiting walls. The past colors your whole picture of life because you have allowed it to dominate your present condition.

In the past, wise Teachers who wanted to help people to expand their consciousness created confession. Esoterically, confession breaks your relation with past failures and points you toward the future. You look to what you want to be and you make a resolution to work toward that picture of perfection.

Without realizing it, we keep our friends and loved ones stuck in the past when we remind them of their past failures. "You are guilty. . . .You always do that. . . .You hurt me so much. . . .You were an ugly boy. . . . You didn't pass the exam. . . .You lied to me. . . ." With this type of treatment, we impress our thoughtforms and visions of failure on our friends' consciousness. When we do these things, we chain them to their past hindrances and limitations.

If we want to help our friends expand their consciousness and lead a more noble life, we need to see beyond what they were before or what they are now.

We need to help them break their prison walls by creating a vision in them: "I was so proud of you when you demonstrated responsibility. . . .You were so kind to that old lady. . . .You have been working really hard lately. . . ."

Help your friends to forget their past failures and show them how beautiful they can become. You will be surprised that their growth will cause growth in you, too.

Criticism of others is another way of tying them to the past or present. "You have really done a bad job.... You shouldn't dress that way....Your performance was terrible...." Don't be a jailer for your loved ones. Be the beauty that releases them into future accomplishment and glory. Help your friends feel the power of their fire, their Divine Self, and gently help them to manifest that Divinity for the betterment of the human race.

How do we begin to see things in our life from the viewpoint of the future? Start by looking at all the things you do. Take each thing separately and ask yourself how important it is in relation to your future. Does it contribute to the vision for which you are striving? You may be happy doing something now, but will that thing make you happy tomorrow? You smoke a pack of cigarettes today, but will it result in your happiness after you develop lung cancer? Take a serious look at the results which you are setting in motion now. Look at your life from the standpoint of cause and effect.

If you think in this way, you will control and sublimate yourself and your actions will be productive. You will expand your consciousness because you have expanded the present to include the vision of future accomplishment, development, and beingness. You will climb over your prison walls and never look back to the place of your limitation and confinement in matter.

There was once a hungry rooster who went into the barnyard looking for something good to eat. He was scratching at the earth, and suddenly he found a beautiful diamond. He looked at it and appreciated its color and cut, but he said, "I am so hungry and I cannot eat this diamond. I wish I could find a kernel of grain."

There are things that are wonderful right now, but they do not help you achieve your goal. It is best to leave them where they are because, though they may be fun, they do not contribute to where you are going. They may even hinder you on your journey since they are just excess weight which you really don't need.

2. The second method to expand your consciousness is to do evening review.[2] In this manner, you stand in the future and align your activities with your vision. You eliminate the things which are not in harmony with the future because you judge them from an elevated consciousness which makes you see your mistakes.

Let's say that you cheated your boss out of some money during the day. During your evening review, you see that this is a bad thing to do and that it does not stand in the light of the really noble person that you envision yourself to be. Your consciousness does not approve of this type of dishonest behavior. The next time you are tempted to steal, you catch yourself and stop because you know that you will have to answer to your consciousness that evening. You see that stealing is not useful for your future, and you decide that it is better not to do it any more.

Suppose that a man is building a house but he goes out and collects materials which are suitable for building a train. He is not a very wise man because he can never build a home with steel plates and iron rods. When you build a house, you must have the blueprint in your mind and collect materials according to its specifications. This is the future for which you collect your materials. If an item does not fit into the picture, why burden yourself with it?

The evening review helps you sort out your materials so that you eliminate those thoughts, actions, and emotions which do not contribute to the plan of the blueprint. You understand the mistakes that you made

in the past so that you will not repeat them, and you see
the jewels which you are collecting. You keep the jewels
and try to enhance their beauty, so that they will be
bright stars which light your path to Infinity.

Soon everything that you do in the present will be
checked from the viewpoint of the future. It will
become automatic for you to stop, take a deep breath,
and say, "Eating this cake will not make me the thin
person I want to be. . . .Telling this lie will not make me
the bearer of truth that I seek to be. . . .Yelling at this
child will not make me the compassionate person that
I long to be." By putting real value in your present you
will expand your consciousness. This expansion of
consciousness will eventually lead you to becoming a
person of real value.

When you see the present from the viewpoint of the
future, you balance yourself and create equilibrium in
your consciousness. Soon your whole life will be balanced and you will be able to clean your garden of all
the weeds that were choking the lovely flowers that
were trying to bloom.

3. The third method of expanding your consciousness is to adopt the viewpoint of the whole picture and
to see things in the light of synthesis. When you take
an object and view it from its present value, you are not
seeing it in the right proportion. If you witness an
event as separate from all other events, you are limited
in your understanding of its real significance.

For example, let's say that you work in a factory
which produces nuts and bolts. Your level of consciousness is equal to these two items until you start
asking where they go. You expand your consciousness
as you find out that they go into a part, which goes into
a motor, which goes into an airplane...and you suddenly know the nut better because you know the function of the airplane. Your consciousness is now more
inclusive and has a greater depth of understanding.

In a similar manner, when you as a human being
think that you are the center of the universe, you are
selfish and egocentric. You want everything for yourself and you do not see the need to share with your

brothers and sisters. In this stage, you try to use everything for yourself.

When a person realizes that he is a member of a family, he starts to expand his consciousness. Instead of concentrating on himself, he expands his area of concern to his family. His consciousness becomes even more expansive as he includes his nation and its problems and future in his scope of interest. This puts a tremendous pressure on him to meet the needs of the greater whole. He starts to think in terms of one humanity and then something very interesting happens: all of his wrong emotions, thoughts and feelings evaporate. His hatred of that religion turns into respect and love. His jealousy and greed are replaced by a willingness to share. He realizes that he was exploiting others for his own comfort and that this was destroying them. Now he feels that he belongs to the whole of humanity. He has cleaned himself of all his separativeness and has expanded his consciousness.

Before you expand your consciousness, you must purify yourself. Purification is detachment from all those things which limit your thinking and prevent expansion of consciousness. You begin to think in terms of the whole and in terms of synthesis.

Your progress and advancement are equal to your expansion of awareness and your measure of synthesis. If you approach the world with 10 percent synthesis, you are a 10 percent human being. This is why everyone eventually hates selfishness; even selfish people hate selfishness. A thief would kill anyone who stole from him.

We had a boy in our school who used to take bread and cheese from other children's plates. He was the most selfish person in the school, but he would attack others, saying, "You are selfish. I hate selfishness!"

4. The fourth method of expanding your consciousness is to look at life from the viewpoint of service and the application of the Teaching to life. We gain a tremendous expansion of consciousness when everything we have and are is given to the service of greater and greater wholes. For example, when you

put your theoretical knowledge into practical application, you have a great expansion of consciousness. You
learn about gratitude, patience, love and simplicity
from your teachers and books, but if you do not apply
these things in your life, you do not expand your consciousness and beingness.

If you say that you know what simplicity is but
you are not simple, you really do not know what simplicity is because you do not have the experience of it.
You say that you know all about gratitude, but if you
are not grateful in all conditions, you really know very
little about it. Your consciousness is limited to theory.
In the application of theory, your consciousness meets
so many obstacles, hindrances and problems that
solving them gradually expands your consciousness.

You have great expansion of consciousness when
you view your talents from the viewpoint of service. If
you have money, do you use it for some humanitarian
purpose? If you have excellent health, do you use it for
some greater good? Do you apply your wisdom and
talents for power, vanity and fame, or do you dedicate
them to the service of humanity?

You also expand your consciousness when your
thoughts are turned toward service. When you decide
to undertake any project for the service of humanity,
you grow in awareness. For example, imagine a very
talented girl who is practicing her music alone in the
garden. Suddenly she decides that she wants to uplift
people with the sweetness of her music and she starts
to make plans to play in a concert hall. She begins to
put a tremendous pressure on herself, so that she will
be able to meet the standards of the concert hall. When
she starts to apply her talents for the service of humanity, she expands her level of accomplishment and
therefore her level of awareness.

The young girl's dedication to the service of
humanity takes her music to levels that it never would
have reached if she were trying to satisfy her own
vanity with it. The service she prepares for expands
the application of her talents. Her field of service puts
her mind in a condition in which her music becomes

radioactive instead of static.

Each movement of consciousness must be directed to the currents of evolution. Each step of life must be considered as inseparable from perfection. A form congealed may be fit for duplication, but the tide never duplicates one wave. . . .[3]

When you are a member of a symphony orchestra, all of your movements must fit into the movement of the whole body. On a larger scale, whatever you do, think, and feel must fit into the vision and progressive movement of humanity. If your actions are hindering or obscuring the current of evolution and the tide of improvement and perfection, you are creating friction between you and the psychic energy of Nature. This is what will eventually bring you sickness, failure, and death.

Put your thoughts, feelings, and actions in harmony and cooperation with the ever-progressing spirit of humanity. Do not make noises which block the orchestra in its expression of unity.

Everything you do, feel, think and learn must have one aim: improvement of your life, steady improvement toward higher and higher levels. This should be the common denominator of all your actions. When you are not frozen — or congealed — you have life; you are always renewing yourself.

People ask whether you must know what perfection is in order to strive for perfection. This question can be answered by a story told by Buddha about a man who was wounded by an arrow. When people came to help the man to remove the arrow, he started asking many questions: "Who shot that arrow? Why did he shoot it at me? How deep did it penetrate? What is the arrow made of?"

The people answered the man, "First let us save your life by taking out the arrow. Then you can ask all these questions."

Who cares what perfection is? The important thing is to try to improve yourself. Expand yourself, and then you will know what perfection is. Perfection is the expansion of your service. Your real value is equal to your service. And before you become a servant, you cannot know what service is.

M.M. encourages us to strive toward a new level of consciousness. He wants us to change our level from that of selfishness to that of service. He says that we must change from the attitude of wanting everybody to serve us to the attitude of becoming servers. We must think more about world problems. Instead of fretting about what we are going to eat and who is going to come to our party, we should be thinking about what creative things we can do for the betterment of humanity. We should be making daring plans which will release humanity into greater beauty. We must do more than read books and play intellectual games with the Teaching.

The disciple must be eager for knowledge. He must really want to expand his consciousness into the ocean of knowable things. A disciple knows his limitations, but he is eager to break them.

It is surprising how many people shy away from knowledge. Some are afraid to reach new levels because they know it will cause a change in their responses, environment, or habits. They are comfortable where they are and with their limitations. A great Sage says that such a person's mind is so full that you cannot put anything more in it.

Expansion of consciousness cannot occur if you live in fear. Fear shrinks you and makes you concentrate upon yourself. Fear makes you identify with nonsense in such a manner that it prevents your expansion. When you break your fear, you drop your identification with the past objects of your physical, emotional and mental worlds. Then in complete fearlessness, you will be ready for the Teacher.

If you are not ready for the Teacher, everything the Teacher says will be opposite to all your physical, emotional and mental selfishness. The Teacher will do the same thing to you that Christ did to the rich man: the rich man said to Christ, "Lord, how can I enter the

Kingdom of God?"

Christ answered, "All that you have, give to the poor and follow Me." Hearing this, the rich man walked away. He was not ready to enter that level of consciousness which was referred to as the Kingdom of God. His fear prevented him from detaching from his worldly goods. The man stopped his progress on the path of perfection. He was stopped not by his riches, but by his identification with them.

M.M. says that it is necessary to be truthful, devoted, and keenly vigilant. Your life is like a field full of hidden explosives. Every moment you are surrounded by sensitive wires — physical, emotional and mental habits, visible and invisible dark forces, and tests from karmic accumulations. You must be very vigilant to pass on to greater unity with your Divinity. Don't be caught in a trap and blown to bits by dynamite sticks of your own creation.

You must be especially careful about your own thoughts. Do not let your thoughts wander back to silly memories of the past — memories which are negative, sensual, or dreamy. Try to keep your thoughts in goal-fitting alignment, so that you are in control of them. Use your thoughts for your future actions, and don't be the slave of your silly flights of fantasy.

It is also necessary to be very industrious if you are going to expand your consciousness. My mother used to tell me that Satan is always present in a lazy mind. If you keep your mind busy with lofty thoughts, Satan cannot enter there. When your mind is lazy, there will always be the opportunity for something negative to enter there. Keep your mind busy with higher things, and negative thoughts will not be able to find a home in you.

M.M. says that the disciple must approach the Teacher with the utmost sensitivity. Sensitivity is the ability to record the needs and visions of others. Sensitivity is the application of the Teaching to the needs of others. Sensitivity is the ability to see something in the dark at the time the lightning strikes. If someone gives you a look, you catch it immediately and act upon it.

You catch the lightning in the fullness of its intensity. When we study the Teaching, it is necessary to change our lives. Old habits must be dropped so that greater light may be focused in our beingness. We must find the path of trust where evil, pain, and negativity cannot tempt us. We must see all events as ripples on the ocean of time and stop being terrified by the destructive events we see around us.

A higher clairvoyant can look at your astral body and see how you are dressed. If you have lots of dark spots in your astral and mental bodies, he says that you are not dressed very well. You cannot enter the subtle levels of consciousness because the frequency there will crack your mechanism.

The path of perfection is steady progress of unfoldment into greater realities. Levels of perfection are stations on the path. You may be a perfect boy, but you must do greater things to be a perfect man. Perfection is a relative idea. If you are a Seventh Degree Initiate, you are perfect on the physical plane. But then a Cosmic window opens for you, and you see that you are only in kindergarten. Life within the Cosmos is unlimited, and it cannot be defined in terms of human conditions and thought.

1. Agni Yoga Society, *Infinity,* Volume II, para. 296.
2. For further information on evening review, see Chapter 80 of *The Psyche and Psychism,* by Torkom Saraydarian.
3. Agni Yoga Society, *Agni Yoga,* para. 36.

CHAPTER 12

LABOR

The achievement of the spirit consists in that amidst earthly difficulties and struggles the spirit develops the higher striving. . . . Therefore the co-workers can prove the strength of their spirit and striving amidst daily labors and difficulties. How could one attain the highest state, attain refinement of consciousness, without spiritual labor?. . .[1]

In the Agni Yoga literature, labor takes on a deeper meaning than the customary definition of work. When we refer to labor, we mean the use of energy and matter to bring into materialization the Plan of the Hierarchy. Whatever you do physically, emotionally, and mentally to build and materialize the Divine Plan on Earth is considered labor in the esoteric sense.

When you are on the path of return to the Father's Home, everything done for your separate self is considered as working against your Self. The only things considered as labor which will bear fruit in the years to come are those things which objectify the Plan someplace in the world.

A plan leads to right action. For example, a contractor buys his materials and instructs his workers according to the blueprints which the architect has provided. Without this plan, much of the contractor's actions will lead in the wrong direction. Without a plan, he may install a shower in the middle of the living room or put the stove where a window should go;

he may make the garage door the entrance to the bed-room. Energy, time, and materials are wasted because of the lack of a plan. Can you imagine the work the contractor will have to do to repair the house once he begins to follow a plan and a blueprint?

To have a plan is the first principle of labor because it results in right action. If you follow a plan in your life, you will conduct your life according to those principles which will result in right action for the Plan. You will not have to go back years later and tear down the wrong structures which you built through greed, gossip, and anger. If you follow a plan, you will not put things where they don't belong; you will not do things in your life which are not goal-fitting. Your "house" will be really beautiful.

We manifest labor in three ways. Many people think that labor means to dig in a trench all day, but this is not the deeper meaning of labor. In real labor or labor for the Plan, you work and build with your *thoughts, words,* and *actions.*

When you are thinking according to the Plan, you are engaged in a great labor. This means that you can be useful no matter what your physical condition is. If you are sick, isolated, or frustrated because your physical environment is such that you have little time and energy for physical service to the Great Ones, you still have the power of your thoughts. In your con-scious mind, you may try to imagine or visualize a great vision of future beauty. This will build a concrete thoughtform for future manifestation.

When you engage your mind in such an activity, you take intuitive feelings and with your mental equipment participate in a great labor which will help to manifest the Plan of the Hierarchy on Earth. You work to build a blueprint upon which those who follow may construct great beauties.

Maybe you work in a factory and do the same manual job day after day. Maybe you are a housewife with children to care for, and it is difficult for you to find time for anything else but cooking, cleaning, and running errands. Where is your thinking during the hours of the day? Do you let it mechanically run wild, from thoughts about your stomach, to your sexual urges, to your jealousy, to anger, to self-pity? You can start to be of real service to humanity and to the Hierarchy if you become a little more conscious about your thoughts. Say to yourself, "For the next five minutes I am going to imagine something really beautiful and think of practical ways and means that it can be accomplished." You can be of great service by thinking beautiful thoughts.

The second way in which you labor is with your speech. People do not realize that with every word spoken, a building starts to form. If that building is not in harmony with the Plan, you inject chaos into your aura and into Space, and you create distortion in your relations with everything in the world. The power of speech carries a heavy responsibility.

Our speech creates etheric, emotional, and mental forms. If you stop and think about your speech, you will be horrified by the forms that you have built through gossip, criticism, and profane language. These things cut your relation with Higher Worlds and insulate you from receiving higher energies. You become isolated, and distortions are created in the energy system within your vehicles. This causes you to become sick, criminal, or foolish. All of this happens because you cut yourself off from the life-giving energies of the universe with your wrong speech.

Imagine that you are going to build a beautiful house. You gather all your materials on Monday and tell yourself that you will begin building on Tuesday morning. During the night, 200 monkeys get into your yard and begin the job for you. They mix everything up according to their own monkey business, and when you arrive in the morning, you find a huge mess.

These kinds of monkeys are inside of you, and they manifest through your thoughts, words, and actions. When you catch yourself complaining that things are not going according to your wishes or plans, look at your monkeys. You will find out that they have been working on your mental and emotional planes to distort things before you even start to build in objective form.

The third way that you labor is with your own hands and feet. Do not expect your neighbor to fix your roof. You must get the ladder and tar and climb up there yourself to fix it.

Your labor must follow a plan, and as you become more involved in the manifestation of your plan, your responsibility becomes greater. If you are the mayor of Los Angeles, you have a great responsibility. If you are the governor of California, you have a greater responsibility. If you are the President of the United States, you have an even greater responsibility. . . . Your labor never decreases as you advance on the path of perfection; on the contrary, it becomes heavier and heavier.

The labor which you do today is a preparation for your labor tomorrow; your labor on one plane is a preparation for the next higher plane. You cannot go to high school before you have finished elementary school. If your first steps are not in line with the Hierarchical Plan, you will not be able to graduate into a higher level of labor for the Hierarchy. Whatever you are doing on any level must really be in tune with the Plan of the Hierarchy.

In order to labor, you first need two things: **preparation** and **purification.**

Your **preparation** must be on the physical, emotional, and mental levels. Physically, you must make your body fit to perform the task which will be required of you. For example, do you try to play a complicated piece of music on the piano without training your fingers first? You must always make sure you have prepared yourself for your task on the physical level.

Emotionally, you must be prepared for the tension and pressure which the labor requires. You must be courageous enough to meet the task with enthusiasm because doubt and fear will act like leaks in the bottom of your boat: they will eventually sink your ship.

If you are asked to lecture or perform before an audience, you must be emotionally ready to do it. If you get up and tremble with so much stage fright that you cannot make your presentation, you are not emotionally prepared. It is not good enough to be able to deliver your speech or sing your song in your own bathroom; you must prepare your emotional body so that it does not panic in front of the audience. You will have to be daring, but you can build your emotional body so that you can perform.

The mental body must be trained so that you will know what to do. If you want to build something, you must know all the procedures. Look at the preparation that a brain surgeon must go through in order to practice medicine. He must have great physical dexterity and stamina, emotional stability and calmness under highly pressured situations and great mental knowledge and control. He must coordinate all of these elements with extreme balance because if one fails, the whole operation could be disastrously affected.

Try to see your life as a study of the science of labor. You will notice that as the responsibility increases, the tension and pressure increase also. On level one, you must learn to practice the virtues of patience and diligence. If you do not learn your lesson well, level two will break you when new trials come; when level two demands that you demonstrate diligence, your lack of patience may shatter you.

Labor is a really delicate science. You must decide to be conscious about the way you live your life and follow the principles of labor in a scientific manner. Then you will proceed on the path with sanity and right direction. You will not waste time or energy and you will not have to go back later to fix what the monkeys in your nature made a mess of.

When you are on the path, there is another kind of preparation which is very important: you must have spiritual preparation. Spiritual preparation means to eliminate any intention to exploit people. Your wish will be to serve them, but not to serve them so that they will serve your greed, pride, or vanity.

You must not deceive anyone with your labor. If your labor leads others in the wrong direction, your motives are wrong and you will one day have to pay a heavy price. Your motivation in serving and dealing with people must always be righteous and pure.

Spiritual preparation for labor requires knowing the Plan. If you know the Divine Plan, you can give proper direction to your labor. This means that you must learn about and study the Plan.[2]

There are three measures by which you can judge if something stands in the light of the Plan. These measures will help you decide if an action leads you and others on the path, or if it serves a separative interest.

The first measure is beauty. Is your thought, speech, or action really beautiful; will it lead to ever-increasing beauty? Or does it stop with showing the beauty of yourself? You must learn to discriminate these subtle differences.

The second measure is the degree of your sensitivity to the Plan. This must be developed as you progress on the path of evolution. Your instrument of sensitivity to the Plan is the heart. If you do something, check it with your heart. If you feel that it is dishonest or ugly, you are not in line with the Plan. This sensitivity must be developed to the degree that it rings in your ears whenever you are contemplating something: "No, don't do that," you may hear. "Stop that. Go back and do it right. . . ." Such feelings are a sign of sensitivity to the Plan.

Once you develop this sensitivity to the Plan, you will be able to conduct your life according to the direction coming through that sensitivity. You will not buy a liquor store even though it may make lots of money. You will not associate with certain people even though they may be a lot of fun. Your sensitivity will lead you toward the Plan, and you will lead a life of beauty, goodness, truth, and striving.

The third measure of whether a labor is for the Plan is its universality. Work for the Plan is work for the Oneness of all humanity. Separative interests of self, race, and nation stand against the interests of the total unit and create a tremendous karmic liability. You and your children will pay for them in this life and in future incarnations.

Those who violate the concept of One Humanity go through great karmic tension and suffering so that they learn the lesson of unity. This is true in the histories of many nations. Take the Roman Empire, for example. They eventually lost everything and had to pay a terrible price for their greed, selfishness and perversion. How different their history might have been if they had tried to enlighten and improve others, rather than exploit them for their own profit.

When there is a note in the symphony which creates a distortion, the composer throws it out. When your body has an element in it that is causing it illness, it tries to throw it out also. The intent of all forms is to be in harmony with the symphony which God is playing. Any distortion in them is a disturbance in the Plan and results in tension between the form and the Plan.

In addition to preparation, the other element needed to labor is **purification.** You must be physically, emotionally and mentally pure before you begin your labor. You must eliminate all those things which stand between you and your task. Imagine a man who is going to climb a mountain but he wants to take his piano with him. We laugh at such a man and say he is stupid, but we never even notice the obsolete forms that we are carrying with us in our mental and emotional bodies. These obsolete forms are preventing us from doing our job on the path.

If there is a past hatred in your heart, throw it out because it will serve you no useful purpose on the path. Try to clear such things out of your nature because you are not on your own selfish path any longer; you have entered the stream of evolution which leads to the Father's Home, where all are united in Beauty, Goodness and Truth.

Physically, you must clear away all those things which do not contribute to your health. Watch what you put into your body, the places you frequent and the people with whom you associate. Make sure that you are really rested and physically in balance.

Physical purification also means to make sure

that your finances are in order, that your house is clean
and neat and that you dress in a dignified way. Everything you do physically contributes to your efficiency.
You must be physically harmonized so that all your
actions and expressions fit your goal. If you do this,
you will never have to waste time, money, or reputation paying off gambling debts or clearing a drunk-
driving record. When you need an important paper,
you will be able to find it right away. You will not miss
work because of illness.

When you enter the path of labor for the Hierarchy, your physical condition must be in order so that
it supports your activities rather than creating complications, congestion and confusion in your life.

On the emotional plane, it is very important to
purify yourself of your glamors and hangups. When
you take a person with excellent qualifications and
credentials and place him in a high position without
purifying him emotionally, he can make a really big
mess there. This is why we have big government scan-
dals: emotionally, something is out of order in the
employees. Those who have hangups and distortions
in their emotional nature make decisions based on
distortions of truth or selfish interests.

One of the most important things to purify from
your emotional body when you are on the path of labor
for the Hierarchy is touchiness. When you are touchy,
the Teacher cannot help you or correct your action.
Anything he says causes a tremendous reaction in
your system and you don't listen. You tell him instead
about all your diplomas and awards. Or you tell him
that you could have done it right if it weren't for so-
and-so, who always gets in the way. The truth is that
you were acting emotionally and not looking at the
reality of the situation. M.M. says that touchy people
cannot advance because they have no ears to hear.

Flattery is a very sneaky vice because it is harder
to notice than the other snakes in your nature. After
you have worked hard to purify yourself, flattery can
remain in your nature like a snake sleeping under a
rock. Then when someone approaches you and cannot

manipulate you through jealousy, hatred, or fear, he will stumble upon that rock and find flattery waiting there for a nudge so that it awakens.

Mental purification is also very necessary on the path. Your mental body must be purified of the things which cause depression, prejudice, superstition, sensitivity to hypnotic suggestions, negative thoughtforms, and laziness. All of these create push buttons in your mind. A push button means that there is a wound in your mental body and when somebody touches it, an old tape automatically starts to play.

People can figure out how to push your buttons for their own advantage and control you and your actions. For example, if somebody wants to make you lose your concentration, he has only to mention your uncle who did a very bad thing to you. You get so mad that you forget what you were doing and talk about your uncle for half an hour.

In our society we all have many push buttons that we are not even aware of. We sit and look at television and the movies for hours on end and think they don't have any effect on us. . . .They put lots of pretty girls around a man at the ocean and make sure that their bodies are half-clothed. They are all drinking beer and having a wonderful time. This is what you want, isn't it — to sit around the beach without much on, drinking beer? So when you go to the market you buy that beer because it now reminds you of other pleasures. You have a mental push button when you see beer in the market.

To purify yourself spiritually, it is necessary to begin a consistent program of right meditation. Right meditation means to sit and think clearly in the light of the Plan. Your thoughts must run parallel to the Plan and you must think of ways and means to put your life in harmony with the Plan. This is real meditation.

Right reading is also an important factor in spiritual purification. Do not read books which create strong pornographic images and thoughtforms in your mind. Do not read literature that creates hatred of certain groups or religions. Stay away from books which will create in you fear, jealousy, or feelings of revenge. These things will eventually sink into your consciousness and become future push buttons.

When you are selecting things to read, make sure that they are in line with Beauty, Goodness, and Truth. If something is truthful but ugly, don't read it. If it is good but there is no truth in it, don't read it. Beauty, Goodness and Truth must always be present together. If one is missing, there will be no balance and you will judge from a lopsided viewpoint.

Spiritually, it is important to develop right motives. First, you must clear away all your wrong motives. This is done by really thinking before you act. Ask yourself, why am I doing this? Am I doing it for my vanity or to exploit others? Is it the right thing to do for all concerned? What will be the result of my action now and in the future? Is this action in line with the Plan? If your action is not in line with the Plan, your motivation is wrong.

In order to be a great laborer for the Plan of the Hierarchy, you need seven virtues. They are:

> one-pointed persistence
> patience
> alertness
> sense of direction
> inclusiveness
> compassion
> courage and daring

One-pointed persistence means that you set out to do something and no matter what happens, you finish it. You persist against all obstacles and difficulties and you accomplish what you intend to do.

Patience in its esoteric meaning is more than waiting for the proper conditions in which to labor. Patience is continuous observation by the Solar Angel of the physical, emotional, and mental bodies, without any disturbance or distortion. The Silent Observer and Inspirer within you *is* patience.

When you have **alertness,** you are aware of what is going on in the world physically, emotionally, and mentally. You see social and global aspects and the signs of the time because you know that your labor will suffer if you do not consider the conditions of the world. You notice changes and patterns and try to see their causes.

The **sense of direction** is sensitivity to the Plan. This is determined by your level of development and evolution. According to this sense, you are able to coordinate your goal and direction with the Plan.

A Hierarchical worker who is going to do something great for the world must be **inclusive** in his thoughts, words, and deeds. In his consciousness, he must see the world as one unit with many beautiful parts.

Inclusiveness is the ability to synthesize many viewpoints and extract the essence or the juice in them all. Inclusiveness does not reject any light that presents itself in the solving of a problem. Inclusiveness takes in those elements of advice, scientific investigation, and knowledge which contribute to the answer of a problem. All wisdom is accepted, regardless of the source.

Inclusiveness does not mean that you collect everything that comes to you and accept it without discrimination, like a trash can. You must learn to look at things and extract the real from the unreal; you must see the beauty of things in a universal sense. If you read a book, you must discriminate between truth and glamor and illusions. Put the truth in harmony with your inclusive viewpoints. Remember, there is no harmony in a trash can.

Compassion is the sign of one who labors as a world server. A world server is one who brings the intentions, the vision, and the revelation of God into manifestation. You must be God-like to do this, and this means that you must be compassionate.

You must have **courage and daring** in order to complete your spiritual building. If you proceed in fear, you will destroy your own work through doubtful or wrong actions. Always try to walk fearlessly, and you will not take wrong steps. Fear clouds your vision with wrong ideas of where to go and what to do. With courage, you act upon the facts in the light of reality.

When you have built your character with these seven pillars of light and wisdom, you will be ready to begin spiritual labor. First, you begin on the mental plane with meditation and prayer. Then through your intuition, you bring the design of the Plan into your mind. Next you formulate your plan of action according to the existing conditions, and you build according to the conditions so that you do not waste your energy or materials.

When I was a boy, we used to carry bags of salt to neighboring towns. We would put the bags of salt on the backs of donkeys and carry them through the river. We never had a problem because there was very little water in the river when we passed through it. One day we gave a new boy some salt to carry to another town. He put the bags on the back of the donkey and started off.

When he had not returned at the end of the day, we went to look for him. We eventually found him sitting at the edge of the river, crying. Without noticing that the water had risen considerably, the boy had crossed the river with the loaded donkey and the water had washed away the salt in the bags. The boy was not alert enough to adjust his plan to the existing conditions, and as a result, he lost the salt.

A laborer for the Hierarchy must be careful not to waste his energy and resources through his stupidity, because he is working for more than just his own well-being; with his stupidity he can destroy part of the Plan. As a laborer for the Hierarchy, there is more to be considered than just yourself; you must consider the scope of the Plan also. As a laborer for the Hierarchy, you have responsibility, and you must be especially careful.

It is also wasteful to give people things which they do not need or which are beyond their level. You must make your efforts fit the needs of the people you are serving; you must give according to the need and the level of the people. You do not try to teach algebra to a first-grader and you do not give a drowning man water to drink.

Laborers for the Plan must have the spirit of cooperation. If this spirit is lacking in you, you cannot work for the Plan and the Plan will not be able to manifest through you.

M.M. says, "Let not evil profit from your labor." Do not work for those who have separative or selfish motives. Don't hold the ladder for such thieves to climb into a window and steal from others. If you want to work for the Hierarchy, you must know for whom you are working and what kind of business they have.

One day a friend of mine came and said, "I don't have a job."

"I thought you were working in a liquor store," I said.

"I don't want to work in that store. A man bought some liquor from me, got drunk and then hit and killed a little girl with his car. I feel as if I had participated in that murder by selling him the liquor."

"Good for you," I said. "You have released yourself from prison and you will have less karma in the future if you quit that job."

Those who are engaged in wrong labor enjoy the fruits of their efforts for only a short while. Those who are engaged in right labor will enjoy the fruits forever. Those who labor for the Hierarchy will enjoy the universe life after life, with clear minds and golden health.

Among the Fiery Servants of humanity should be particularly noted those who take upon themselves sacrificial labor. The spirit of these servants of humanity is like a fiery torch, for in its potentiality this spirit contains all the qualities which can uplift mankind. Only a powerful consciousness can take upon itself sacrificial labor. Each task of a servant of humanity reflects the quality of his spirit. . . .Each manifestation of a Fiery Servant of humanity is creativeness for the good of mankind. . . .

On the path to the Fiery World let us be affirmed in the understanding of sacrificial labor.[3]

1. Agni Yoga Society, *Fiery World,* Volume III, para. 37.
2. See *Hierarchy and the Plan,* by H. (Torkom) Saraydarian.
3. Agni Yoga Society, *Fiery World,* Volume III, para. 71.

CHAPTER 13

BEAUTY

Turn thy mind toward the joy of creation. . . .[1]

One of the nicest things in life is to be in contact with Nature. The closer our contact is with Nature, the more beautiful, healthy, joyful, and creative we are. Most people do not appreciate the wonderful benefits that may be derived from physical, emotional, and mental contact with Nature. Unfortunately, they stop at the physical contact and miss the richness of the experience. It is like eating a delicious tropical fruit without being able to taste or smell it; you just fill your stomach and that is all.

Watch a baby discover a flower and you will see a vivid emotional contact. The child is delighted with the color and fragrance. He laughs and shows it to his mommy with great glee. His heart and soul have met with something beautiful and he wants to share it.

Mentally we contact Nature when we start to think about these beauties. If you are being refreshed by the glory of Nature on a summer afternoon, you may stop by a mountain stream. You may pause to watch the fish as they swim along and notice representatives of each kingdom in the water. You may think about the minerals, plants, animals, and humans nearby and their interrelation with each other. If you are really in tune with Nature, you may let your thoughts rise to advanced humans and to the deva kingdom. You may even see and feel the oneness of

143

Creation by just observing the life in this one tiny section of the Earth.

You may even contact Nature on a spiritual level. You may wonder about the reality behind Nature and how these beauties came to be. You may wonder about the Creator and what He is expressing in a leaf, in a bird in flight, or in a brilliant emerald. You may wonder about His mind and beingness and begin to feel a growing respect for the magnitude of His beauty. You breathe deeply and in some way fuse with this beauty. You have identified with the reality which you have contacted in the beauty of Nature, and an electrical energy has passed into you. This electrical energy is called *joy*.

Joy is an electrical energy which circulates in Nature. When you contact Nature in the right way, you feel this joy, the electricity of Beauty, Goodness, and Truth. Your fusion with these elements of Creation is registered in your being as joy.

I was visiting a friend one day and he asked me to help him cut down a tree. I was shocked by his request because the tree was so beautiful. It was big with lots of branches that birds had built nests in. There was so much life in this tree that I was hurt that anyone would want to cut it down. I asked my friend why he wanted to cut the tree down.

"I don't like it," he said.

We talked about that tree for one hour. After pointing out many beautiful things about the tree and about Nature, I asked him to sit under the tree for a while and try to contact the energy in the tree. I asked him to talk to the tree and see if he could feel anything. I left him alone and went home.

The next day he called me and thanked me for not letting him harm the tree in any way. He said he had contacted the joy of Creation in the tree and learned to appreciate Nature. Now he can feel the joy in all Creation since he had that one contact. The joy of Nature now gives him a great joy in living.

The beauty of Nature refers to everything in Nature. It means the unfolding of a flower, the sound of the ocean as the waves pulsate, and the colors in the evening sky. It also means the beauty in human beings. So many times we forget to look for the beauty in each other. There is such a joy that we can get from each other. It is sad that we don't appreciate each other more.

Look at his smile; watch as she feeds her baby; listen to a child at play. . . .There is such beauty in humanity that we miss by not taking time to notice it and fuse with it. When was the last time that you really looked at those near you and noticed something beautiful about them? Did you sit all day at work and complain about the boss, or did you take one little moment and notice the cheerful expression on a customer's face? Did you appreciate a friend's beautiful eyes or the dance that your brother did when he was happy? Did you feel the joy of Creation in humanity today? If you didn't, you missed out on a lot.

There is such a creative, constructive influence that we can have on each other. You can begin to feel others' peace which radiates out from them. You can fuse with the brightness of their emotional bodies. You can appreciate the diamond in each human being and polish the jewel within your own being.

When we focus upon the darkness of others, we become like clouds full of acid rain. But when we see the light in others, we become stars which guide them through the night. It is so simple: look for light, and you become the light. Observe the joy of Creation, and you will become one with that joy.

In order to see the beauty in others, you must adopt an impersonal attitude. If you have been sitting all day thinking about how much someone bothers you, you must stop it and take a new look at him. Pretend that you have never seen him before and treat him in a really impersonal way. Don't block your mind with the ugliness of past thoughtforms. The beauty will never be able to penetrate through these walls of smog which block the Sun.

By taking an impersonal attitude, a sense of value develops in you. This growing sense of value establishes a line between you and the joy of Nature. It creates a channel of contact between you and the beauty of Creation. Just as a child has a cord connecting him to his mother, we too must develop a cord connecting us with Nature. This link nourishes us just as the link with the mother feeds the child. Look upon Nature as your mother and learn to love Her and relate with Her.

Go to a quiet spot in Nature and relate with it. Lie down on the grass and smell the freshness. Kiss the green in the blades of grass and thank God for creating such a beautiful field. Listen to the song of the birds and the harmony which the waterfall plays. Try to see how the trees serve the other forms in Nature. Look at what the water is doing for the fish and how the grass has its function, too. Think about the role of the Sun in all of this. Learn how each does its job without any expectation in return. The Sun doesn't ask for five dollars from the grass, and the water doesn't give just one cup of itself to the fish. Nature is so wonderful; learn how to live like it does, and you will be the most joyful person ever. Like Nature, your life will have real value in the scheme of Cosmos.

Once I went into a shop to do some business. I asked the owner how things were going for him. "Cross your fingers," he said. "I am doing so much business that the money never stops flowing."

"Good for you," I said. I was happy that he was doing well. "How is your wife?" I asked. "Certainly she must be happy with your success."

"She is so mad at me. I work 18 hours a day. She calls me and complains that I am never home, and she worries about my heart. She doesn't understand that we have a really big bank account now and we can buy new furniture. Last night we had a big fight about it. I wish she understood about money a little more."

This man was so busy making money that he didn't have time to live. Other people are so blocked by their interests, worries, and fears that their lives are like trash cans: they are full of junk and they cannot look out. They have no room for beauty. They are ready to die for their troubles.

Learn to enjoy life. God doesn't want you to be weighted down with worry, fear, and trouble. Run on the beach for a few minutes and feel the sand between your toes. Follow a butterfly through a patch of wild-flowers. Feel the Sun kissing your cheek and try to share love with a passing bee. Don't die for your troubles all day long. Leave them for a few minutes each day and try to communicate with Nature. Turn your mind toward the joy of Creation.

> ...*learn to overcome irritability.*
> *My pupils must have a sympathetic eye....*[2]

There is a close relationship between the ideas in these two sentences. Love, sympathy, and compassion prevent irritability. Irritation really kills you. Negative emotions create a poison in your system that settles on your nerve channels, blocking the electrical energy which is trying to get to your system. The life is cut off from your organs and glands, and the body begins to slowly degenerate.[3]

Irritability causes many diseases which you would not ordinarily contract. You really make yourself sick with your emotions and thoughts. Your emotional reactions become physical reactions, too.

These things can be prevented and overcome by a sympathetic heart. Sympathy, compassion, love, and understanding can stop irritability and the poison which pollutes your system. A pure heart will result in a pure constitution and a healthy life.

Watch yourself when you are irritated. Say that you are eating lunch and your co-worker complains about the boss and the job. You begin to get annoyed and vent your frustrations. Then both of you talk of nothing but the horrible work situation which you must endure. Later, do not wonder where your bad breath and headache come from. Do not wonder why your eyes are blurry and you seem to be developing trouble hearing. You are failing because of your irritation.

How many times have you caught a miserable
cold after being really angry at someone or something? Irritation kills all the antibodies in your blood
so that germs can find a nice home in your system.

Test yourself and you will notice that you have
much more energy when you protect yourself from
irritation. Irritation really saps your energy, and the
effects begin to show after the age of 55. People who
live in irritation begin to shake after this age. Give
them a cup of water and watch their hands as they try
to keep it steady. They will spill it because the sediment
from irritation — imperil — has settled on their nerve
endings and they cannot control their muscles any
more.

Christ emphasized love over and over again. Love,
compassion, and a sympathetic eye are the greatest
remedies for irritation.

Once I was invited to dinner at a friend's house.
We were talking and it was getting a little late. The
wife seemed to be getting nervous as time went by. At
11:30 the daughter came home. Her mother flew at her
when she walked in. "I told you to be home at 9:30," she
yelled as she dragged her daughter into another room.
The girl didn't have a chance to open her mouth.

The mother kept yelling at her for a long time and
said some really ugly things. I wouldn't have talked to
the devil like that — it was awful. When the mother
came back, she said "I really fixed her!"

I said, "You really fixed yourself. Look at how pale
you are. You are shaking all over and your face has a
big scowl on it. You look terrible. Did you ask her why
she was late? Did you find out what happened?"

She called her daughter into the room and asked
her why she was late. The daughter, who was now very
upset, started to cry and explained through her tears.
She had been at her girlfriend's house just as she said
she was. The girlfriend's brother had a terrible accident and needed to be rushed to the hospital. She was
the only one who could drive him as her friend didn't
have her license yet. Her girlfriend was close to hyste-
ria, and in the rush and confusion she didn't have an

opportunity to call home. The brother, a little boy, was now very sick in the hospital. The mother felt so badly when she heard the story that she started to cry, too.

An understanding, sympathetic eye does not jump to conclusions. It calmly asks questions and tries to see things as they are. A sympathetic eye doesn't waste the energy of others by putting complicating doubts and false conclusions on the path of the truth.

In order to overcome irritability, it is good to take positive steps against it. Find the things in your life which upset you and make plans about what you are going to do about them. Remember that whatever you do must be done in the light of Goodness, Beauty, and Truth. If your neighbor always parks so that you cannot get out of your driveway, you are not going to hit his car or let the air out of his tires. This will result in increased problems for you. Instead, you are going to talk to him and show him in a gentle way the trouble that his inconsiderateness is causing for you.

If the boss always picks on you in front of everyone in the office, you are not going to talk behind his back. Go to him and point out what he is doing to you. Do not be shallow and attack him behind his back. Act like a wise person and find methods to remove irritating factors from your life in a beautiful way.

Many people do not realize that negativity makes you leak energy from your system. Negativity feeds the germs which try to penetrate into your mouth, lungs, and throat. Like flies which are nourished by filthy conditions, germs gain power from your negativity. Stop the negativity in your system, and the germs of disease will not use you as a feeding ground.

> *. . .As through a magnifying glass behold the good, and belittle tenfold the signs of evil, lest thou remain as before.*[4]

This is the key to developing a sympathetic eye. When you increase the beauty of others, something in you is touched and you feel beautiful also. When you see the evil in others, ugliness is touched and increased in you, too. Concentrate on the good which others have and don't think about their irritating qualities. Soon you will notice that they will manifest the good more than the bad. Whatever is reinforced in a person will have the energy of manifestation. So help others to manifest their good by reinforcing it in them.

When I was young, I would go to the docks to look at the ships as they came into port. There was one Italian liner that was magnificent. It moved with such power and grace that I was thrilled watching it. It was painted white and it looked wonderful as the Sun hit its decks.

Once I was with a friend watching the same ship. After expressing surprise at my admiration he said, "The ship is dirty."

"Where?" I asked in disbelief. I was just enthralled by the beauty which the whole structure created as it sat in the water.

He pointed to one little spot on the side of the ship where a tomato had been thrown. Well, when you look for ugliness, you will find it. I was really surprised that he was condemning the whole ship for one little flaw.

My father taught me the joy of increasing the beauty in others when I was very small. He did it in such a tricky way, but it really stretched my mind. One day we were walking near a lake and there was a girl of ten or eleven walking in the distance. She had on a colorful dress and her hair looked very special.

My daddy pointed out to me how neat and pretty she was. Then he magnified her beauty in my mind when he said that she moved like a deer in the forest. It made such a nice impression on me! I could just picture a little deer running among the trees on a sunny afternoon.

Suddenly my father said, "Bless her mother and father for making her such a beautiful girl." My thoughts immediately went to the girl's parents and I sent them kind thoughts. My father increased my ability to see beauty tenfold that day. Now when I see a beautiful garden, I think of the care of the gardener and bless him for his efforts.

It is interesting that M.M. says "...belittle tenfold the signs of evil, lest thou remain as before." He is saying that no one improves if he sees dirty and ugly things. He identifies with ugliness, which is distortion and degeneration. If a person wants to grow and unfold into new levels, he must identify with beauty. Beauty unfolds into greater manifestation.

Ugliness becomes a thoughtform in your aura and shapes you in its image. Focusing on ugly things is like inviting poison into your system: it penetrates into every cell and affects the entire body. Ugliness can be seen by people who are ugly. They identify with the ugliness and seek to increase it in the world.

In one of Khalil Gibran's books, there is a beautiful story about Christ. It shows us a good way to keep ugly thoughtforms from developing in us and thereby increasing the ugly things in the world.

One day Christ and some of His disciples were walking into a town. At the edge of the marketplace many people were throwing stones at a dead dog. They were cursing the dog because it was awful-looking and full of disease. But Christ didn't focus on the horrible side of the situation. He looked at the dog and said that it had beautiful teeth, "teeth like pearls."

The disciples were really amazed. This was a great lesson for them. It taught them not to emphasize ugly things. It taught them to find beauty in everything.

Say, for example, that you have to work with a person whom you do not know very well. When you are new to the job, you notice many things about the person. Some of these things may not be nice. Maybe he is a gossip, or he doesn't clean up after himself. You notice these things, but you don't focus upon them. Find things about him that are valuable and compliment him on them. "That was a really complete and original report that you gave." Or, "You're in a good mood today. I like working with cheery people."

You will be surprised. Your fellow employee will become a friend because he will develop a positive attitude toward you. Later, if there are things which are not good for the job you two are doing, you can talk about them in a noble manner. He will be eager to change for the good of your friendship and for the betterment of the work which you must do together.

When we constantly pay attention to ugliness, we increase it. The nightly news is a good example of this. Pay attention to the increase in the crime rate over the years. Every night people feed themselves on bombings, kidnappings, murders, and liquor store hold-ups. What good does knowing about these things do? It only feeds our fear and stimulates bad images in our minds.

Why not find good news to report? "Ten children donated three afternoons a week to cleaning the neighborhood." "Woman babysits for free while mother goes to work." Why aren't these kind of stories in the nightly news? Why must we hear about every gang rape ten times over? Where is the mind of the nation that supports such reporting?

It is especially important to talk about beautiful things when eating. Tell cute stories to one another and try to be really light-hearted when you eat. When you bring trash to the dinner table, your food becomes poison in your system. You pay ten dollars for a big steak and pour acid all over it with your negative thoughts and ugly emotions.

Talk about culture, great heroes, or the joy of living. Don't complain about the boss or tell how bad the children were in school. If you change the quality of your family life in this one area, you will see how your love for each other will increase.

Learn to approach Our Heights pure of heart.
Our Ray will shine upon thee to exalt thy daily
*   life....*[5]

The great heights that a person reaches spiritually are measured by the degree of his compassion, love, and universality. If he holds great ideals and ideas in his consciousness, he will be a person of achievement because he always holds the best before himself.

A person has a pure heart when he loves. The measure of a person's purity of heart is the percent of his love. If he loves ten percent of the time, he is ten percent pure. If he loves seventy percent of the time, he is seventy percent pure.

A person with a really pure heart has no bad motives. He is really harmless. People with bad motives can never raise themselves to the heights of spiritual giants. They will never be able to walk with Great Ones.

Many people wonder how they can keep a pure heart in this crazy world. In Eastern countries they have a very nice practice. After the evening meal, the family does not gather around the television and watch criminal programs for three hours before going to bed. The family sits together and tells stories about great heroes who exemplify strong virtues. The father might sing a song while the little girls make a pretty dance. In this way, everyone thinks great thoughts before sleeping. No matter what happened during the day, their dreams are sweet because their minds are uplifted with stories of courage and hope for the future before sleeping.

One night I was invited to a man's house for dinner. I did not know him well and did not know what to expect. To my great pleasure, after dinner he brought out a book of poetry. For three hours we sat before a nice fire and read Walt Whitman. As I walked home, I hardly felt my feet on the ground. I felt so uplifted. And it was so interesting — the next day I awoke feeling really joyful.

Have you ever noticed this? You go to a beautiful symphony and the next day you are charged. You feel different at work and bring joy to those around you. You uplift others, and they see you as a really magnetic person. They want to be around you because you brighten their day.

When you have a pure heart, you radiate joy and release a special feeling of freedom throughout your body. This makes you magnetic. Once a boy in Texas wrote me a letter saying that nobody loved him and he was very lonely. He wanted to know how to make people love him. I told him that you cannot force people to love you; you cannot buy the love of others with expensive presents either. Love comes to you when you make yourself magnetic and joyful. People love you when you are harmless and pure. People love you when you stand for something great and noble.

Once I told another young man that the simplest way for him to be loved was for him to stop feeling sorry for himself. I told him to change his reaction and attitude to life. It is a great secret of Nature that when you change, Nature will change toward you. It will have a response similar to yours. If you leave the house with a frown in the morning, don't expect a hundred smiles before lunch. But if you leave the house with a really happy face, you will lose count of the happy faces you see.

If you want to be loved, be loving. Have a pure heart and seek the beauty in others. They will look for yours, too.

> *Follow the simplest path, ere you ascend the mountain. . . .*[6]

Simplicity is the result of tremendous inner richness. When you are simple in your relationships, you show that you have inner wisdom and that you are in contact with reality. People complicate life through their stupidity. Something needs to be done, and they do five extra things because they are not sure of their goal or they are in doubt about the right approach. When you are simple, you don't waste time, money, and energy.

Some of the greatest Teachers whom I had as a boy were men of tremendous simplicity. They wore simple clothes and ate simple food. They did not complicate life with things which they did not need.

I remember going to visit a very holy man once in the mountains. My friend and I were passing through the forest and we saw a little deer. We became very still and watched it play for half an hour. When we reached the holy man, I told him about the deer. He laughed with delight as I explained how the deer nibbled at a bush. He had so many questions for me because he was really enjoying Nature through my story.

My friend kicked me because he thought the man was too important to bother with the details of our silliness in the forest. But the holy man, in his simplicity, thought it was magnificent. He felt the beauty of Nature and he did not block his joy.

Notice how Nature does things — in simplicity. The simplest things are always the most beautiful.

> . . .*The power of vision requires pure conditions*
> *amidst prana.*
> *Christ's deeds were consummated amidst the beau-*
> *ties of nature.*
> *Never did He dwell for long in cities.*[7]

Just think, at that time the cities were very clean and beautiful. Look at the pollution we have now. Smog clouds the physical and spiritual vision. Pure prana is needed for spiritual ascent. When you breathe poison, your vision is really blocked.

And as you ascend spiritually:

> *Know how to love as you ascend.*
> *Only later wilt thou realize how gently and lov-*
> *ingly I strive to shorten thy journey in the*
> *assigned sphere of action.*[8]

Have you ever noticed that some people close their hearts as they progress in the world? They start looking down on others because they have superior wealth or knowledge or position. They become critical because others don't have as much as they do. This is such an ugly thing because it means that these advancing people are using their progress for their own self-interest.

M.M. is speaking of ascent in a collective way in this verse. He means intellectual, financial, moral, and spiritual advancement. He is telling us that the way to avoid misusing our expanded position is to develop our love nature. This will keep us in balance.

Increase your love proportionately. Try to love more strongly and deeply because this will be your only source of grounding. It is just like grounding an electrical wire so that you may have light. Love grounds you. It makes all your money, positions, knowledge, and progress a benefit for humanity and not for your self-interest. Love is like an insurance policy that ensures that you pour your light on humanity. With love you are protected from the greatest danger on the path — self-interest.

Look at the love that Christ pours on humanity. Look at the love that your Solar Angel has for you. Do these Great Ones have a private bank account, or do They keep things from us because They want them for Their own use only? They are really Higher Beings, and this means that Their love is profound. You cannot even imagine the depth of it. They want you to progress and succeed. They never belittle you by showing everyone how great They are in comparison to you. This is such a petty thing to do; it is so small.

Don't puff yourself up by showing how much bigger you are in comparison to others. Increase your love; increase your beauty. Learn to ascend with dignity, solemnity, and nobility. Learn to love as Nature loves. Be free with your heart. Don't keep what you have for just your own interest.

Know to spread happiness — condemn not.[9]

When you condemn others, you spread negativity through your whole system. Do the opposite and make people happy. You will see that soon you will be happy, too.

Make it your duty to make others happy. Keep a spiritual diary. Every day mark in it what you did for others. Make it a point to reverse the ugliness in the world with your beauty.

Some people are so miserable that it is an automatic reaction for them to try to make others miserable, too. It is like a disease with them. Kindness, compassion, sympathy, and a loving heart can sometimes crack the flow of their negative energy. If you know such a person, stop being critical of him and change your reaction to him. It may take a long time, but meeting his attacks with kindness will result in his eventual freedom. Slowly a smile will replace the frown chiseled on his face.

The saddest thing is to let an opportunity to do good for others pass you by. Once I was on a plane and a big television star was sitting next to me. He seemed very sad, so I asked him what the matter was.

"My brother was in Germany and he wired for $2,000 for an operation. I didn't send it to him even though I had the money. Now he's dead, and I can never bring him back. If I had only known....If only I could go back and do it right...."

This man's life was a real hell for him. He never enjoyed his money again, even though he had a successful career and lots of money.

One night I was called to the bed of a very wealthy man who was dying. There were tears in his eyes, so I tried to console him. I thought he was afraid to die.

He said, "I don't care about dying. I am crying because I had many opportunities to do good with my money during my life, but I let them pass by. Now I cannot go back and do the good that I could have done."

What a terrible way to die — full of regrets and remorse. Instead of loving relatives, he had bad memories with him as he prepared for his passing.

Learn how to spread happiness, so that you leave a path of goodness behind you. This will keep your pillow soft at night. Spreading happiness increases your love. It expands your heart so that you are not bothered by the silly things people do; you just seek to serve them.

M.M. gives another hint on how to increase our love:

Thy faith should be aflame,

And thou shouldst look forward without expec-
tance.
Expect naught, yet be cognizant of the motion of a
blade of grass.[10]

Let your faith be a beacon in the night. It will guide you through all the storms that life brings. Have faith in the power of your love, but do not look for reward. Just live and do the best you can. Like a blade of grass, you will have enough water, air, and Sun to grow and prosper. Keep the flame in your heart bright, and you will always walk on lighted paths.

---

1. Agni Yoga Society, *Leaves of Morya's Garden*, Volume I, para. 19.
2. *Ibid.*, para. 32.
3. See *Irritation, the Destructive Fire*, by Torkom Saraydarian.
4. Agni Yoga Society, *Leaves of Morya's Garden*, Volume I, para. 32.
5. *Ibid.*, para. 43.
6. *Ibid.*, para. 51.
7. *Ibid.*
8. *Ibid.*, para. 66.
9. *Ibid.*, para. 83.
10. *Ibid.*, para. 209.

CHAPTER 14

BATTLE

The essence of the Teaching is directed to the inner struggle between the self and the Self. The most famous treatment of this battle appears in the *Bhagavad Gita,* with the terrible conflict of Arjuna. The battle of Arjuna represents the battle which each human being must fight against himself when he enters the path of perfection, the path to his Father's Home.

In the opening chapter of the *Bhagavad Gita,* Arjuna is standing on the battlefield midway between two opposing armies, his forces and the army of his kinsmen. He is confused and does not think that he should try to defeat family members who threaten his survival. This opposing army represents his personality, composed of his physical, emotional, and mental desires and illusions. The spiritual army, the army of the Soul, wants him to stand for right human relations, goodwill, and the unity of all life. This army wants him to live a virtuous life of self-sacrifice for the furthering of his evolution.

These two sides of man clash on the battlefield of daily life. They will continue to fight until either the soul or the personality is victorious. Man either falls into terrible crime and inertia, or he is released to a life of sacrificial service for the advancement of the race.

It may seem funny that the physical body always wants to be lazy, while the spiritual principle always wants labor. The spiritual side of a person wants to create labor because through hard work he meets many difficulties and obstacles which make him grow.

The emotional body wants pleasures, but the spirit wants joy. Pleasure is something that comes to you, while joy radiates out of you. When you run after pleasures, you try to attract physical, emotional, and mental objects to yourself. You try to collect things for your own gratification and amusement. But when you are joyful, you are radioactive; you give of yourself because of deep love.

The mental body also likes to collect things. Intellectually developed people who do not feel the pull of the spirit want more and more possessions. The spiritual body does not want to be cluttered with all these objects; it wants to give and sacrifice.

These two armies are within each of us. Victory is achieved when the spiritual side conquers the physical, emotional, and mental mess that we are living in. The physical body becomes spiritual when it becomes really industrious. The emotional body becomes spiritual when it tries to give joy and happiness to others. The mental body becomes spiritual when it tries to think of sacrificial things the person can do so that others have more striving, courage, and daring.

In giving the Teaching, M.M. is sounding a great call to all of humanity. He is presenting humanity with the challenge of the spirit, which is the call to battle against the fierce enemy of the personality. M.M. is not giving a Teaching that tries to pacify you like a narcotic drug. He is presenting a Teaching that will challenge you to strive for more light and love.

The real Teaching makes you so angry at your silly life that you work really hard to change. When you find a teaching that tells you everything is beautiful and you are a king or queen, leave that teaching. Sooner or later it will take your money and your free-will, too.

You will know the real Teaching because it is a call to battle. It tells you that only through sacrifice, labor, daring, and heroic works will you progress. False teachings tell you to stay where you are because everything is so beautiful. The real Teaching says, "Get up. You have a lot of work to do if you are going to evolve into a higher kingdom."

> *A messenger being overtaken by pursuers throws himself with his horse into the broadest part of the river. The pursuers stop in the hope that the messenger is drowning, but he instead rides out to the opposite shore. The pursuers, in their haste, rush to a narrow place, and drown in the current. Verily, where it is narrow, there it is dangerous. This consideration should be applied everywhere. Seeking the mirage of alleviation does not lead to achievement. The most difficult is the most accessible. People do not wish to understand that persistent quests awaken powerful energies. Therefore let us not strive for the narrow, let us prefer the broad principle.[1]*

Let's examine this verse a little more closely. A horseman is taking an important message. It could be a war message, a peace message, or an important message from the Hierarchy. He is being followed by men with evil intentions. When he comes to a river, he shows great courage and daring. He and the horse jump right into the river at the broadest point and swim across. He risks his life to keep the message from the enemy.

The pursuers stop to see whether he is drowning. They don't want to risk their property or lives for the completion of their mission. When they see that he is safe on the other side, they try to find the easiest way to cross the river. They think about their own skins first, and they get trapped. The narrower part of the river has the stronger current, and they are not strong enough to stay afloat. They drown because "where it is narrow, there it is dangerous."

Whenever you are looking for an easy way out, you are entering the most dangerous path.

"*Seeking the mirage of alleviation does not lead to achievement.*" Alleviation refers to things that are comforting for you, things that are pleasing for your physical, emotional, or mental nature but which don't lead you into achievement. Comfort flows with the current and eventually carries you over the waterfall of wasted energy.

The Teaching flows against the current. The Teaching leads to the path where you must fight against laziness and comfort. Common and comfortable things make you give up your quest for a higher path because you surrender yourself to your lower nature and say, "Take over; I give up." But when there is a steep path in front of you, the Teaching challenges you to climb against all difficulties. This is when you really progress.

Hard work and striving are the real Teaching. When you start to accept the Teaching as a nice Sunday morning lecture, you have stopped your progress on the path. The Teaching tells us that the only way to progress is to create difficulties in our lives. For example, tell yourself that you are not going to eat a certain food for one year, and then keep your resolution. Or tell your body that you are not going to smoke or drink for a week, just because it wants these things so badly. Eventually you will find yourself the master of your bodies instead of their slave. You are going to be victorious over your bodies.

Easy paths may lead to destruction. Difficult paths collect your energies so that you keep awake and keep striving. Eventually, you must achieve a great victory over your nature. If your friends and associates seek the easy way, you will know that they do not stand for improvement. They are headed down the path of destruction, which may be very attractive at first but always ends in death. Misuse always breeds ugliness.

M.M. says that when a new person wants to join your organization, he should be tested. Give him heavy labor and make him do things that he hates to do. If he refuses or complains, you know that he is not one of you. Tell him to leave. When he tells you that it is a free country and he doesn't have to work just because the Teacher told him to, know that he is not on the path to the Hierarchy.

The Teacher, Master, or Chohan is there to make you work against your lower self. They make you progess in such a way that you become the master of your own instrument.

The path toward the Hierarchy is not paved with sweet words of false praise and encouragement to enjoy life. The path toward Hierarchy tells you that we are living in a dangerous time and that strong-minded workers are needed to do heavy work with no payment or reward. We need people who will fight and labor for the salvation of humanity.

"The most difficult is the most accessible." We think that the most difficult thing is the hardest task to accomplish. But it is just the contrary! With one heroic action, you have accomplished a victory.

I remember once when I was with a group in the mountains and we thought that a big bear was going to kill us. We were running very fast and we came to a huge river. I didn't think about the river; I just jumped in and swam to the other side. I got stuck in a little mud, but I got out just fine.

Some of the boys stopped by the riverside because the river was so wide and they were afraid to jump. They stood there and thought about finding an easy way across the river. The bear got them and injured them very badly. I saved myself only because I jumped into the most difficult place. Just jump, and you will see that the most difficult thing can be the easiest thing in the long run.

Ask yourself what the most difficult thing to do is. Sooner or later, you will realize that it is being a Divine Being. You will realize that you don't need complicated philosophy, psychology, physics, and chemistry. You will see that you are Divine and that you must act according to what you are. When you realize this, you will have achieved a great victory.

"People do not wish to understand that persistent quests awaken powerful energies." A quest is searching, digging, striving, analyzing, and penetrating. The hidden energies that are buried deep within you will never manifest if you do not awaken them and use

them. When the quest becomes persistent, the energies will be at your service. They will be ready to be used in your persistent quest because you overcame your physical, emotional, and mental bodies so that your spiritual beingness and reality could reveal itself to you.

The persistent quest in the battle against your self awakens powerful energies of heroism, austerity, solemnity, concentration, control, simplicity, and beauty. All of these things are awakened when the spoiled child — the physical, emotional, and mental bodies — are under the control of Arjuna — the fighting warrior and disciple.

Striving reveals your Inner Divinity because through striving you master your instruments. Striving is the radioactivity of your Inner Divinity which annihilates personality obstacles. Striving is the building up of spiritual muscles so that all of your internal enemies are destroyed. These enemies disguise themselves, but the disciple observes himself very carefully and exposes them. He notices the coyote-gossip and smashes him with respect for other's rights. He finds the mouse-laziness and beats him with a beautiful vision of the future. He finds the scorpion-touchiness and shoots him with detachment. Thus the disciple becomes Soul-infused and transfigured.

In this way, the disciple becomes a real help to his fellow man. His associates notice that he is really in control and they look to him for guidance. By setting an example of victory, the disciple shows others that they can conquer their lies, gossip, and hatreds. He shows them how beautiful life is when it is lived in a simple form without these ugly personality habits. In this manner, the disciple loves his enemies. He says, "You are beautiful in your Divinity. I love you, but I don't love your lies. . . . I love you, but I hate your gossip. . . . I love you, but I cannot tolerate your prejudice. . . ." The disciple gives these people courage to fight against their distortions and sicknesses so that they can become Divine Beings.

Buddha said that blood could not be stopped by

blood, but that it could be stopped by love. Love crushes the accumulation of energy being directed against you. Love generates its own force so that you do not have to violently attack others who are hurting you. If someone is spreading unkind lies about you because of their jealousy, treat them with kindness and love. You will be surprised at how a little positive attention from you will make them see part of their own beauty and make them want to be beautiful. They will feel so ugly and awful the next time they start to tell a lie about you that they will be ashamed and want to do kind things for you.

The advice, "Do not resist evil," means that you do not lie when someone else does, even if he lies against you. When someone does something wrong against you, you do not take revenge on him. The best approach is to do something good back to him, so that you overcome the evil in him.

Recently in a political campaign, the man who was running against the governor called him all sorts of dirty names, to which the governor did not respond. The governor stuck to the issues and maintained his dignity by not calling his opponent dirty names back. By ignoring the bad comments and sticking to the issues, the governor crushed the accumulation of negative energy and stopped the formation of negative karma between him and his opponent.

Someone must say, "This is enough. I will stop the accumulation of karma between us." People don't realize the significance of karma. In the end, your karma and his karma are one; so by eliminating the karma of someone else, you are eliminating obstacles on your own path. Why should you accumulate more karma on your path? Help your brother and help yourself by not continuing with the karmic accumulations which will later come back and haunt you.

Some people may think — how easy it is for the Lords, when They have passed beyond the boundaries of earthly burdens! But whoever says this does not know the scope of reality. Precisely as it is upon Earth, so also in Heaven. The earthly burdens pass away, but incomparable cosmic cares take their place. . . .[2]

I used to think that since the Masters had taken care of all Their karmic accumulations, They were free to do whatever They wanted. But it is not this way at all. On our level, we worry about our children. But Masters worry about all of humanity. As you advance, your problems multiply. On one level you go to a university and earn a degree so that you can get a good job, make lots of money, and exploit people. But there are higher universities which graduate you into greater responsibilities and burdens; there are planetary, solar, and galactic universities. As you achieve, your burdens become greater because there are greater challenges and difficulties which weigh on your path.

> . . .*Truly, if it is difficult on Earth, then so much more difficult is it in Heaven. . . . You suffer from darkness and chaos. In all abodes it is as difficult from many aspects of darkness and the same chaos. . . .*[3]

In this case, darkness means the ignorance people manifest through their behavior. If we were not ignorant, we would have no problems. Look around and you will see the result of our ignorance in the pollution of our air, earth, and water. Look where our ignorance is bringing us. If an earthquake happens, what guarantee do we have that the reactors built on the fault lines will not explode and spread radioactivity for many miles? If I were a cartoonist, I would draw a cartoon of humanity hanging itself with the rope of its own ignorance.

> . . .*When the destructive subterranean fire tries prematurely to pierce the earthly crust, or when layers of gases poison the space, the difficulty surpasses all earthly imagination. . . .*[4]

The Masters are working to make this planet a university for humanity so that mankind may pass to another stage of evolution. But humanity is destroying the planet with its fumes and chemical pollutants.

These pollutants make it difficult for the Masters to send messages to humanity because the earthly atmosphere is so filled with dirty gases that Their telepathic messages are distorted, if they are received at all. Instead of seeing a clear picture, you must look through snow and fuzz on the screen and you can hardly see the image being projected.

> ...For ignoramuses think that hymns and harps are the lot of Heavenly Dwellers. Such error must be dispersed. Nowhere are there indications that it is difficult only upon Earth; in comparison it must be said — if here one is annoyed by devils, the Archangel is threatened by Satan himself....[5]

If you are bothered by little devils now, remember that greater devils are awaiting you as you progress. The true Teaching says that more and more difficult times are ahead of us. It is these difficulties that will bring out latent energies within us so that we master the world.

> ...Thus one must understand action and the everlasting battle with chaos. One must realize it as the only path and grow to love it as the sign of the Creator's trust.[6]

It is best to understand that the battle is never going to end because you are battling against imperfection. You are a person now, but you are not yet a Master. You work and become a Master, but you are not yet a Chohan. When you become a Chohan, you are not yet a Planetary Logos. When you are a Planetary Logos, you are not yet a Solar Logos. When you are a Solar Logos, you are not yet a Galactic Logos. . . .

Wherever there is imperfection within you, that is where your battle is. If you become satisfied with your position on the path, you commit suicide because you are not moving forward toward greater battle. Greater battles take you to greater levels on the evolutionary spiral. The Teaching must manifest in your life as practical guides which direct you during the long battle.

Chaos is disorganized activity. This type of activity works against itself and against its own welfare. There is no geometry, harmony, or rhythm in it. Chaos exists on all levels of life because of the misuse of energy.

Chaos is not only a problem for humanity; it is not limited to our level or even to our Planetary Logos. Chaos is a condition in all of Nature. We are told in the Teaching that not only do human beings die prematurely because of their karmic conditions, but sometimes whole galaxies are blown out of existence prematurely, causing severe disturbances in the solar and galactic atmospheric conditions.

The universe is in the process of construction; it is not yet completed. We have a fallacy in our minds that God created everything in seven days and then sat down to watch the universe spin around. This is not true. The universe is in the process of creation. What we have now is only a small part of what is going to be. How deep is God? How infinite is God? The things we have now are only shadows and echoes of coming beauty.

Battle is directed toward all those forces which prevent the spiritualization of man and do not let the human soul proceed on the path of perfection. The weapons used against the human soul are many: hypocrisy, totalitarianism, fanaticism, slavery, bribery, flattery, pornography, greed, ego, vanity....There are also the weapons which are used against humanity: disunity, hatred, confusion, separatism, and love of materialism. Also, there are the weapons of chemical and noise pollution, electrical waves and radiation, electrically produced sicknesses, and brain and mind distortions. Man must fight against all these, preserve his freedom, and protect his survival.

This is not only happening on the physical plane; man must also fight more subtle forces of chaos or Satan. All of this fight is carried on in the light of Christ and His disciples, the group of Victorious Ones which is called by esotericists, the *Hierarchy.*

1. Agni Yoga Society, *Fiery World,* Volume II, para. 324.
2. *Ibid.*, para. 30.
3. *Ibid.*
4. *Ibid.*
5. *Ibid.*
6. *Ibid.*

CHAPTER 15

THE PATH OF PROBATION

Let him not approach for whom the probation seems too long.[1]

In speaking about probation, M.M. is referring to the tests that one must pass before he has an expansion of consciousness. When he passes these tests, greater responsibilities are given to him.

Probation is a time of physical, emotional, and mental testing. We are tested to determine the quality and character of our creativity, ability, and talent. Our solemnity, patience, tolerance, and other virtues are put under severe pressure. We are tested to see whether there are any microbes hidden in our nature, such as anger, fear, jealousy, greed, or hatred. Past temptations are presented to us over and over again, to see if we have really conquered our drives and blind urges.

After a long period of testing, we have an expansion of consciousness. This expansion leads us into heavier responsibilities. If you examine your life, you will notice that every time you were given greater duties or responsibilities or every time you became more creative and successful, there was a probationary period first. The probationary period is the path of testing and crisis; it is a long path on which you meet yourself and slay that in you which limits your freedom and your Divine expression.

The most important thing on the path of probation is the foundation upon which you are building your

170

future. On the path of probation you test your materials for strength and durability and lay your foundation. You can have a really strong foundation, or it can be rotten. A rotten foundation will only earn you lots of hard work for cleaning and repairing later on. But with a solid foundation, there will be no fear in the future. You will never have to go back and rework the same blueprints again. Everything will be in order and in a proper state of repair.

As you progress on the path and are given greater responsibilities, your period of probation becomes longer and longer. For example, when a person learns how to fly an airplane, he must log so many hours in the air with his instructor before he can fly solo. Then he must log even more time in the air before he can take a few passengers. When he accepts the responsibility of 500 passengers, he must be really tested and have much experience in the air. Then look at the years of added training he must pass through for one space flight. As your responsibility increases, your period of probation becomes more strenuous.

If you do not have the patience, stamina, and fortitude to withstand the tension of these tests, M.M. says that the path of probation is not for you. It is better to drop out than to continue. For example, an oceanliner is tested before it is put in the water. Imagine that a little crack goes undetected and the vessel is approved for sea travel. At two or three miles per hour, the crack will not be noticed or cause any complications. But at 30 miles per hour, the vessel will be in great danger, and all the cargo and human life involved may be lost. All because one little crack in the structure was not detected.

M.M. says that we must test our physical, emotional, and mental nature so that hidden things will surface. We must find them before the time becomes critical. In this way they may be sealed and repaired so that tragic loss and damage do not result.

Imagine that you are the leader of a small group and the members entrust you with small donations and personal information. As the money adds up, do you take out small amounts for personal expenses that no one will ever notice? Do you use their confidence and personal information against them in small ways, such as by telling their secrets to others who ask, for reasons unknown to you? The path may become very difficult for you. You may lose a great deal of money through accident or injury to a family member. A person in your group may be promoted over you when you know that the secret information which you hold will win you the job. The path becomes extremely difficult and puts your vehicles under tension. Do you stand steadfast with your principles and virtues, or do you give in to the energies of the moment and take the easy way out? What is the fabric of your character made of — flimsy plastic or unblemished marble?

If you can withstand the physical, emotional, and mental pressures of the testing period, you are ready for another round of responsibilities. As the new responsibilities come to you, watch your bodies. If the emotional body begins to fall into fear, stop it before it enters the black abyss of unnamed doubts and agonies. If it reflects fearful emotions, calm them and heal the centers before they crack. Be ever-watchful for weaknesses in your vehicles and repair them with all due haste. When everything is in order and running smoothly, it is an indication that you are ready for greater responsibility and greater testing.

The emotional body is very tricky and must be kept under constant guard. It must be kept really calm, beautiful, and serene. Any shock in the emotional body reflects in the centers and can cause a center to crack. When a center is cracked, the mind does not function properly. Also, energies are accumulated and translated in a distorted manner, causing trouble to the whole system. The time of probation must be long enough for everything in your nature to be checked.

During the probationary period, you must educate your mind. Imagine that a great inspiration comes to you and you are highly enthusiastic about it, but because of lack of knowledge you cannot form the thoughtform in your mental body; you do not have the education and capability to bring the idea into actualization.

Such people are like cars with flooded carburetors: their minds are flooded with energy but they cannot go anywhere. In the marketplace you can find many people with flooded minds. Many psychics, witches, and drug users are flooded and they don't know what to do or where to go; they mislead so many people. When the mental, emotional, and physical bodies are not ready, the probationary path becomes longer and longer.

The path of probation is an indication or a symbol that you are preparing for an entrance into your spiritual heritage. Ninety percent of humanity is living the life of suffering, hating, and exploiting each other for physical, emotional, or mental concerns. Those who enter the path of probation are challenged to surpass the life of the revolving merry-go-round and make a breakthrough into higher levels of consciousness.

As your consciousness expands, so does your field of responsibility. Instead of five pounds of pressure, you graduate to fifty pounds of pressure. A person with a really expanded consciousness can withstand a million pounds of pressure. As your responsibilities increase, the smallest cracks show within your nature.

This is why M.M. tells us to be careful when carrying the Chalice.[2] One little shock can break the Chalice. The Chalice is the repository of spiritual consciousness and contact with higher forces. It is the seat of greater contact with the creativity within one's Self. It holds the contact with the Genius Who is sleeping within your nature. When you touch this center, you release a tremendous amount of energy and electricity into your system. If your vehicles have small cracks in them, they will not be able to hold the energy and it will escape. You will be out of control and at the mercy of the unleashed energy which is exhausting itself in one of your vehicles.

The Chalice is also the repository of the individual's duties and responsibilities. Man must be very careful to carry his Chalice with self-respect and dignity. He must carry it very carefully because as his duties and responsibilities increase, the attacks upon him will multiply. He will have many challenges and crisis points to pass. He must meet each conflict as a warrior of spirit: steadfast, daring, and powerful. Because of his strenuous preparation, all cracks will be sealed and not one precious drop of energy will be wasted on self-pity, anger, doubt, or fear. The Chalice will be held upright because it contains the most sacred accumulation of precious jewels in the kingdom.

What are some of the tests on the path? You are tested in your ability to write and speak for a great cause. It will be determined if you can face greater difficulties with fearlessness, courage, and daring. Your ability to use time wisely and to work goal-fittingly will be tested. Your capacity to forgive and not fall into the rage of anger and revenge will be tried to the limit. When greater responsibilities are given to you, your attitude will be carefully monitored. Do you say, "I have too much to do right now; find someone else." Or do you respond with the spirit of achievement and say, "Bless this project and those who deemed me worthy of it. I shall try my best in a spirit of joy." Are you able to make the necessary adjustments in your life so that the group effort takes precedence over personal concerns? What are the materials that you are building your higher bodies of, and upon what foundation are you arranging them?

This is the secret behind the legend of the Virgins who were waiting for their Bridegrooms to come. Some of them were vigilant and kept their lamps glowing all night, while some were lazy and went to sleep. The lights of those who fell asleep went out and the Bridegrooms couldn't find them. In other words, the lazy ones were not prepared because they did not respond to the call. The others responded with a sense of responsibility, energy, and preparation. This is the probationary path. It is more important than the path of discipleship because it is the path upon which you build your foundation.

Probation puts your machine in order. Some years ago a young man came to visit me. I remember thinking what a healthy and strong server he could become if he worked on himself. He told me that he had read *The Science of Meditation* and that he wanted to study with me. I was very happy about this, but as we walked toward my office, I could smell a strong odor of marijuana about him. When I asked him if he had smoked before our appointment he said, "What's the matter with it? A little marijuana now and then doesn't hurt anyone."

I said, "Marijuana creates big cracks in the minds of those who are doing meditation. Go away and come back in six months after you have not smoked anything at all."

Marijuana and drugs, as well as disco, rock, and acid rock music create many problems in our systems that are very difficult to repair. They damage the brain, so that when heavier pressure is put upon it, it cracks. The problems do not always show up right away in the person. But later as he starts to advance and progress on the spiritual path, they appear as wounds and sores which have been festering unnoticed for years. They are like ulcerated sores that eat away at the fabric the person has been weaving.[3]

Your system may be doing fine in your service to humanity until a big crisis comes and you find yourself face-to-face with your ulcer. Then you cannot meet the challenge because you have a hidden crack within your nature caused by the effects of drugs and low-level music, and your system cannot stand the tension of the moment.

It is extremely important that everything that we do contributes to our physical, emotional, and mental well-being. We must have healthy food, emotions, and thoughts. We must maintain pure relationships with others. Life prepares us for service to humanity on a sliding scale of heavier and heavier responsibilities. This is the destiny of each human being: ever-increasing progress through ever-increasing responsibility. This is our entry requirement into the next kingdom of

Nature.

On the path, we all fail many times. The important thing is to turn your failures into future successes by learning from them. Don't get discouraged and sit down on the path because you made a mistake or did not pass the test. Don't quit! Learn and keep going. Eventually you will triumph. It is your destiny. You must have faith that you will be victorious; you must keep treading the path with hope, confidence, and joy.

One sign that you are expanding your consciousness is that you start to control your habits or break them. As a child outgrows his toys, so you outgrow those things which do not contribute to your ever-progressive evolution.

The second sign that you are expanding your consciousness is that you enjoy serving others more and more. You serve others in a spirit of joy without any expectation.

A third sign of expansion is growing humility. You see how ignorant you are, and you decide that you really want to learn and progress. You look to those who are ahead of you on the path, and you strive to be like them.

Another sign of expansion of consciousness is that you see things more clearly. You begin to recognize causes and to become a cause in your own life. In your job, you are given increased responsibilities because you become a responsible person. You expand your range of authority because you are capable of greater responsibility. This simply means that you have demonstrated that you can be a leader because you can see clearly and solve your own problems.

It is very important that you recognize that you are on the path of probation but that you do not look to where the path is leading. You do not say to yourself, "If I pass this test, surely my Master and my Solar Angel will notice me and give me a big reward." You do not try to play games with Them or impress Them. You just get out of bed every morning and try to do the best you can and in some way make things better than the day before. If yesterday you were able to hold your

tongue when someone insulted you, today try to forgive him, and tomorrow try to love him. Don't look too
far down the path; just look at your actions today, and
everything will fall into place naturally. Try to make
an effort every day to increase Beauty, Goodness, and
Truth in the world.

Trying to constantly improve will graduate us
from the human kingdom to the Divine kingdom. If we
do not take this step in evolution through our service
and sacrifice, we will suffer more and more. Increased
suffering will eventually make us awaken to the pitiful
state we are in and say, "I don't want to live like this
any more. I want to evolve and be really spiritual."
This will lead us to greater concern about the welfare
of our bodies and about the degree of our service and
sacrifice. We will take a positive stand for evolution
and see all of our actions in relation to it.

When we accumulate more suffering, we are wasting our time, energy, space, and creativity. Imagine
that the Owner of the planet says to you, "Here is 5,000
dollars." You take it and enjoy it for a while. Then He
calls you back and asks you what you did with it. You
hang your head and say, "I went to nightclubs and
danced to disco music with some of it. I smoked a little
dope with part of it, and the rest I spent on drinks for
my friends."

Do you see the pain and suffering you are going to
be in for when you waste your resources in such a
fashion, feeding your lower nature and living just for
the satiation of your senses?

In the future, we will learn and progress through
joy. This is a natural conclusion to our conquering of
our lower selves. When we become the masters of our
physical, emotional, and mental natures, then we will
release ourselves from pain and suffering and enter
into joy. Your joy starts when you take command of
yourself and get out of the miserable condition in
which you are living. When you learn how to keep your
balance, you enter into joy.

Joy is communication with higher planes. Other
types of joy are temporary experiences and actually

false joys. Real joy lasts because you have conquered
yourself and have entered into greater states of awareness.

> You already know that neither goodness nor intel-
>   lect alone leads to Us,
> But the evidence of spirituality is needed.
> This quality comes the moment the spirit is ready.
> Naught can hasten the affirmation of the path.
> Even a Call is useless. . . .[4]

Intellect alone is not the only way to progress
because the intellect usually works for self-interest.
Goodness alone is not a way of progress. So many good
people are misled. Their acts of sincerity very often end
in evil results because they were not mindful and they
were used by dark ones with evil intentions.

Take, for example, a woman who decides to help a
needy family by driving them places and buying them
little things. In her concentration on being good, she
does not see that the family is not developing their own
sense of responsiblity. Every time they need or want
something, they simply call the nice lady, knowing she
will provide it for them. Soon the family will weigh as
heavily on her as an iron weight around her neck.

The spirituality that M.M. is talking about has
three components. The first is striving toward greater
heights. You must always try to go forward through
dedication, service, sacrifice, and expansion of consciousness. You must make conscious efforts to grow in
every way possible. You must not be happy where you
are. You must want to be more loving, dedicated, and
sacrificial. You must want to grow in your service.

The second aspect of spirituality is sacrificial service. When someone asked a Master how a person who
is approaching the Hierarchy could be recognized, He
replied, "By his field of service." If his field is one mile,
he is equal to one mile. If his field is a whole country, he
is equal to a country. But when his service includes all
of humanity, he has really become universal and he is
approaching the Hierarchy.

The third aspect of spirituality is the sense of

universality and inclusiveness. When you have these three qualities, you are a spiritual person. But you must have these qualities 100 percent of the time. One little lie or a small bit of gossip diminishes your degree of spirituality, and you are not a truly spiritual person.

We must again remind ourselves that our service grows through a long period of preparation. A person does not decide that he is going to be a doctor one day and put his name in the phone book as Dr. So-and-so, brain specialist, the next day. He must go to medical school, learn by degrees, and pass many tests before he can accept patients. Only by hard work, preparation, and probation does he become able to serve in such a way.

He who is with Us has oft an hour of battle.
But he knows that he is ever victor.[5]

If you decide to stand with the Hierarchy, you will have many battles to fight, but you will also know that you are always going to win. The real battle is within your own nature. You are going to conquer your separative interests and stand for humanity in everything that you do. The light will increase in you, so that eventually the two armies within you will face each other on the battlefield. Like Arjuna, you will wage the battle of the Higher Self against the lower self and win a great victory.

Your lower bodies will pull together and fight until death. The battle will last a lifetime or lifetimes, but you are going to win. Your Higher Self will shine through as you increase your light through sacrificial service. The battleground is filled with your doubts, fears, negative emotions, hangups, and blind urges and drives. Eventually you will conquer each and every enemy the lower self puts in your battlefield. The action will progress according to your own pace, but you will win. That is certain.

The most important thing to watch for in your battle is laziness. Laziness is like having 1000 donkeys in your nature who won't move, but just sit down and rest. Battle is the only way to fight these donkeys.

Our psychological nature is so tricky; when you are at your laziest point, you complain of being too busy. Have you ever noticed that you get the most accomplished when you are really busy? Making excuses is just an illusion most of the time. Put carrots in front of your donkeys and move! Do something; create something to do. This is very important.

"But the evidence of spirituality is needed. This quality comes the moment the spirit is ready." This means that you have passed your period of probation and now you are ready. For example, if I need to hire a typist, I will give all the applicants a test. If a person can only type ten words per minute, her "spirit is not ready" for the job. But if she can type 100 words per minute, she will get the job because her "spirit is ready."

Unfortunately, we live in a society that encourages laziness. Once I went to Santa Barbara, California, and spoke with fifteen boys. I asked them what they were doing to improve their lives and they told me that they were smoking dope and thinking about how beautiful God is!

Where was the going-forward, the striving? They were only becoming a load on society's back. Some of them asked me for a ride, but I told them that I did not want them to be a burden on my car. "Work. Make something of yourselves. I am not going to contribute to your laziness."

They accused me of not being a spiritual man. I told them that a spiritual man would challenge them to become something great. "You can walk," I said. They were not very happy.

Daringly raise your shield. I ask one thing: not to weaken your strength with gold. My Teaching does not like gold.[7]

Money can really weaken you. When you serve and expect reward, you lose your strength. When you expect reward, selfishness enters the flow of service and sacrifice coming from your Innermost Self. Self-ishness stops the flow of light, love, and power which is trying to flow from your actions. When you begin to sell your service, the service stops and you become a mercenary. Your power leaves you.

> Love the solitude of thought, when the sparks of understanding weave a wreath of knowledge. And as I have vouched for you, so entrust yourselves to Me. With the Hand of Power I affirm the path to the Heights. Apprehend the Good when My Envoys will bring the tidings: "He has come!" The hour of happiness is ordained, and on the way there are flowers.[8]

If you do not give yourself totally to Him, you are not entrusting yourself to Him. You are not in a state of total, sacrificial givingness. You must renounce yourself to Him, to the Teaching, to the Plan and the Purpose. If you hold something back for yourself, then you are not really entrusting yourself to Him. Entrusting yourself to Him means to really give yourself to Him.

In the *Koran,* a Moslem is defined in its original translation as one who gives himself totally to God. He has at-one-ment with the aims and goals of God, and he lives a life of dedicated sacrificial service.

Many people give 60 percent and keep 40 percent for themselves. If you really give everything, you function physically, emotionally, and mentally for the cause of humanity. Then you are really entrusting yourself to Him, and no matter what happens you will be all right. You achieve a state of total givingness.

The solitude of thought that M.M. is speaking about suggests that your physical, emotional, and mental noises no longer penetrate into your secret chamber of contact. You have hushed your glamors, illusions, hangups, and urges. There is no imposition on your vehicles by these things. You are like a hermit going into a cave. The solitude is an inner state. It is a state of total concentration in which you create a vacuum around yourself and become one with the vision you have.

In esoteric literature, flowers have a double meaning. They stand for the actual flowers we have in our gardens. We should plant and care for these flowers because they help to beautify and purify our atmosphere. The devas love them and like to be near them. Flowers on the path also stand for blooming people. This includes Great Ones Who have transformed Their natures, as well as anyone in humanity who is actively working for the spirit and not for the separated self.

> *Possession devoid of the sense of ownership*
> *will open the path to all without conventional*
> *inheritance....*[9]

Those who will have power over the resources of the earth will be those who do not feel that they possess these things. They will see themselves instead as custodians whose responsibility it is to provide for the right distribution of God's bounty among His people. There will be no gold found in the safe-deposit box of the custodian of electricity, and there will be no secret bank account found for the custodian of natural gas. These things will be like folk songs and other forms of folk creativity: there for all of us. There will be no "copyright with all rights reserved."

When we do not approach life with the attitude of possession, we have all the abundance needed for survival and comfort. Christ says to learn to be like the lilies of the field. Food, sunshine, and water will be provided for you, but you must not hoard these things so that there is nothing left for your neighbor. Possession eventually results in the removal of things from your hands. If you are a good gardener, take care of the land, but don't think that you possess it. It belongs to all of humanity.

1. Agni Yoga Society, *Leaves of Morya's Garden*, Volume I, para. 287.
2. See Chapter XII, "The Chalice and the Seeds," in *The Science of Becoming Oneself*, by H. (Torkom) Saraydarian.
3. For further information see *The Fiery Carriage and Drugs*, by H. (Torkom) Saraydarian.
4. Agni Yoga Society, *Leaves of Morya's Garden*, Volume I, para. 311.
5. *Ibid.*, para. 337.
6. See the *Bhagavad Gita*, translated by H. (Torkom) Saraydarian.
7. Agni Yoga Society, *Leaves of Morya's Garden*, Volume II, page 14.
8. *Ibid.*, page 17.
9. *Ibid.*, page 35.

CHAPTER 16

QUALITIES OF AN AGNI YOGI

In esoteric literature, Agni Yoga is called by three names. These names are the yoga of synthesis, the yoga of life, and the yoga of the Innermost Self. M.M. also calls Agni Yoga, the yoga of utmost sacrifice.

Agni means fire. Fire has three different aspects. These are fire by friction, solar fire, and electrical fire.

Fire by friction is the fire which acts in the personality. It is a physical, emotional and mental fire. Your body has heat, your emotions are warm, and your mind is fiery. Fire by friction is one fire which acts through the vehicles of the personality.

Solar fire is the fire of your Soul. This is the fire of your Transpersonal Self.

The third fire is the real fire within you. It is the electrical fire, the fire of Spirit.

These three fires are aspects of the one flame. You are a Spark which manifests through the personality, the soul, and the Spiritual Triad.

Fire by friction integrates the personality. It works through the physical, emotional, and mental vehicles and molds them into a symphonic masterpiece. The personality vehicles are synthesized into a beautiful harmonic expression of the perfection within.

Solar fire fuses the personality with the life of the human soul. People who have reached this stage are called Soul-infused personalities.

Electrical fire makes the Soul-infused personality enter his own Core. This is when he becomes Himself.

184

The first fire, working through our personality, identifies us with one humanity. We work for humanity and we serve humanity. By molding and synthesizing us, solar fire opens those centers and intuitive processes which bring us in contact with the Hierarchy. Electrical fire puts us in contact with Shamballa.

These three fires do not work only on the planet. They are found in the solar system, in the galaxy, and in all of Cosmos. On one level of the spiral, the first fire puts us in contact with the Planetary Logos, the life of this planet. The second fire puts us in contact with the Heart of the Sun. The third fire puts us in contact with the Central Spiritual Sun. On a higher level of the spiral, the first fire unites us with the Sun. The second fire unites us with Sirius, and the third fire unites us with the Great Bear.

Agni works on different levels and in different fields. We are in existence in all of this fire because we *are* fire.

Yoga means much more than unity. It means progressive unification with a higher level on the evolutionary spiral. Unity is a process which results in progressive at-one-ment.

The first step of progressive unification is to become one in your personality. You must create unity within your physical, emotional, and mental bodies so that they function as an integrated whole. In some people, there are splits and gaps which cause the bodies to actually work against each other. For example, the mind wants something but the emotions are against it and the body rejects it. There is separation in the person, and he cannot make up his mind. Sickness and unhappiness result. The energies work against each other, and the person cannot find any direction in his life.

When the bodies are united, the first grade of Agni Yoga is achieved. This is unification through "fire by friction." The second grade of Agni Yoga is unification of the personality with the Transpersonal Self. This is unification through "solar fire." Unification through "electrical fire" is the third grade. This unification comes when you sense your Divinity and you conduct your life not from the personality or Soul level, but from your Innermost Core.

As you unite on the personality, Soul, and Innermost Core levels, you unite with humanity, Hierarchy, and Shamballa. This is a process of progressive unification. M.M. says in the Agni Yoga literature that your unification with your Divinity will be so complete that one day you will feel that your heart is the Heart of Cosmos. When you reach this stage, you are an Agni Yogi.

How can we achieve this level of realization? How can we become an Agni Yogi? Let's be very practical and consider points which we can incorporate into our lives. There are eleven qualities which we need to develop.

The first quality to be developed is **purity.** There can be no unification until there is purity. Start with the purification of your personality vehicles. Try to make your body, emotions, and mind really pure. Clean them of all the factors which are preventing your health and well-being.

After you clean your vehicles, try to increase your depth of purity and eliminate all obstacles and cleavages which form barriers between you and Cosmos. This is a very difficult thing to do because it requires purification by love. You must replace all the darkness in your nature with the light of love. This means that you do not hate anyone because of their racial, national, religious, or ideological differences. You become so fiery that you touch the essence of things and the outer phenomena do not limit your consciousness. You find the common denominator in all things and discern the real from the unreal. Love purifies you of all those obstacles which separate you from the whole of Creation.

Purity means much more than physical fasting. Purity involves mental and spiritual fasting as well. These lead to deeper and deeper levels of purity. You start with one little point in your nature and expand your field from there. For example, you say that you are not going to lie to your wife any more. Soon you include your friends and boss on the list of people to whom you are not going to lie to. After a while, you really stand for honesty. You are honest in all of your dealings at home and at work.

If you have purified your system of all that is separative, you have been purified by the fire of love. As the depth of your love grows, the more the radiance of your purity will glow in the murky sea of separation which tries to engulf you.

On the mental level, anything which blocks your understanding is an impurity, an imperfection. Clean it, and your consciousness will be really unified. You will be able to penetrate into the core of any problem and solve it. With the purity of your mind, you will be able to find the essence in other things and relate to that essence.

It is very important to purify yourself. You can start physical purification by taking regular showers, by dressing in a becoming manner, and by eating only pure food. Do not take anything into your system which will pollute it. Find those things which are healthy for you and those things which create disturbances in your system. Eat only those things which contribute to your health, and eliminate those foods which cause anger, greed, and other emotional excitements in you.

Emotional purification is more tricky than physical purification because you must watch yourself very closely. Try to determine what controls you emotionally. Then make a plan of how to change your reactions or how to detach yourself from those situations. Emotional purity is very difficult, but once you master it, you jump a major hurdle in your evolution. When your emotional body is coordinated, you will express only those emotions which are in harmony with Agni Yoga.

Once you decide that you will have only those emotions that are in line with Agni Yoga, you will be tested. During these tests, watch yourself. For example, if someone you know calls and is very nasty to you, do you react in a nasty manner, or are you able to hold your temper and composure?

There is another kind of purity which is extremely important to those who seek the path of the Agni Yogi. Many people fail here because it requires alterations in patterns of behavior as well as changes in associations. This is the purification of relationships. You must be very careful about the people with whom you interact. M.M. says that even a handshake may pollute your life for many years. When you become an Agni Yogi, your purity can burn the impurity in others, but until that time, you must be careful about whom you touch.

An Agni Yogi is so pure that every vibration within his group creates a reaction in his instrument. This is why they say that "an Agni Yogi feels the weight of a cloud upon his shoulders." He is extremely sensitive, and he can feel the wrong motives of those in his group. His absolute sensitivity is necessary because only with a sensitive instrument can he reach higher sources.

The next level of purification is mental purification. Mental purification means that you will have only pure thoughts and motives. There should be no lust, envy, greed, or jealousy in them. You will have to learn how to respond to hateful things with compassion and love rather than with anger and revenge. Purity of thought is based on synthesis, sacrifice, and the oneness of life.

Lazy people of small vision and effort will never dare to enter the path of the Agni Yogi. Only those who really strive and struggle can find the entrance to the path; then they must be willing to work harder than they have ever imagined. But they know that their striving will lead them to attainment of oneness with life. This is the blessing that motivates their every action.

The second quality which needs to be developed on the path to becoming an Agni Yogi is **striving.** An Agni Yogi strives by trying to improve himself. He tries to make himself as perfect as possible by maintaining constant vigilance over his actions, emotions, thoughts, motives, and creativity.

The path of an Agni Yogi is the path of improvement; the Agni Yogi works every day on all the expressions of his life in order to reach perfection. He learns how to do this with great solemnity and joy. If he makes a mistake, he simply tries again and learns from his error. He does not become grief-stricken and give up. Soon the Agni Yogi learns that perfection is an ever-expanding reality. Once he reaches a certain level, he does not stop there. This leads to degeneration. He must constantly struggle and strive to improve himself. This is the life of an Agni Yogi.

An Agni Yogi may be very excellent in what he does, but he still strives for betterment. Stopping on a level of achievement means that he won't be accepted into greater realities.

Striving is an effort to make breakthroughs in your life. You must try to break out of all those limitations which bar you from the next level of the spiral of life. If you are in school and you want to drop out because the work is too much or you have lost your motivation, remember that giving up is not a sign of an Agni Yogi. An Agni Yogi would write the paper or study for the test. He would make a game of it and joyfully say, "I can complete this project. It is possible for me to achieve." He approaches the task with enthusiasm and the spirit of adventure. The fire in him does not allow him to sleep in matter, to become paralyzed by negative emotions, or to be defeated by low-level thoughts. The fire in him revives him so that daily he may renew his struggle. Yoga means continuous striving on the path of perfection. It is a cyclic unification with perfection on ever-expanding levels of Divinity.

The third quality upon which those wanting to enter the path of Agni Yoga must work is **fearlessness.** Fearlessness has three degrees.

The first degree of fearlessness is that a person identifies with spirit and not with matter. As long as a person is connected with his possessions, position, and body, he lives in the fear of losing them. When a person is identified with the Self, he is able to overcome fear. He can never lose or damage the Self, the Reality within. The person who lives in the light of his Divine Self lives in Beauty, Goodness, and Truth. He becomes one with these principles because they are Life. He is not afraid because he is one with life itself and he knows that though his form may be damaged, nothing will happen to the life in him. An Agni Yogi is a person of total fearlessness because Agni Yoga is the yoga of life.

Most people we meet today are not Life itself. They are bodies, cars, houses, and dollars. They are stuck to the objects of their desires, and they find their identity within them. The cost of their home, boat, or automobile is the measure of their worth in the world. They live in fear of diminished value. Those who awaken realize that they have nothing to be afraid of if they learn to focus their attention on the oneness of all life.

The second degree of fearlessness is the ability to penetrate into the mysteries of the Cosmos without any fear of the darkness, the unknown, or the mysterious. You must be able to challenge the mysterious with the spirit of conquest because you want to know what life is and discover the principles of Cosmos. You must want to know who the Great Ones are and whom and what They serve.

When I was a boy in Asia, my Teacher told four of us once that we were to meet a great Teacher whom we had heard much about. The others started to tremble, but I said, "What's the matter with you? Why are you afraid?"

One replied, "Are you crazy? He is such a great Teacher!"

"No, I'm not crazy. I love him and I will be very happy to finally see him. You are the crazy ones to be so afraid!" When he came, I went up to him and kissed his hand. The other boys trembled at a distance, but I sat right by him. I was not afraid because he and I were one in spirit. He was me and I was him. We had a bond of unity in the spirit. My fearlessness allowed me to penetrate into this mystery without any hesitation. I wonder if the other boys ever learned this truth. Their fear prevented them from experiencing the beauty of this deep reality.

The third degree of fearlessness is the ability to make a sacrifice without any trace of fear. You will notice fear on the faces of people when you ask them to donate one penny for a great cause. They may tell you that it is a really worthy cause which they believe in with deep sincerity. But when you ask them to back their conviction with an action, their hearts tremble and stop them from giving or doing anything. Fear paralyzes them into inertia. This fear comes from attachment to matter.

Fearlessness develops in a person when he gives matter sacrificially and when he gives up matter because it is not contributing to the achievement of his goal. He develops an attitude of not caring about matter because he realizes its true value. Either the matter can be used better elsewhere — as in the case of excess money — or the matter is better off not being used — as in the case of drugs and cigarettes. When you see the true value of an object, you control it and do not associate any fear with it.

When I was a young man, I was traveling through the mountains alone. A thief stopped me and said, "Give me your money or you will be killed."

"Why are you doing this?"

He said, "I need money."

I said, "I will give you everything I have, then." I started to take off all my clothes. I was joyful. He was so happy because he was going to get a lot of material goods. But then a puzzled expression came over his face as he thought about my action. After a while, he said, "You are the most fearless man I have ever met."

"What should I be afraid of?" I asked. "You asked me for something and I am giving it to you."

Suddenly he got up and said, "Here are your things. I am not going to take anything from you." You could see that he was stricken with respect for my courage and fearlessness.

A long time ago, there was a man in Greece who was fascinated by geometry. The country was at war with Persia and his city was under siege. But he was near the solution of a very important problem about triangles. He was working very hard at his desk when a huge soldier came up behind him with a dagger in his hand. "I am going to kill you," he said.

"Wait," the man said. "I want to finish this problem."

The soldier didn't wait but stabbed the man in the back. The man laughed a little before he died and said, "Look, you killed my body but I am taking my mind with me. You can never kill that!"

Fearlessness continues on an ever-progressive and gradient scale. Fearlessnes is an attitude of identification with spirit and a giving up of matter in every form. If you have a dollar, you can give a dime to a worthy cause, but if you have a thousand dollars and only give a dime, you are too attached to matter. Your generosity should be in proportion to your means.

Fearlessness rests in breaking your identification with matter so that when you give, you are not giving anything up. You are merely sharing with others the life which you have been the temporary custodian of for a time. You lose your sense of "I and mine" so that you feel that another's need is your need. You are one with the life in others.

The fourth quality to develop in order to become an Agni Yogi is **beauty.** Beauty is the ability to manifest your Divinity, the Inner Essence. In each creative act, the artist tries to give expression to his Divinity. When this Divinity is translated in a form, we say that it is beautiful. When the Innermost Divinity of the artist is expressed in beauty, he is born in that beauty. He is given new life through his translation.

Through expressing, evaluating, appreciating, and working for beauty, you are bringing your Innermost Self into manifestation. You are giving birth to yourself. You are bringing Agni into manifestation. This Agni is your Spark, which reflects the beauty of God. Thus through beauty, you become an Agni Yogi.

The fifth quality is the **sense of universality.** An Agni Yogi is not separative in any of his actions. His thoughts, conversations, writings, and actions stand for unity, for universalism, and for one spirit and one existence.

The Agni Yogi knows that all life is one existence. Now we see the stars and planets as separate and distinct bodies. But the great Sage, D.K., says that if you go far into Space, the whole of Cosmos appears as one lotus which is slowly opening and expanding into the universe. . . . Existence is one little lily in Space.

An Agni Yogi is a person who unites this Cosmic perception with his smallest experiences. His Cosmic understanding is proven by his respect for the Divine, which permeates his smallest action.

Christ once said that those who are faithful in the smallest acts will be given greater things. This faithfulness in the minutest of details is part of the Agni Yogi's character. He sees a great vision and unites with it. He brings this vision into his conversations, relationships, and daily life. You feel his universality when you are with him. Though he may be speaking of simple things, you know that the whole Cosmos is behind him.

Try to work for universality. Don't be separative in your thinking, in your actions, or in your emotions. Try to unify others and stand for unity. Remember that ugly criticism does not fit into the life of an Agni Yogi. Gossip and dirty remarks extinguish the fire in our systems.

Try to radiate the purity of your spirit. When you stop emitting dark, dirty things, your spirit will be pure. Be fiery and make a decision that you are going to be universal. Don't wait for tomorrow; make a decision and begin right now! Decide that you will not say anything nasty or separative about anyone or anything.

If you should make a mistake, don't give up. Start over with renewed determination. A great Yogi said that sometimes we strive for years and years to reach the mountaintop. Then just as we reach the top, we slip and fall down to the bottom again. An Agni Yogi must get up and start to climb again. An Agni Yogi recharges himself and begins again with energy, enthusiasm, and inspiration.

Sometimes a little thought may make you miserable. For example, you may feel that you are not adequate for the heights. You must crush these thoughts which diminish you. Any time a separative thought comes into your mind, try to overpower it with your Beauty. Radiate your Beauty to every cell in your body, and let it shine out for the whole world to see.

The sixth quality which we need to develop is **Love.** People say, "That's easy. I know what love is." But real Love is so deep. It is the ability to sense the Heart of the Sun. It is not personal, family or national love. It is not even international love. This Love means that you are devoted to something abstract and Divine. You are spiritually intoxicated with bliss.

One day when I was in Asia, I was taking a walk and I saw a yogi. He was smiling. I could tell that his joy was very deep and real. I went over to him and asked him a few questions.

"Your questions are not important. Are you happy?"

"I don't know," I said.

"You have many questions, but you are not ready to understand any of my answers. Try to understand that only in Bliss, only in utmost Joy and Love, can you understand the mystery of life."

The seventh quality we need to develop is **transfiguration.** Transfiguration means that your physical, etheric, emotional, and mental bodies become dynamically radioactive with the beauty of your Spirit. We think transfiguration is very far away from us, but it isn't. We can achieve this state through sacrifice, dedication, meditation, and love. We all have the ability to transform and transfigure ourselves, so that eventually we will stand as shining flames.

The eighth quality is **enthusiasm.** Put energy and joy into your actions. As you proceed through your daily routine, put fire and compassion into your actions, emotions, and thoughts. Approach the world with an enthusiastic attitude, and put the light of your spirit into everything you do. Try to charge your objects, friends, work, and ideas with the spirit of fire. You will learn that as you give fire, you become fire.

Enthusiasm is the ability to bring into manifestation within you the spiritual fires from the higher planes. This is done through your words, emotions, thoughts, and actions. As you become a transmitter of fire, the fire goes through your vehicles and purifies, energizes, sublimates, and transforms your personality. Through channeling fire, you transform yourself.

There was a girl who came for counseling one day. She was filled with sorrow because her whole family had been lost in a tragic accident. I spoke with her for a while and then asked her if she had a few hours to help us. She said that she didn't mind helping, so I told her to paint the wall. She began the task and soon was singing a lively song. It was raining outside and she made a happy tune out of the rhythm of the raindrops hitting the roof. Suddenly she turned to me and said, "You just released me."

This girl overcame her grief with the fire of enthusiasm. During the next few weeks I gave her many other jobs to keep the grief from returning. She labored day and night and became very enthusiastic. This was a test for her, and she passed.

The ninth quality to be developed is the **sense of Infinity.** Many people do not realize that one of the causes of depression is being stuck on the same track all the time. You cannot see beyond the end of your nose because you think that this is all you are and have. Your focus is limited to the past and the present. You think that your present problems are everlasting. The result is that you get depressed and give up. You cannot conquer your problems because you are so attached to them.

When you start looking at your life from the viewpoint of eternity, your problems melt away. Your essence is Eternity. There is no time, space, matter, force, or form in your essence. You build these things and relate to them only in confined areas which we call

time and space. You are not these things; you merely
use them for a specific purpose and a specific time.
Your essence is eternal. When you can feel yourself in
the realm of eternity, you are a real conqueror of life
because you master the technique of seeing your progress in terms of your essence. The eternal viewpoint
releases you to the joy of a progressive, ever-expanding
life.

The tenth quality of an Agni Yogi is **self-sacrifice.**
If you want to become an Agni Yogi, you must begin by
making small sacrifices in your daily life. Eventually
a time will come when you give all that you are and you
have for the service of humanity. Self-sacrifice is like
an avalanche: once you begin, you can hardly stop
yourself from doing and giving more. Suddenly you
realize that all the world is yours and that it is impossible for you to give anything up; everything belongs
to you. You are able to enjoy what you have and use it
for the time being. You feel the relief of not having to
worry about your objects because they cease to own
you.

Your level of sacrifice is related to your level of
consciousness. First you start by being nice to someone you don't like, and you consider this to be a great
sacrifice in your life. Soon being nice to others becomes
such a habit that you really start to love everyone;
being "nice" becomes part of your nature.

The eleventh quality of an Agni Yogi is **observation.** In the Agni Yoga Teaching we are advised to
develop observation. We are told that observation
helps us to expand our consciousness. We must be
awake and conscious in order to observe. Observation
must be carried on in all our relationships and communications. Through observation, we develop first a
seeing eye. An eye that sees brings a great amount of
knowledge to its owner.

Observation is not a mechanical process, like a
video camera which continuously takes pictures of people and objects. Observation is a *conscious* registration of life events, plus an observation of the causes
and effects of the events. The person begins to observe

also the physical, emotional and mental undercurrents related to outer events. Also, the formation of inner currents is observed as an effect of outer currents.

Observation is an effort to see and understand how a cause creates an effect, how an effect is annihilated by a cause, how a cause turns into an effect, how an effect annihilates itself. . . .Observation is the faculty of seeing and understanding how life functions in all departments of nature and how a person can consciously cooperate with it.

All knowledge is the result of observation. No skill is developed without observation. Observation uses not only the eyes, but all the sense organs and the intuition. Observation starts with physical objects and develops with emotional, mental and finer objects. Eventually observation becomes four-dimensional. It is after you develop four-dimensional observation that you can operate your "all-seeing eye."

It is the human soul who carries on the process of observation. The more advanced he is, the greater is his field of observation. Observation leads to synthesis. The sense of synthesis enables a person to see an object in relation to the physical, emotional, mental, and spiritual worlds, and also in relation to individuals, groups, nations, and humanity.

We must remember that the human soul becomes himself through the process of observation. The more he observes, the more he becomes himself, because through observation he disidentifies himself from the object of observation. As he finds himself more liberated from the limitations of the objects of observation, he becomes freer, more himself, until he reaches the point where he becomes the *observer.* At this point, he observes with disidentification all that is going on within his own world and the outer world.

There is a very mystical principle behind this. You increase your sacrifice to such a degree that eventually you will be able to sacrifice your whole self. This is the hidden meaning behind what Christ meant when He said that unless a man loses himself, he will not be able to find his Self.

This all begins when you decide to make one little
sacrifice. Choose an area that is a problem to you in
your family, national, or international life and decide
that you are going to be giving with your money, emotions, kindness, thoughts, or abilities. You will see how
your little sacrifices grow into big sacrifices for the
Plan and for the Hierarchy. Eventually, you become
united with the sacrificial principle.

Our Solar Logos is called the Great Sacrifice
because He built this solar system so that little bugs
like us could become human beings, Masters, and
angels.

In your sacrifice you must make sure that your
main motivation is the achievement of unity. Ask
yourself if you are working for right human relations,
goodwill, and the spreading of light. Ask yourself if
your life is molding itself around principles which will
last throughout all eternity. Hierarchy gives you the
laws and principles to follow, but it does not tell you
what to do. Hierarchy wants you to apply the laws and
principles according to the level which you are on. A
real disciple will never give you advice directly about
what action to take. But he will remind you of certain
viewpoints which you might have overlooked in your
analysis. He will tell you to collect yourself and stand
for something which is lasting and rooted in the light
of Goodness, Beauty, and Truth.

I used to wonder why the Masters never came and
solved all of humanity's problems. But if They did
that, we would never stretch beyond our present level.
We would still be like animals and never be able to find
our own solutions. They give us Their light and wisdom through laws and principles. These are the bea-
cons for us to follow in our efforts to solve our own
problems.

These eleven qualities will be with you in future
incarnations. The Ancient Wisdom teaches that whatever you sow, you reap; you never lose anything. Life
after life, your capabilities and attributes accumulate.
Since nothing is ever lost, your character becomes like
a big jigsaw puzzle. In each life, you find another piece

or maybe even a couple of pieces. Eventually, you make the puzzle complete; you become a complete being.

We are told that even a glass of water given in the name of the Hierarchy is not forgotten. Even the gift of a glass of water is registered in the Book of Life. This is why the most important thing is sincerity of motive and a spirit of sacrifice and service to humanity. Your main motive should be the liberation of humanity. Eventually, you grow to a point where you work only for others and not for yourself.

In your service to humanity, you must be aware of your level and your ability to serve. You must use common sense so that your service will be of value. There will also be times when you may need to protect yourself. If you don't have power, strive until you are equal to the task.

Along these same lines, we have the dark night of the Yogi, not to be confused with the dark night of the soul.[1] This is something different.

The Teaching says that an Agni Yogi makes himself so purified that he becomes extremely sensitive physically, emotionally and mentally. He starts to pick up the thoughts and emotions of others, and if he is not protected and shielded by the Hierarchy or his Master, his solar plexus, digestion, and health degenerate. He becomes like a sponge which picks up the dirt of everyone he sees. When these negative vibrations accumulate, the Yogi becomes depressed. But he does have techniques to overcome it. With meditation, prayer, and contemplation, he can come out of his dark night. M.M. says that the greatest thing to help conquer all these accumulations is unification with the Hierarchy. One second of alignment can cure the problem.

Protection comes to the student when he is making great efforts in the deepest sincerity. Then the protection is always there, even in small places. A disciple becomes so accustomed to protection that he begins not to notice it. He may be driving on the freeway and narrowly miss a terrible accident.

The disciple is always protected if he is sincere in

his heart that he is going to serve the Divine Plan and humanity. The frequency with which we tune into the Hierarchy is love. If you move and breathe in absolute lovingness, you are on the same frequency as the Masters of Light.

---

1. See *The Hidden Glory of the Inner Man,* by Torkom Saraydarian, p. 126.

CHAPTER 17

MAITREYA AND THE AGE OF WOMAN

There are two subjects emphasized in the Agni Yoga Teaching which are not mentioned in other yogas or teachings of the East. These subjects are the foundation of humanity's future.

The first subject of strong emphasis is the reappearance of Maitreya, or **the Christ.** The second subject is the **Age of Woman.**

When Great Ones thought about how to make people progress on the path of evolution, they created myths, legends, and heroes using the dynamics of the mind. The dynamics of the mind are mental images charged with spiritual aspiration, which create a strong drive toward spiritual evolution and beingness.

The Great Ones created myths, heroes, and legends, and They even sent legendary figures to humanity. The spiritual, mental, and emotional health of people depends upon how much they assimilate these images. The more they assimilate, the more they advance. The more they advance, the greater is the beauty they bring to the world and the deeper is their penetration into Cosmos.

The health of the physical, emotional, and mental bodies is related to a vision toward which you strive. This vision creates a polarization in your atoms, cells, emotions, and thoughts, and a rhythmic and harmonious configuration begins to build in your nature.

All sickness is the result of disharmony of the

energies and forces in your body. It is the result of conflict within yourself, in which the survival potential is giving in to the powers of degeneration and death. Images created by the Great Ones are antidotes to this "giving in" process.

Worship is a scientific technique to polarize you toward the images of great heroes and eventually mold your life upon the principles of those images. Worship is a technique to make you equal to the object of your worship. The worship of an image of greatness eventually creates such a heat in your bones, muscles, emotions, heart, and mind that the hidden Christ within you is released. An intense moment of worship is a moment of release of the divine electricity within you. The moment of striving in which your image is lost in the image of your worship is the moment of transformation, the moment of overcoming yourself.

One of the greatest of these images presented to humanity is the image of Christ. In the Agni Yoga Teaching, there are thousands of verses related to Christ. Why is Christ emphasized so much in this Teaching? There are five reasons:

1. Christ stands as the purest symbol of perfection.

2. Christ stands as the real symbol of striving. The whole foundation of His Teaching is continuous, steady progress toward improvement and perfection. "Be perfect as your Father in heaven is perfect," He said.

3. Christ's love for humanity is not surpassed.

4. Christ lived in the consciousness of oneness with all of humanity.

5. Christ kept Himself totally pure from materialism, hypocrisy, flattery, and corruption and stood for beauty, dignity, solemnity, purity, and synthesis.

> *The Brothers of Mercy could enter into the worst nests of pestilence without being contaminated, because they had committed their consciousness to Christ irrevocably and undividedly. Such communion of consciousness created flashes of fire for unassailable purification....*[1]

When one commits his consciousness to Christ, he

magnetically attracts His radiation. That radiation turns into a shield in his aura, into flashes of fire which purify any contamination. Many saints and Holy Ones throughout the ages have demonstrated such an immunity.

Commitment to Christ also protects one from dark attacks. Those who have irrevocably committed themselves to Christ stand like towers, and the attacks of darkness do not approach them. It is also known that the arrows of slander and malice thrown at dedicated ones turn back and smash their source.

One may build a city, one may give the best knowledge, but most difficult of all is to reveal the true Image of Christ. Think, how to cleanse the Image of Christ. . . .²

This is a very difficult task — to cleanse the Image of Christ — because in order to know what that Image is, you must *be* like that Image, at least in a certain degree. You must become something higher than yourself.

Different churches, cults, and individuals without faith present Christ in their own image or through their own interpretation. Christ must be presented by words or writings only after one has had a contact with Him; a contact which is proven by a life of great beauty and creativity. It is only after such a qualification that one must dare to speak about Christ. For such a person, it will be a great labor to expose all those presentations which are the result of decayed consciousness or mediumistic revelations.

When the world is convulsed, the sign of Maitreya is given as an antidote. When the foundation of Our Works has been laid, the forces of the spirit have been strengthened. Thus the sign of Maitreya has been affirmed. And in Our Day, when the manifestation is affirmed, one may repeat — how vitally the power of the spirit has entered into life and how greatly this new power has been affirmed in consciousness. Hence one must apply

the consciousness to a mighty understanding of
Hierarchy, which holds the chain of all strivings.
Thus each manifestation of beauty placed at the
foundation of Our works must be acknowledged as
a vital action. Thus the power of the foundation
consists in beauty, and the striving to the fulfill-
ment of the Higher Will will lead to the predes-
tined Victory. Thus, Our Towers should be built —
verily, in beauty![3]

When Christ starts to manifest within you, all the
trash that is within you will come to the surface and
burn away. This has happened many times: when
people make a contact, they are horrified because contact is a mirror in which you see exactly what you are.
You cannot fool yourself any more or hide from yourself after contact with a great Image.

Contact with this great Hero creates a vitality in
you — "*. . .how vitally the power of the spirit has
entered into life."* In the Agni Yoga Teaching, spiritual
vitality is called striving. Striving means steady effort
toward perfection, and service plus striving lead to
expansion of consciousness.

*"Hence one must apply the consciousness to a
mighty understanding of Hierarchy, which holds the
chain of all strivings."* All heroes do one thing for us:
they create striving within us, in every aspect of our
lives. The Image of Christ is a light through which we
can transform ourselves. This is why Christ said, "Let
your light shine," so that we transform ourselves into
lights.

> *. . .Fate can be overcome if thou manifest the
> Christ, Who sacrificed Himself for Truth.*[4]

Fate is the accumulated effects of your thoughts,
words, and deeds which can be overcome only through
the power of Christ, if you let Him manifest through
you — which means, if you start living a life of truth
and sacrifice yourself for truth. Such a condition raises
you above the layers of life where you are bound to the
effects of your actions.

A pure thought ever ascends.
At the feet of Christ it blossoms, radiant. . . .[5]

Beseech Christ.
Search for the joy of inner exaltation.
Discover and unlock the Gates of Knowledge,
And affirm thyself in the understanding of God's
plan.[6]

...I proclaim love. My disciples must realize
happiness in the love of Christ.[7]

Smile — I grant thee the joy of spreading the
Teaching of Christ, . . .[8]

In the Agni Yoga literature, great emphasis is put upon the Teaching of Christ and upon His sacrifice for the good of all humanity. Christ is called Maitreya and also the Great Wayfarer in the Agni Yoga literature.

Maitreya sends courage. Maitreya will accept
the gift. Maitreya feels its love. Maitreya sends
blessings upon the joyous labor. Maitreya bestows
labor upon Earth in the name of miracle. Walk
joyfully. It is a joy to Me to lead the smiling ones.
Discern the Teaching of Light in each manifesta-
tion. Resourcefulness is a quality of My pupils.[9]

Why does Maitreya send courage? Because the disciples of Christ today and in the future need courage. Just like the twelve disciples of Jesus Christ, the disciples of today are presenting a new Teaching to the world, and this requires a great deal of courage.

A new Teaching always meets every point of resistance which it is possible to have directed against it. It meets resistance from family, established traditions and beliefs, and the contemporary educational system.

The courage which disciples of the new Teaching must have is not emotional excitement which grows cold when night comes. Their courage is a steady, burning flame in their hearts which warms them during storms of protest, attack, and prejudice. It is an intellectual and highly charged courage which gives them the strength to meet each and every obstacle thrust in their way.

It is a great art to present the Teaching in a way that it does not create any more resistance than that which already exists. In order to do this, you must consider the values and dignity of those to whom you are presenting the Teaching. Don't say to someone, "You are a holy-poly follower and that is old-fashioned. You must stop it and follow my way." The new-age method is to see the merit and worth of the "holy-poly follower." This establishes a common ground between their beliefs and the Teaching. It creates in them an interest and a predisposition for acceptance instead of rejection. New-age teachers build bridges instead of walls.

It sometimes takes great efforts to crack the cement in which many traditions and belief systems encase their followers. These beliefs are not necessarily good or bad; people are just stuck in old ways. When your mind rigidly follows one direction, you cannot break those limitations which are imposed on you. Your direction becomes the curse of your life. Your mind becomes cemented, and you cannot go beyond the level which you have attained. You think that whatever you know is the truth and it is all there is to know.

Imagine that every day you take the same route to work. You never try other roads which are available to you. On your same route every day you see pretty carnations. You think they are the most beautiful flowers in the world without realizing that there are other flowers in God's garden. When people tell you about roses and daisies, you tell them that carnations are enough for you. This may be true, but what a limited bouquet your table will have.

The new-age Teaching embraces all the flowers of God's creation. Nothing is rejected. A new synthesis is formed, and the old is expanded upon.

"Maitreya will accept the gift." The new Teaching which you are presenting is a gift to humanity. With

the presentation of this gift, you are preparing humanity for the coming of Maitreya. In preparing His path
of return, you are giving Him a gift also. Maitreya
accepts your efforts and the progress you are making
in trying to align humanity with the principles of
Goodness, Beauty and Truth. Your efforts have value
for Him when they are given freely, without expectation.
"Maitreya sends blessings upon the joyous labor."
It is so important to be joyful when you labor. How can
you expect to dispel the darkness when you are cursing
and complaining about your work? A negative attitude will not reap any blessings.

A blessing is an increase of energy which flows
into your nervous sytem. This energy makes you more
joyful, healthy, and free. You feel independent, open,
and sincere. Do something in the name of Maitreya
with joy and enthusiasm, and a blessing will come to
you. You will feel energy which heals your body as well
as your relationships with others. You will notice that
your joy increases your magnetism and that you suddenly accumulate more co-workers around you.

*"Maitreya bestows labor upon Earth in the name
of miracle."* Spiritual progress proceeds only through
labor in all fields of human endeavor, so that life in its
complexity advances like a symphony. The kingdom
of God cannot be established in the world unless the
world is highly organized in all its fields. All this needs
intelligent and dedicated labor. Only such a labor can
produce miracles, which we can see, for example, in
many fields of research and creativity.

The king, or the kingdom of God, which we call the
Hierarchy, believes in labor. All Great Ones are the
product of heavy, self-sacrificial labor in the world. No
one can advance toward perfection without labor, and
the gift of labor is a miracle. Through labor man
emancipates himself from darkness and enters into
light.

We see such a labor in the life of Christ and in His
ministry. He was in His Father's business every minute during His life. The miracle was His example of
love, sacrifice, and vision for one humanity.

"Walk joyfully. It is a joy to Me to lead the smiling ones." M.M. says to bless your obstacles because they are the elements which make you grow. Keep your joy strong when obstacles block your path.

There was a priest who called me one day and explained that he was going to San Francisco to give a big seminar. He insisted that I give him two cases of *The Magnet of Life*[10] so that he could sell them to the people who attended. He was going to pay me a percentage for them when he returned. We had a gentleman's agreement, and since he was a priest, I thought he would honor it.

When a few months went by and I did not hear from him, I called and asked if he had sold the two cases of books. "What books?" he asked. He denied ever taking the books to San Francisco and even began to curse me. I just hung up the phone and put my attention to something else with a big smile.

Five years later, I went to San Francisco to give a seminar. Many people attended. To my amazement, they all had *The Magnet of Life* tucked under their arms. "Where did you get those books?" I asked.

"A bookstore had a special sale on them a few years ago. We bought them for only two dollars, and we have been studying them ever since."

It was strange how the books had gone out five years earlier to prepare listeners for my seminar. Life uses strange ways to make you successful. Sometimes things don't work out this nicely, but you must always keep your smile in spite of any difficulty. Try especially not to fall into self-pity or feel sorry for yourself.

When I was a very little boy, I noticed that during the most critical times my father would smile, make a joke, and get others to laugh. One day we were riding in a carriage and the horses became very frightened by a car passing by. They had never seen an automobile before. When they heard the noise, they started to jump. I jumped out of the carriage because I thought it was going to turn over. I fell near the wheels, and the carriage ran over one of my toes.

My father finally got the horses under control and

rushed over to me. The first thing he said was that he was glad that the carriage didn't run over all my toes. He started joking with me and making me laugh, so that I didn't feel any pain at all. Today I do not have the nail on one of my toes, but I really learned something that day about joy.

Gloomy, depressed, and negatively oriented people cannot be led by Christ. I have a clear experience in my life that those who have a true contact with Christ and are led by Him have five distinct qualities:

1. They are joyful and they never let that joy disappear from their hearts.
2. They are patient.
3. They are optimistic.
4. They are enthusiastic.
5. They are open-minded.

It is through such qualities that the energy or spirit of Christ can produce miracles.

I met a few such people in my life, and they were amazingly peaceful in crises and dangers because the Lord was with them. Three of them were highly advanced women. Another one was my Teacher. Another was my Father.

"Father," I said once, "what is the secret of your peace and joy?"

He answered in a curious way. He said, "Stay in His presence, love, and work hard."

"*Discern the Teaching of Light in each manifestation. Resourcefulness is a quality of My disciples.*" Once for three days there were three of us who dug a ditch so that we could lay a pipe. It was very hot and the work was hard, but we were laughing and having a lot of fun. There was so much energy running through us that we never became tired. We touched a reservoir of energy and were able to continue with complete vigor until the job was finished.

If you dedicate yourself joyfully to whatever you are doing, hidden reservoirs within you will suddenly open and replenish your system. M.M. says that these reservoirs can be felt only in the highest tension. You need to pass through this tension so that your centers open and you have a higher contact.

Those who walk in Joy do not let negative feelings penetrate into their hearts. They remain optimistic and keep their position as fighters for light. They keep striving to do their best because they know that if they do not spread the light, the darkness will eat them. They spread the light by first maintaining their own light.

> *My Hand sends rays from the mountains. We shall begin the New Era without delay. I teach not a dream but to harken to the flow of events.*[11]

The "New Era" is the era of Christ and the era of woman. We are told that this is the Age of Woman and that women will inspire Beauty, Culture, and Nobility in the human race and help great achievements to be realized. It is interesting to notice that in the last 100 years, the Teaching was brought to humanity by the labor of three great women — H.P. Blavatsky, Alice Bailey, and Helena Roerich. They gave the deepest Teaching that mankind has ever received — the Teaching of the Hierarchy.

"I teach not a dream...." World events are the manifestations of an inner plan and purpose. When you open your mind and watch world events in a detached way, there is nothing to fear. Fear is an emotion which controls many people because of propaganda in the news and because of attachment to material objects. When people are kept in fear, they can be controlled. They will act for the preservation and pleasure of the ego and forget those things of real value. People who are fearful place value on the false, the unreal, and the not-self, and they are easily manipulated by their attachments.

Our television and radio condition us to live in fear. "Crime increased ten percent last year. . . . Fighting on the border. . . . Inflation eating your salary. . . ." Learn to look at events and see the causes behind them. Don't be conditioned by the fear that sensational approaches to the happenings of the times try to stimulate within you. Your fear makes lots of money for someone else, so be more aware and more awake.

Nothing can be cleaned unless the trash comes to the surface. Take, for instance, all the cults, mediums, witchcraft, and false prophets we see in society today. These false values must come to the surface and be accepted by some for a while before people become disappointed in them and seek the real and the beautiful.

Once a man told me that the meditation exercises in *The Science of Meditation*[12] were no good. Then he complained about his lack of attention and his inability to concentrate at work. I asked him what kind of meditation he was doing.

"The best. It is a very advanced form of meditation," he said.

"Show me," I said. "I want to know about this."

He stood up and clutched one foot behind him like a crane. Then while trying to keep his balance, he held one nostril shut and forced air out of the other nostril. Then he started to jump up and down on one leg.

"That's meditation?" I asked.

"It is so advanced. Really! The thinking methods in your books are no good because thinking only created atomic bombs and inflation."

We sat and had a long talk, and I made him see the lack of logic in his statements. I also explained the difference between thinking for your own selfish ends and thinking in the light of your Soul for the good of all humanity.

The trash must come to the surface so that people see it for what it is and clean it. Once I received an advertisement in the mail from a yogi in India. He was going to come to the United States to show 10,000 people how they could be transformed into masters in one day. He was also going to show people how to raise their kundalini fire in five minutes. . . . He was going to do all this for a mere 1,500 dollars!

M.M. says about women:

> *The lofty mission of women must be per-*
> *formed by the woman. And in the Temple of the*
> *Mother of the World should abide the woman.*
> *The manifestation of the Mother of the World*
> *will create unity. The task now is to create a*
> *spiritually sovereign position for the woman. And*
> *the transmission to woman of direct communion*
> *with the Highest Forces is necessary as a psycho-*
> *logical impetus. Of course, through the new reli-*
> *gion will come the necessary respect.*[13]

The Age of Woman refers to leadership by the feminine principle. The feminine principle is the principle of love, compassion, and intuition. In the Ancient Wisdom we are told that the second solar system (our present solar system) is feminine; the feminine principle is the dominating factor. Women dominate as agents of greater wisdom.

The new religion will bring to women the respect necessary to make the feminine principle influential. It will show that the equality of women is not to be found in going to bars and drinking with the men all night long while the children watch television at home. The new religion will give many beautiful examples of women who have achieved much for humanity with their beauty and simplicity. It will be shown that the Mother of Buddha and of the Christ were the same. She is the Mother of the World. She is not a symbol, but a Manifestation of great feminine achievement.[14]

Women will bring about a true spirit of brotherhood in humanity. Women will be the transmitters of the spiritual light of the Hierarchy to humanity. They will bring illumination and guidance from their Innermost Cores and lead humanity with love, compassion, and intuition.

Woman's mission will be to be the spiritual leaders of humanity. Woman will treat the world as her child, and through her children woman will point humanity in the right direction. She will inspire the children of the world by bestowing vision and inspiration. It is women who will teach about heroes, nobility, and virtues. It is women who will teach the sanctity of life and the glory of spiritual manifestation. In spiritual and creative endeavors, women will prepare the way for the greatness of humanity to flourish.[15]

1. Agni Yoga Society, *Heart*, para. 582.
2. Agni Yoga Society, *Leaves of Morya's Garden*, Volume II, page 75.
3. Agni Yoga Society, *Hierarchy*, para. 201.
4. Agni Yoga Society, *Leaves of Morya's Garden*, Volume I, para. 3.
5. *Ibid.*, para. 21.
6. *Ibid.*, para. 24.
7. *Ibid.*, para. 27.
8. *Ibid.*, para. 153.
9. *Ibid.*, Volume II, page 37.
10. Written by T. Saraydarian, currently available in revised form as *The Hidden Glory of the Inner Man.*
11. Agni Yoga Society, *Leaves of Morya's Garden*, Volume II, page 43.
12. By H. (Torkom) Saraydarian.
13. Agni Yoga Society, *Leaves of Morya's Garden*, Volume II, page 65.
14. See Chapter 89, "The Seven Principles in Man," in *The Psyche and Pschism*, by Torkom Saraydarian.
15. See Chapter XII, "Torchbearers," in *Woman Torch of the Future*, by Torkom Saraydarian.

CHAPTER 18

THOUGHT

Agni Yoga literature says that thinking is mental speech which can be heard by those who have ears to hear. Thoughts travel through the air and affect other people; they are substantial, so it is very important that we pay attention to our thinking.

There are many kinds of thought discussed in the Agni Yoga literature. For example, there are **base thoughts:**

> . . .*The best thing is to destroy the germs of base thoughts, which are more infectious than all diseases. One should be careful not so much about uttered words as about thoughts. During one word ten thoughts are born.*[1]

Base thoughts are thoughts that are harmful to people, thoughts that prevent the progress of other human beings, thoughts that divide people, thoughts that obscure the minds of people, thoughts that create conditions in our life in which we become stagnated.

It is important to remember that whatever we think, we become. When we start thinking base thoughts, we become base human beings. Base thoughts limit the freedom and progress of humanity. They create degeneration, separatism, and mental and emotional pollution. These thoughts must be thrown out of our minds or, better yet, burned out because whenever you are thinking base thoughts, one part of your mental body is degenerating.

214

There are also **mean thoughts:**

> *Mean thoughts have been compared to crawl-ing reptiles. Nothing is more analogous to this scum of the consciousness. Can one sit calmly in an armchair, knowing that beneath him crawl poisonous snakes and scorpions? One must free oneself from reptiles, and first of all along the path to Hierarchy. Condemnation and blasphemy against the Lord are irreparable. Thus each one who condemns the Hierarch must remember that his levity and crime will infect his karma for many ages. Verily, if there is only one way — through the Lord — to the one Light, then only extreme ignor-ance will allow destruction of this single path. One must assert striving to the Highest as the essence of life and assume a reverent attitude towards this striving for salvation. By diminishing the Hier-arch one may condemn oneself and inflict peri-lous harm to many near ones. It is time to remem-ber this![2]*

Like scorpions and vipers, mean thoughts and penetrate the minds of people and cause infection there. Mean thoughts are like insects which carry poi-son. When they touch your mental body, they create infection. There are many people who are physically healthy but mentally infected with various germs. This mental infection will eventually make them sick physically.

If you have mean thoughts charged by hatred, jealousy and revenge, try not to release them because they will carry poison with them and infect people. When you infect other people, they will infect you. Automatically the infection will come back to you through the thread through which you sent the mean thought to them. Mean thoughts are like boomerangs.

Mean thoughts paralyze a part of your mental body. Those who have mean thoughts have fewer view-points. When someone has fewer viewpoints, he fails because he always forgets to take into consideration an important point that is related to his decision.

Mean thoughts create cleavages in your aura and prevent you from seeing things holistically. Then because of one important screw or nut, your whole engine falls apart.

You don't need to destroy people who have mean thoughts; they will eventually destroy themselves.

"One must free oneself from reptiles, and first of all along the path to Hierarchy." To be on the path to Hierarchy means that you are preparing yourself to be a perfect human being. You cannot increase in Light, Power, Beauty and Wisdom and you cannot approach your true Self if you are still manufacturing mean and base thoughts.

As you come closer to the Hierarchy, the light within you will increase so much that pressure will force the smallest defects in your aura to appear. On the path of greater responsibilities and tests, you must beware of the smallest mean thought so that you do not infect your aura.

For the average person, mean thoughts are not too harmful. But an advancing person who is coming closer to the light has a grave responsibility to be more pure in his thoughts.

"Condemnation and blasphemy against the Lord are irreparable." When you condemn or blaspheme, you cannot repair the damage you are doing. The "Hierarch" refers in this verse to Christ. When your actions, words, thoughts, and emotions are opposite to what He is trying to do for humanity, then you are creating blasphemy against Him, and your crime will follow you for ages.

Only through Christ can you reach the Source of light, love, and power because He is the Hierarch. Any base thought against Him creates a tremendous wound in your body.

The Hierarch is also your true Self within you. Within the planet, it is the Christ. Within the solar system, it is the Sun. This is why in old religions it is said that you cannot work against the light.

Can one imagine people as thinking only of

that which is useful? Of course one can; harmful and undisciplined thoughts are primarily useless. One can accustom oneself to useful thoughts, and such an exercise will be the best preparation for the Fiery World. The habit of thoughts for Good is not attained quickly; still, it leads to fiery realization. Thus, not in the manifestation of a special world, but through the quality of daily labor do we approach the Fiery World.[3]

Those who have **selfish thoughts** always use people and opportunities for their own selfish egos; they use everything for themselves. Selfish thoughts create vanity — which is a mental tumor — and pride, which is mental cancer. Maybe one day the medical profession will find the relation between selfish thoughts and various sicknesses. If they do, they will find that the roots of all sicknesses lie in the mental body because man is a mental animal.

The word man comes from the Sanskrit word, *manas.* Manas means to think. Man is a thinking animal. If you do not think, you are not a human being.

Then there are **good thoughts:**

If thought in itself contains creative energy, then how useful it is to direct good thought into space. When mankind shall agree to send forth good thought simultaneously, then the infected atmosphere of the lower spheres will at once clear. . . .[4]

Good thoughts are those thoughts that help you and other people to grow, unfold, and be prosperous. Try to have good thoughts because when you have good thoughts, you energize and fertilize your mental body. Good thoughts are vitamins for your mental body.

Good thoughts do two things. First, they enrich your mental body. Second, they prevent bad thoughts from doing greater harm to you or to others. This is why Christ emphasized blessing your enemies. To bless your enemies means to send them good thoughts. If you send bad thoughts to your enemies, you energize them along negative lines. Try to isolate them with your good thoughts.

Good thoughts also give you energy. When the great religious leaders like Christ and Buddha prescribed to humanity to have good thoughts, They were actually giving a science through which we could be healthy, beautiful and creative.

What happens if energy increases in your body? First of all, energy fights against germs and microbes. I was in Holland, and I visited the garden of a certain man. There was not a single insect in his garden. I said, "Don't you have any bugs here? What do you do with the bugs?"

He said, "We found another way to deal with them. We give the plants natural fertilizers, and when they are healthy, the bugs do not come around them at all."

The same is true for the human being. When the human being is healthy, bugs do not come around. Only when you are weak do bugs come to you. If you have base or mean thoughts, you will see that the bugs are coming to you. These fleas are messengers of God. They are saying, "Hey, bug, you are doing something wrong, and we came to tell you about it. We are picking at your skin so that you pay more attention to your thinking."

In Nature nothing happens by accident. Why is it that some people are not attacked by fleas and you are attacked? — Because you were doing something wrong.

Then there are **selfless thoughts.** When you have selfless thoughts, you are mostly occupied in helping other people through your writings, speech, actions, service, activities, emotions and thoughts. What percentage of our time do we devote to helping others? Half a minute or three minutes daily? That half a minute or three minutes is equal to what you are because *you are equal to your selfless thoughts.* Your greatness comes in your givingness, in making other people grow and unfold. This is done through selfless thoughts.

Selfless thought is not a state of consciousness in

which you ignore yourself. You are the trustee of your body, emotions, and mind. You must handle them in such a way that you do not degenerate them, harm them, or make them diseased. You must use them to radiate Beauty, Goodness, and Truth.

Selflessness is a state of consciousness in which you use your mental powers benevolently for everything existing around you, including yourself. You must be an example of beauty in order to teach beauty to others. You must be really healthy in order to teach people health. You must be very charming in order to show other people how to be charming.

Then there are **creative thoughts:**

> *If thought in itself contains creative energy, then how useful it is to direct good thought into space. When mankind shall agree to send forth good thought simultaneously, then the infected atmosphere of the lower spheres will at once clear. Hence, it is necessary to take care, even a few times daily, to send out thought not about oneself, but about the world. Thus the thinking will accustom itself to disinterested strivings. As the Savior of mankind thinks only of the entire world, so in emulation of him we can apply our thoughts for the manifestation of creative energy. . . .*[5]

Creative thoughts are those thoughts that help the Plan and Purpose of God to manifest on Earth. The Plan is that humanity must be one humanity. If you are working in this direction or thinking this thought, you are really helping the life of this planet and you are living as a human being.

Most of humanity are living like beasts. You must conquer the beast within you and start living as a human being. A human being doesn't need locks, guns, or knives. If you need such protection, it means you are surrounded by nonhuman beings, who have just entered the human kingdom and are exercising their bestiality.

Creative thought helps the Plan, the human cause, to make the planetary humanity become human beings

— loving, tolerant and free, not criminal and selfish. A human being is selfless, beautiful, full of goodness and righteous. If you have the opposite qualities within you, you are a beast.

Nature creates a great symphony, and a human being must add to that symphony. Human beings are the extension of the forces of Nature and the creativity of Nature. As a human being, you must add something to the creativity of Nature.

The vegetable kingdom brings a new beauty to Nature. The animal kingdom brings another beauty. Human beings bring another beauty. God is unfolding and flowering through the kingdoms. Humanity must decide to unfold a rare flower of Beauty, Goodness, and Truth, to unite and synchronize with the creative forces of Nature so that it becomes a creative force.

With creative thoughts, you fuse and unite with the creative forces of Nature. When you are united with the creative forces of Nature, you are always new and refreshed; you are always changing into beauty, goodness, and light because the psychic stream, the great river of Light, Love, and Power streams through you. You become part of that great creative river; you are not separated from Nature.

When you become one with the creative forces of Nature, eventually you will achieve the degree of perfection in which those forces will renew your body and create a new light around you — all because of your creative thoughts.

Then there are **healing thoughts.** People must be educated how to think thoughts that are healing physically. If this were told 50 years ago, people would have laughed. But now doctors are using meditation to heal cancer and different sicknesses.

Healing thoughts are those thoughts that create a prototype of Beauty, Goodness, and Truth and impose this rhythm on decaying organs and tissues. For example, if your stomach is not working, think that your stomach is really beautiful, healthy, and vitalized. You will see that this thought will eventually replace the other thoughts you had about your stomach, and your stomach will be healthy. Because we don't know yet the technique of thinking healing thoughts, we can get only two or three percent benefit from trying to do it. If we really learn the technique, we will be able to heal ourselves.

The secret of thought is that everything in Nature is the crystallization of thought. Everything in Nature is manufactured, built, and engineered by thought. Whatever you are thinking now is exactly what you are going to be in the future. Thought is a real magician, and if we know how to work with thought we will become *magis*. A magi is a person who can control the forces of Nature with his mind. There are two kinds of magic: black magic and white magic. Black magic uses thought for the destruction of other people. White magic uses it as a service.

Only by the tension of all strength shall you conquer. One must remember this and apply it. We have decided on complete success, it depends upon you to accept it. The entire garden of doubt, suspicion, fears, offenses, condemnations must be cast aside. If you desire to accept victory then every treason must be avoided, because the consequences of the manifested doubts and lack of respect to Hierarchy will disrupt all threads. When the ship is holding by one anchor during the tempest, it is stupid to begin to change the chain. Guard the foundation and ascend only by the growth of the foundations. I shall be tireless to repeat about Hierarchy until you will realize it. It is not enough to nod your head, it is time to think and to apply. I have reasons for repeating this.[6]

Tension is the concentration of your energies on to one point, so that the strength of your energies is felt and the work is performed by that focus. If you are half-hot, half-cold — or lukewarm — you cannot achieve anything. If you really want to do something, you must gather together all your physical, emotional, and mental strength. This is the difference between success and failure. You fail if you do not concentrate all your energies into extreme tension.

If you are unified and synthesized within yourself, you achieve your goal. If you are not synthesized within yourself, you fail. This is also true with groups. If a group is really dedicated to bring a great beauty into manifestation, they will succeed. But if even one person in the group is creating distortion with his doubt, that group will gradually be weakened more and more.

In man, in a group, in humanity, and in the whole solar system, success is achieved through focus and tension. This idea must be remembered and applied in daily life. If you are drinking a cup of water, drink it consciously. If you are driving, drive consciously. All your strength and focus must be there. One of the most difficult things to do is to bring yourself into focus in whatever you are doing.

"*Guard the foundation. . .*" The foundation is Honesty, Beauty, Goodness and Truth. Guard these things, so that you attain victory.

> *Certainly, the evolution of the spirit requires refinement, without which it is impossible to build. Each one who considers himself a server of Culture must accept the affirmation of the manifested synthesis, for how are the steps of Culture to be built without a cautious attitude? Therefore, each foundation must be guarded for affirmation to the world. Culture is built not with an attitude of coarseness towards the subtle energies and thought, but by a creative attitude of caution and responsibility. Hence, while constructing, one should remember about refinement and about striving to the higher spheres. Thus the evolution of the spirit is reached.[7]*

The "manifested synthesis" means to feel within yourself that you are a spirit, an immortal being; to feel within yourself that humanity must be one; to feel within yourself that there is one Plan for the whole Creation; to feel that behind all this Creation, the Plan, and Purpose, there is only one God. You must adapt your life to these concepts.

There is a verse that says that those who act against great saints and holy people will eventually be destroyed through very bad deaths and sufferings. They will not only suffer in this life, but their karma will follow them life after life. For example, when a person commits a crime and later dies, his crime is repeated for maybe 10,000 years in the astral plane. This is the hell Christ talked about: you will be caught within the hell you created for others and you will burn in that fire.

The worst suffering you can have is in the fire of conscience. That fire burns you day and night. We must not do certain things because of fear, but because they are not right. Because we want success and victory, we are going to clean ourselves, purify ourselves, and make ourselves beautiful, starting with our thoughts.

> *Each thought gives birth to action. The most insignificant thought creates a tiny action; therefore think broadly, in order that even in failure there may remain a potentiality sufficient for substantial consequence. Even if people do not know how to act well, at least they could cultivate good and broad thoughts within themselves. I am emphasizing cultivated thoughts, because the dark dust annihilates the beauty of creation. It is difficult to ask for a thought about righteous creativeness when a mist of blood clouds the consciousness. But sooner or later one will have to turn to the force of purified thought. Therefore it is better to begin sooner.[8]*

---

1. Agni Yoga Society, *Leaves of Morya's Garden,* Volume II, page 80.
2. Agni Yoga Society, *Hierachy,* para. 57.
3. Agni Yoga Society, *Fiery World,* Volume I, para. 307.
4. Agni Yoga Society, *Heart,* para. 300.
5. *Ibid.*
6. Agni Yoga Society, *Hierarchy,* para. 136.
7. *Ibid.,* para. 249.
8. Agni Yoga Society, *Heart,* para. 127.

CHAPTER 19

THE TEACHING OF LIVING ETHICS

Living ethics are the outcome of your experiences. When you have continuous experiences about something, eventually you find out what is right and what is wrong, and you form rules.

Experiences eventually turn into a rule in your life. If you choose to follow that rule, you don't need to go through those experiences anymore. For example, if you were going in the wrong direction on the freeway and you had a crash, you say, "That was the wrong path. The rule is that I am not going to get on the freeway going in the wrong direction anymore."

The purpose of the rule is to prevent you from the agony and suffering of the second, third, fourth, and fifth experiences. But people are not really aware of this. They have millions of experiences. They say, "This is wrong; I shouldn't do it." Then they make a rule, but they do not obey it. But if they would obey the rule that is the outcome of their experiences, they wouldn't need any more of those experiences and they wouldn't need to spend any more time, energy, pain, and suffering with those experiences.

When the experience and the rule become digested by your nature, eventually you digest their wisdom and the wisdom changes in your subconsciousness and your soul into a living ethic. It becomes a subconscious urge, drive, and instinct within you that makes you act ethically. Where did that ethic come from? It didn't come from anybody else because if you learn

224

ethics from anybody else, they are only as good as a piece of paper hanging on the wall.

Esoterically understood, ethics must come from your own soul and consciousness; you must do exactly the things that your heart tells you to do. You may have many experiences that bring you suffering, pain, and failures, and you can realize you are doing wrong; but if you don't make a rule and try to follow it, all your insight will be forgotten. Only when you try to start following that rule is it digested by your system and does it become a living ethic.

A living ethic means that your experiences and your rules are now controlling your actions, your words, your thoughts, your mouth, your feelings.... Your experiences and your rules have become a living process now, not like something you buy at the store and put on the shelf to sit for months. When you don't have living ethics, you are like a person who brags, "I have ten thousand dollars hidden in a box," but he doesn't have ten cents in his pocket to spend for food.

Living ethics continuously bring into action Light, Love, Power, Beauty and Goodness from your inner resources. Living ethics are not dead objects on the shelves of your consciousness. If the shelves of your consciousness are full of these dead materials, you are really in corruption. Living ethics must be brought into activity.

Let's take five important points in living ethics. If we try to live these points in our lives, we can progress ten or fifteen lives in one life.

1. **Self-protection.** You have insurance for your car, your home, and your body; but do you have insurance for the most precious thing that you have — your true Self? Everything else that you have depends on that real Self. If He is insured and safe, everything else is safe. If you "lose yourself" and "gain the world," everything else is lost.

This means that we must insure ourselves with Self-protection. What is the Self? People think that their body is the Self. They say, "I am hungry." That's your body who is hungry; it's not you. Then they say,

"I am angry." That's your emotions; it's not you.

The Self is the Divinity within you, the creative Center within you. The Self is the source of Light, Love and Power within you. How to protect that Self? There are five methods that you can use to protect your Self and prevent attacks on your real Self.

The first method to protect your Self is not to allow yourself to fall into self-deception. Any time you are in self-deception, you are in danger. People cannot deceive you unless you start deceiving yourself, and once you start deceiving yourself you think that it's the best way to live. This is why it's so difficult to get rid of self-deception.

You must first of all ask yourself, "Am I thinking in the right way; am I feeling the right way; am I acting in the right way?" If you are doing wrong and you are trying to convince yourself that you are on the right path, you are in self-deception.

Groups and nations are also victims of self-deception. A self-deceiving person is a soldier without guns and without protection; he is in the hands of enemies. When you are in the stage of self-deception, you receive lots of attacks from the subjective and objective worlds. You must protect yourself, your fortress, your inner castle — which is your Divine Self within you. You can destroy the walls of the fortress through self-deception. You must continuously tell yourself, "I am going to protect myself physically, emotionally and mentally so that the fortress inside is really safe." If you are not protecting your physical, emotional and mental nature, eventually enemies will creep in and reach the core.

Ask yourself, "Am I doing something wrong which is destroying me? Am I doing things which I don't approve of?" This is the best way to destroy yourself. If you are doing things which you don't approve of, you are creating a conflict or a cleavage within yourself. The worst war is the war which a person fights against himself. Christ said something very important about this. It is not a religious statement, but a scientific statement: "A house divided against itself cannot stand." Self-protection, unity within yourself, is the greatest protection.

The second method to protect your Self is not to allow yourself to fall into inertia. Inertia means that you do not strive to improve yourself any more. People think that inertia is a state in which you sit down and become crystallized and change into a statue. Actually, you can be in inertia on any level, in any enjoyment or pleasure, in any activity or business in which you are no longer progressing. Whenever you stop at your limit, your ring-pass-not, you are in inertia.

If your limit is reached and you cannot make a breakthrough, you are in the worst inertia because you have the glamor that you are doing things while you are not doing anything — because you are trapped in your own success. Inertia is a state of consciousness in which you cannot make a breakthrough to a higher state of consciousness, in which you cannot make a new evaluation of your life, and in which you do not grow and expand in your service and dedication.

The greatest inertia is the state in which the human soul, instead of expanding his Light, Love and Beauty, shrinks and contracts. You must be radioactive because anything that does not progress is in the process of retrogression. This is a physical and supernatural law. If you are not progressing, you are going backwards.

Also, sometimes if you are going forward at the expense of your spiritual unfoldment, you are going backwards. This is what Christ meant when He said that if you gain the whole world and lose your soul, you have lost everything. Don't be like a person who takes a gun and shoots himself, saying, "I am learning through an experience." What kind of experience is that?

The third method to protect your Self is to avoid hatred. Hatred is the most poisonous arrow that one can direct to himself. People think that their hatred mostly affects others; this is not true. Your hatred degenerates your own heart and bones and eventually makes you a zombie, in which you do anything foolish to satisfy your hatred. Then you become a plaything in the hands of those who are calm; they laugh at you and use you. You make yourself a slave and an object of the amusement of others through your own hatreds.

In my life I have seen people who are full of hatred eventually going through dangerous experiences of pain, suffering and loss. In hatred you lose your Self because hatred is separatism, while the Self is unity and oneness. You cannot work against oneness. You cannot separate or divide oneness because if you divide oneness, you don't have the Self. The Self stands on the foundation of unity, synthesis and inclusiveness. If you want to protect your Self, don't become the slave of your hatred.

Who is going to understand these things? People say, "If we do not hate each other, we don't have business." That's right, isn't it? But you have a business that is killing you; you have had a business for many centuries that never gave you greater happiness and progress into the subjective world — which it is your destiny to enter.

It is your destiny to achieve immortality and continuity of consciousness. We have kept ourselves so busy with the trash of life that we have forgotten our direction toward the Father's Home. You worry so much about your life in these 50 or 60 years, but after that, do you know where you are going? When you enter the subjective world, is your flame going to be protected? A great Sage says that there are Cosmic winds that can attack your flame if it is not protected. This is why the golden Chalice exists — to protect your flame from Cosmic electrical storms. Protect the self by not hating — but by loving.

The fourth method to protect the Self is not to fall into depression. Depression is identification with your silly or petty interests. "My boyfriend didn't call me today." Big deal. "My girlfriend is going with somebody else." Let her go. So what? And you take the gun and shoot yourself, or you take lots of pills…and you are depressed, and you mess your whole life.

Try never to allow yourself to fall into depression. Try to get over it immediately and start dancing. Do something. One way to overcome your depression is to visit a hospital. I did this at a time in my life when I was passing through a heavy depression. When I saw the sufferings of the people there I said to myself, "I am so healthy, why am I depressed?" I started to feel the blessings in my life, and slowly I couldn't find any more reasons to be depressed.

There are other techniques to overcome depression. Run. Run one or two miles daily. You will be so tired that you won't have the energy to be depressed! Play music and dance with yourself.

This is not to say that people do or do not need psychiatrists or psychologists, but the greatest doctor is within you. We don't have too much faith, but faith heals. If you have faith in yourself, you will heal yourself.

The fifth method to protect your Self is to never try to escape from your responsibilities. Anyone who escapes from his duties and responsibilities leaves the gates of his fortress open to his enemies. Don't run away from your responsibilities, no matter how much it is going to cost. If you run, you are going to pay 100 times more for it. You will see that lots of thieves are entering your fortress, and it will be so difficult to throw them out.

Do not escape from the responsibilities that you have. Nobody will tell you what they are; your own heart will tell you what your responsibilities are. People have headaches, sudden changes in blood pressure, weakness.... Usually such people are those who have escaped from their responsibilities, now or in the past. They are now ill because escaping from responsibilities distorts the balance and equilibrium of Nature, or the harmony between them and Nature. When this harmony is broken, a person is open to any kind of attack. This is why Blavatsky once said that *the first sign of awakening and entering into higher consciousness is the sense of responsibility.*

2. The second point in living ethics is **Self-discov-**

ery. You must regenerate yourself and discover yourself physically, emotionally, and mentally. Are you
eventually reaching your Innermost Self and discovering that Self?

Our focus of attention and concentration is out-
ward—toward our personal affairs, showing off, physical, emotional and mental activities and relationships....All these outer activities consume our time,
but do we make any kind of effort to find out who we
are?

What are the signs that you exist? What are the
signs of your true Self? What are the signs that are not
coming from your true Self? Can you detect them and
eventually find your true Self? Once you find your Self,
it will be very easy for you to know what other people
are. When you know your own heart, you will know the
hearts of other people and what is going on in them.

Don't forget that you pass through all the things
that are going on in the hearts of others. When you
know the mechanism of your heart and the secrets and
mysteries of your heart, you will know the hearts of
other people. Even when they walk, move, or make a
gesture, you will know what is going on in their hearts.
You will be able to know because you have gone
through experiences and recorded them and studied
them, and now you know what your heart is.

Are you like a little child trying to swim in the river
but is caught in weeds? Your duty is to find out where
you are caught. Who is catching you? What is it that is
trapping you, and can you break that trap? Go home,
sit down, and ask yourself, "Am I trapped in something?" Do you say: "No, no, I am so beautiful. As long
as I have my beer, my television, and my girlfriend (or
boyfriend), I am so happy." Try to go a little deeper
beyond this attitude and see if something is trapping
you.

If you are trapped and you cannot expand in your
Creativity, Light, Love, Energy and Beauty, find out
why. A human being is naturally a radioactive beauty.
This is why Christ said, "Let your light shine." There
is light in you, and the light must shine out. If the light

is not shining out, there is something wrong. What is that light? That light is your joy, your creativity, your energy, your service, your honesty, your simplicity, your solemnity, your endurance, your serenity....

3. **Self-regeneration.** People depend on outer things, but the first thing you must do in any situation is to depend on yourself. Don't immediately go and beg for help. If physically you are sick, try to regenerate yourself. If emotionally you are sick, try to regenerate yourself. If mentally you are sick, regenerate yourself. This is the message of all the religions and philosophies of the world: look for your help within yourself; regenerate yourself.

When you have this self-regenerative attitude, you become a fountain of energies that flood your actions, emotions, thoughts, and activities. You become a help and a service for humanity. You must let your light shine and look for help within your own self.

Your true Self is the window that opens into the Almighty Self. Instead of thinking from morning to night that you can't do things, that everything is a mess, that you are going to die, that you are going to be sick, that the world is sick...change your attitude and say, "Everything is a mess, but I am not a mess." This is not self-hypnotism. This is a command coming from your own true Self and saying, "Hey, body, get well. I have a duty....Hey, throat, get well; I am going to speak." If you do this, your body will obey. Try to learn the secrets of giving commands to yourself.

Self-regeneration gives you courage and hope. Don't say, "Today something is wrong with my knees; I know it's cancer." Even if it is, don't think about it. Say to yourself, "It's going to be healed, if it's necessary." Try to depend on your inner resources to regenerate yourself.

This Teaching is the Teaching for heroes and warriors. You must put in your mind that there are lots of things to be done, and you are one who is going to start to do something.

4. The fourth point in living ethics is **Self-liberation.** Even if you are a king sitting on the throne, even

if you are a millionaire surrounded with millions of dollars, you can be the worst slave — a slave who is always full of hatred and limitations. No one can liberate you unless you liberate yourself.

The first step to liberation is detachment from the things with which you are attached and in which you are lost. Eventually you must find out where you are lost. Are you lost in your dollars, in your sex organs, in your stomach, in your lies, in your deceits, in your fears, in your properties and possessions, in your glamors and vanities...? When you find the place where you are lost, then there is hope that you can find yourself.

When you find yourself, that's the spiritual marriage, the spiritual feast — because something was lost and you found it. The greatest treasure you can find is your Self. Whenever you find anything that is not your Self, you are losing whatever you are finding; your find is a loss.

Try to liberate yourself from the habits of your speech, from the habits of your thinking, from the habits of your body. And to do this, first of all you must find out where you are hidden.

Discover yourself. If you are more advanced, you are hidden in more subtle areas, and it will be very difficult for you to find yourself. Because of your advancement, you have so many methods to hide yourself. Simple people can be discovered easily. This is why Christ said that the poor will inherit the kingdom of God — which is your true Self.

5. The fifth point in living ethics is **Self-examination.** Try to find out what percentage of Self you are, and what is the proof that you have become the Self. Show it; manifest it; prove how much Self you are now. If you are not manifesting the Self, you are losing. If your light is becoming smaller and smaller but you are becoming more and more expanded, physically, emotionally, and mentally, you are losing — just like a person who plays cards and collects lots of cards in his hand, but still loses the game.

Try to gain yourself through self-examination. Self-examination means to take yourself into account daily and see where you are doing wrong, how you are doing wrong, what is the reason you are doing wrong, where you can correct these things....Maybe you cannot correct everything at once, although it is better to correct everything at once. To negotiate with the enemies is the worst politics in the world.

You must have energy and daring to do this. For example, if you want to stop smoking, instead of saying, "Tomorrow I will smoke five cigarettes; the next day four..." and so on, can you throw the package of cigarettes on the floor, crush it with your feet, and say, "I have finished with cigarettes"? Can you tell yourself: "I am the Self. You, my body, are not going to smoke from now on, and I don't want any trouble."

The Self must demand, command. If you start working this way, you will see how beautiful life is. Instead of becoming a puppet of your physical body, you will become the master of your physical body. This is living ethics.

In the Agni Yoga literature are found all those principles by which your life can bloom and flourish. This is why it is called living ethics—whose principles never pass away.

CHAPTER 20

THE TEACHING OF LIVING
ETHICS AND DISCIPLESHIP

*Let us talk about the accepted and destined
disciples, and about discipleship in general.*
*In their unawareness, many imagine that so
long as they are reading the books of the Teaching,
and have some desire to become disciples of this or
that Great Teacher of the White Brotherhood, they
will be accepted and quite welcome.*
*But almost no one ponders what he has done
in his life, or rather, lives, to deserve this greatest
of privileges. Truly it is the greatest, and before we
expect to receive this privilege we should realize
what it means....[1]*

Living ethics is one of the names of the Teaching.
When we exercise certain rules and experiences throughout our lives, they become living ethics. For example, if
you have an experience and then forget it in two or three
days; if you do not live that experience, observe it, and
apply it to your life, it is not a living ethic. If you have a
rule that is based on many experiences and you do not
apply it, it is not a living ethic.
Living ethics are those experiences and rules that
you apply to your life to transform your life and the
lives of others, no matter what kind of discipline you
use to transform them or yourself.
One of the greatest topics in living ethics is discipleship. Discipleship is a life in which you do things

234

that your personality and the friends of your personality do not like. You have millions of friends of your personality who want many different things. They are not necessarily human beings; they are also glamors, illusions, desires, hallucinations. When you obey these things and block the power and will of your Soul, you cannot be a disciple.

Every time you see that you are becoming a better person or that you are transcending yourself, if you observe very carefully you will see that it is because you did something against your personality. You didn't try to make your personality and the personalities of others take control and satisfy their own blind urges, drives, and vanities.

Discipleship means to obey your innermost drives, aspirations, and striving. In doing this, you are creating trouble within your own nature. One part of your nature says, "I want to go toward independence, Light, Beauty, Goodness and Truth." The other part says, "No, let's do it this way...that way..." and there is a conflict. Discipleship is the ability to conquer your personality, in no matter what shape or form the personality appears to you. To discipline the personality means to tune the personality with the music of your Higher Self.

Living ethics means that you want to see fragrance coming out of your actions, thoughts, and words; you want to see a living dynamism coming out of yourself. That dynamism is created through your discipline and through living the experiences and rules you have discovered throughout your life.

Unless we do these things, we become hypocrites and lizards. A person who is a lizard doesn't have too much aim. He doesn't have a spine; he can turn any direction he wants because there are no principles or rules in him.

It is impossible to create disciples and people who are really dedicated to the living Teaching unless they have a foundation. If they don't have a foundation, it is impossible to build anything in them. You can build a tall building on a weak foundation, but eventually it will fall on your head. The foundation in your life can be built only through suffering, heavy discipline, betrayals, refusals, rejections, and your victories over your limitations.

What percentage spirit are you? That's your foundation. How many tons of knowledge do you have? That's your trash. How many diplomas and certificates do you have? They are your loads, your burdens. There is only one foundation: that you transform yourself in such a degree that you become spirit instead of matter. This is the heaviest discipline, and it cannot be built in one life.

Do not deceive yourself. Use discipline to see what you are. Then change your materialism, your materiality, your connections with your personality, your self-pity and your self-centered activities, and eventually turn to your Innermost Self. Say to yourself, "I am going to dissipate everything that is not God within me." Thus you will become a foundation upon which great things can be built.

In our level of evolution, discipleship has eight major requisites.

1. The first requisite of discipleship is strict obedience to principles. There are four very important principles that a disciple should obey; they should be guidelines in his life.

The first principle is **righteousness.** Righteousness means to live in the frequency of your Inner Divinity. If you are unrighteous in your thoughts, you create a mess in your mental plane. If you think unrighteously, you cannot be a creative person because you are distorting your mental body in such a degree that you will never be able to see beauty, understand beauty, and manifest beauty.

> One should not hesitate. Walk like lions! Righteousness adorns your armor.[2]

The second principle is **gratitude.** A great Sage says that a person is equal to his gratitude. You must be grateful for the opportunities that are given to you.

Every opportunity, whether it is painful or joyful, is a chance to increase the Light within you. Through such opportunities you build your foundation for the future.

Who cares how many years you lived, how many tons of food you ate, and how many times you enjoyed sex? Then you go and bury yourself in the ground to cover your pitiful self. Gratitude means to see the opportunities and be grateful to the giver of the opportunities that can make you awake, stand on your own feet, and build your foundation.

You must be grateful for the opportunities to know yourself. For example, something happened and you realized you were really ugly. Don't start cursing that moment and the people who caused that moment. Say, "Thank you. I am so grateful for that moment which, like a light, revealed some darkness within me." It is only with the pill of gratitude that you can digest the lessons that you are eating through your life. You will never digest them in cursing the moments that should be causing you to be grateful.

Be grateful for different kinds of help — physical help, emotional help, mental help, spiritual help, direction, illumination, a book, a paper, even a word that really awakens you and puts you in line. Only in being grateful will you assimilate the Teaching. Anything valuable that you find cannot be assimilated until you express gratitude to the source. If you don't know how to express your gratitude, you will never digest the things you receive.

> ...The quality of gratitude is likewise the finest purification of the organism....Great is the healing power of the emission of gratitude....[3]

The third principle is **solemnity.** Solemnity means to respect yourself and others. To respect means to really care for others' joy, happiness, prosperity, and growth. Respect means to cherish the flame that is within you and others and do everything possible to make that flame radioactive.

If you examine yourself closely whenever you fail,

you will see that your failure was probably a failure of self-respect. Whenever you don't put yourself in the right position or in respect, everything shatters around you. Are you respecting yourself when you are doping your body, when you are killing your body with wrong food, when you are dealing with your body as you would deal with a slave or enemy? You must also respect your heart and your brain.

Your respect will prove that you think I exist. I exist for you because you respect me. Similarly, if you respect yourself, you exist; if you don't respect yourself, you don't exist.

> ...The best expression of gratitude will lie in the realization of the greatness of the Mission. The Service is so great that each step already constitutes an achievement. Each day, with each thought, something significant is done. A great manifestation gives rise to innermost solemnity. In this solemnity there is also expressed gratitude. Solemnity is one of the best magnets. Hence, let us think about the greatest, for by this measure all else can be covered.[4]

The fourth principle is **responsibility.** Responsibility means that you are really careful about the consequences of your words, deeds, and thoughts.

> Think of yourselves not as inhabitants of Earth, but of the Universe. In this way you will assume a greater responsibility. Likewise, you will apprehend how strenuous is the battle for each victory in the realm of Infinity....Responsibility is a duty to oneself and to the Highest....[5]

2. The second requisite of discipleship is meditation. We come back again and again to meditation. In Armenian they say that the bear has one song and he sings it 365 days of the year. Meditation is continuous, regular, scientific thinking. Meditation means to have a daily period of serious thinking.

Most of our thoughts are efforts for self-deception.

Real thinking is not self-deception; thinking is making yourself awake to reality.

3. The third requisite of discipleship is study. A disciple must learn how to study. To study means to carefully observe, watch or read events, books, etc. To study means to penetrate into the causes of things and see how they are forming results.

4. Discipleship requires that a person be self-supporting and not hanging on the necks of others. A disciple must stand on his own feet, physically, emotionally, and mentally. Immediately when people have problems, they go to each other and yak-yak, so that they receive a little emotional or mental support. But a disciple must stand on his own feet; he must develop an independent spirit.

Independence does not mean not to respect those who are radiating and have beautiful fragrance, but you do not hang on them.

5. The fifth requisite of a disciple is striving toward higher states of consciousness. Try to create some kind of measure and start measuring your state of consciousness. It doesn't matter what kind of measure you choose; the important thing is to create your own measure and start using it.

Are you expanding your consciousness? If your consciousness is not expanding, you are wasting your time and your life. People think that evolution takes care of you and no matter how you live, you are doing something great. But you are actually living like a mouse running in a wheel: you think you are running two miles, but you are in the same place as you were before.

No one is going to measure you; you are going to measure yourself. Sometimes expanding is not growth. The same thing is true in playing cards: sometimes to accumulate more cards in your hand is victory; sometimes to lose all your cards is victory. You must ask yourself what is your own measure.

Find a way to know whether you are growing or not. Service is a measure. Beauty is another measure. Sacrifice is a measure. Devotion is a measure.

6. The sixth requisite is the ability to control your mouth. The first aspect of this requirement is not to talk about things you don't know about. Observe yourself when you are speaking: do you really know why you are talking? We start talking, and suddenly we find ourselves racing toward Niagara Falls...and how we came there, we don't know.

The other day a man came and was talking about atomic energy. I looked at him. He didn't know what he was talking about. Then suddenly he realized it. "I guess I don't know what I am saying."

"Well," I said, "it's good you realized, but you already spoke."

This is the one thing that people must know—they already spoke. You cannot take an eraser and erase what you said.

When Jesus was crucified, the high priests wanted Pontius Pilate to change what he had written on the tablet over the cross. But Pontius Pilate said, "What I have written, I have written."[6] The important thing is not to write anything if it is not correct. Once you write it, once you say it, it's gone; it is recorded in the archives of the universe.

Millions of people are writing, talking, and expressing things they really don't know about, and this is why we are in chaos. When we are talking about things we don't know about, we are creating exhaust fumes. Everything that is not reality is like an exhaust.

The second aspect of this requirement is not to talk about things which are not your business. If you speak about things that are not your business, you create problems, disturbances, and difficulties. You may ask, "What is my business?" You find it out.

The third aspect of this requirement is not to speak about things entrusted to you. If you speak about things which are entrusted to you, you prove that you don't have foundation and you are not a human being because you don't have principles and nobody can trust you. A person is a human being when he is trustful. If you cannot trust someone, he does not exist; only your trust in him makes him exist.

7. The seventh requisite of discipleship has to do with karma. If you don't have good karma, no matter what you do, you are going to fail. Karma here means that you have money in savings and when you go to the bank they will give it to you.

When you are asking for something that is not given to you and nobody is helping you to have it, you don't have this good karma. You didn't work for it; you didn't sow anything, so how can you think you are going to reap something? You are like a person who goes to his garden and says, "I want tomatoes." And your garden will laugh at you and say, "You didn't plant tomatoes. How can you expect tomatoes?"

> In the question of the acceptance of a disciple, his karma plays the main role. Precisely, in connection with discipleship it is most essential to realize the law of Karma and to comprehend it in all respects. Thus, a person overburdened with karma cannot hope to become a close disciple. Only those whose earthly karma is almost completed can be accepted among the closest disciples."[7]

A person who is overburdened with the wrongs he did, with the debts he created, and with the mess that is behind him cannot expect to be a close disciple. You must create your discipleship with your tears, sweat, and striving. You must get rid of your debts. If you do not try to get rid of them, karma will continue to bite you forever.

> ...There are few who realize what a heavy burden the Teacher takes on by accepting a disciple....[8]

Every time the Teacher makes a contact with a disciple, it is a tremendous responsibility. With his contact he is building a magnetic line between himself and the disciple. Every time the disciple does something wrong, thinks a stupid thought, or has negative imagination, vanities, etc., the pollution immediately comes to the Teacher's aura. What a heavy karma the

Teacher is taking on to accept a disciple among the chosen disciples.

8. The eighth requisite of discipleship is devotion to the Teaching and the Teacher.

The Teacher will not forget to accept every sign of devotion. Devotion and alertness forge the union between worlds.[9]

Respect is shown only in demonstrating a life lived according to principles, virtues, and creative beauties.

1. Agni Yoga Society, *Letters of Helena Roerich,* Volume I, page 283.
2. Agni Yoga Society, *Leaves of Morya's Garden,* Volume II, page 24.
3. Agni Yoga Society, *Agni Yoga,* para. 31.
4. Agni Yoga Society, *Fiery World,* Volume II, para. 465.
5. Agni Yoga Society, *Aum,* para. 593.
6. John XIX: 21-22.
7. Agni Yoga Society, *Letters of Helena Roerich,* Volume I, page 284.
8. *Ibid.*
9. Agni Yoga Society, *Agni Yoga,* para. 349.

CHAPTER 21

THE PATH OF PERFECTION
AND THE HEART

If the Teaching cannot be assimilated in our lives and expressed in our deeds, emotions, expressions, and even thoughts, then we do not live the Teaching. To have a live Teaching, it must be expressed through our lives.

A living Teaching is a creative Teaching, a Teaching that expands our communication, compassion, and inclusiveness. A living Teaching is Joy expressed through everything we do. A living Teaching is Love that binds people and brings them together. Most importantly, a living Teaching is a life that unites humanity and brings the concept of God into people's lives.

This is why Christ said that if you love God but do not love your brother, you are failing — because God's love must be expressed through love for your brother.

Living ethics leads people into improvement. If you want to start to live the Teaching, you must improve day after day in all that you are doing. Improvement takes you into the process of perfection. Man has one goal in life, and it is so pitiful that people don't know that goal; people think that sex is the goal; people think that the accumulation of money is the goal, people think that accumulation of lands and possessions is the goal, that to be powerful and ruling is the goal. These are not goals; they are traps. There is only one goal: to perfect yourself.

243

Christ emphasized this in such a beautiful way. He said, "Be perfect as your Father in heaven is perfect." This means that you are going to strive day after day to improve yourself in all aspects. If you are ever trapped in anything, you are stopped on the path of perfection and you are not living the true goal of your spirit.

The true goal of your spirit is to be perfect, so you must at least try to improve yourself. Perfection comes stage by stage; the path of improvement is an endless path.

> *Sickness rises from sin — says the Scripture. We say that sickness comes from the imperfections of past and present. One should know how to approach the cure of sickness. To the regret of physicians, the process toward perfection is the true prophylactic measure. It can be understood that the process toward perfection begins with the heart, and it has not only a spatial but also a narrow material meaning. Mothers carry their children close to their hearts as a panacea for calming them, but usually one is unaware that this holding close to the heart creates a powerful reaction. Thus, also in the Subtle World we gather people close to the heart for strengthening and for cure. Of course, the heart loses a great deal of energy through such strong application. But, then, more than once has the heart of a mother been represented as transfixed by swords and arrows, a symbol of the acceptance into the heart of all actual pains.*
>
> *Not only in developed sicknesses but at their inception is the cure through the heart especially potent. At present, this remedy is almost forgotten, but it is no less powerful than a blood transfusion, for through the reaction of the heart the finest energy is transmitted without the unpleasant low admixture of blood. When one thinks about the process of perfectment, one must not forget solicitude for the heart that gives.[1]*

This verse tells us that if you did something imperfect in the past, you are going to have a headache now. That wrong is like a seed that is going to grow and eventually make you face it. If you are not perfecting yourself — your body, your emotions, your mind — now through education, discipline, and purity, you are going to have problems in the future.

Life is like swimming against the current. Immediately when you stop swimming, the current pulls you backwards. Either you are going to improve, or you are going to go backwards. If you are not really making great efforts to improve and perfect yourself, then you are trapped in matter, in self-interest, and in your vanities and glamors; you are really serving matter without serving your spirit.

To improve human life, expand the human consciousness, and eliminate sicknesses and diseases, the road suggested is the road of steady striving toward perfection. One must try to improve his physical body and its environment, his emotional body and its environment, his mental body and its environment, and his spiritual goals and expressions. These improvements are the steps toward perfection. When you are improving, you are becoming attuned with the Cosmic intentions. God needs perfection, and life is created to make you perfect.

Let's say that you are a great artist. If you stop on your present level of achievement, you are degenerating. Life is going forward like a river, and if you cannot go forward you create friction and slowly degenerate.

People think that if fifty of us do not advance, life is not advancing. This is a great illusion. This Planetary Life is advancing. The Soul of this planet is in the process of development and improvement. He is taking great initiations in Space. If that Life is going 10,000 miles per hour, you must go at least one mile per hour, so that the whole clock of the universe is synchronized.

This is the secret of life. When life is advancing, life radiates more energy. If you are not advancing parallel to that advancement, you are flooded with energy and your carburetor will not work. You also need assimilation of energy and creativity with that energy so that you synchronize yourself with the advancement of life.

Sitting and hallucinating doesn't help. Working day and night for your sexual pleasures, your stomach pleasures, your drinking pleasures, your moneymaking pleasures, and your buying and selling pleasures doesn't make sense if you are not progressing toward spiritual perfection.

During the war, once there was a terrible fire and we had to collect many children from a school and drive them out of the area to safety. I had a truck, and I told all the children, "Jump on the truck. The fire is coming!" All of them jumped on the truck except for one little boy who was busy digging a hole and filling it with pieces of straw. I shouted at him again, "Hey, jump on the truck!"

"No," he said. "I am busy playing. I don't want to come."

I said, "You are playing, but the fire is coming."

The boy refused to move. Finally I grabbed him and dumped him in the truck. He was furious. He started to curse me. He scratched me with his fingernails so hard that he drew blood on my face. I had to slap him and hold him down to make him come with us. Three or four miles later when we came out of the fire, he was still cursing me for taking him away from his game.

Are you like that boy? You are in danger. The fire is coming, and you are busy making money. Be careful. How many millions of times did you lose that money? Don't you realize that yet? Don't keep yourself too busy with such things. Money is important; your land and your house are important; but none of these things must hinder your progress on the path toward perfection.

"It can be understood that the process toward perfection begins with the heart...." This is so important, and we often forget this advice. We teach our children algebra, geometry, and physics; how to race together; how to exploit each other... but we don't teach the virtues of the heart.

There are ten steps you can take to train your

heart.

1. **Feeling for others.** If you do not have feeling for others and you think you are advancing, you are deceiving yourself. Eventually you will see what kind of pressure you are cultivating around you and how people will eventually rob you of whatever you have because you don't have feeling for others. Your God is one God, and everyone is a child of God. If you do not have feeling for others, you are already separated from God.

2. **Compassion.** What are we teaching to our children? Are we making them criminals instead of teaching them to save this world and make people their brothers? You can never improve if you do not have compassion. Compassion means deep love for the sake of the loved one. If I love you for myself, that's love, but if I love you for yourself, that's compassion.

3. **Humility.** Humility means the recognition of where you are and what you are. You must stand outside and look at the sky and the beautiful stars and galaxies and know what you are. Think about Infinity, and you will see what a bug you are. What are you so proud of? If you deepen this concept in your mind, you will see that humility is unity with God. Pride is separatism; pride separates.

4. **Patience.** Patience is a great quality of the heart. If we watch our lives, we will see that from early in the morning until night, we are not patient. And because we don't exercise patience, we always do things imperfectly. Patience leads our steps toward perfection. Patience takes us toward improvement. In everything you do, try to be patient, and you will see how much you will improve.

5. **Tolerance.** Tolerance means not to keep yourself occupied with the stupid things that people do. Give space to others, so that they can improve, through their own failures and successes.

6. **Wisdom.** We must teach wisdom in our schools. At this time, there is no class that teaches you wisdom. There is no class that teaches ethics; there is no class that teaches right human relations and goodwill. These

are now considered obsolete, unnecessary ideas.

You will never be successful in life if you are not spiritually beautiful. When we learn the Teaching and do not apply it in our lives, we become hypocrites. A hypocrite is a person who is divided within himself. If a person is divided within himself, he eats himself. He becomes weak; he degenerates; and he destroys himself.

Try to bring light into your life and try to live in that light. Even if you fail, it doesn't matter. As long as you make efforts to see that you are wrong and you want to improve, that willingness to improve will save you from hypocrisy.

7. **Sacrifice.** The heart must be cultivated through sacrifice. You must start doing things sacrificially. Every day at least once or twice you must do a sacrificial deed. Once or twice a day, sacrifice something for your husband, your wife, your children, your friends.

Children must be taught to do sacrificial deeds. Whenever you do something sacrificial, you open the heart. And when the heart opens, you are on the path of perfection. This is very important: unless your heart is open, you cannot enter the path of perfection. All rivers of life come from the heart, say the Scriptures. From the heart issue all virtues.

8. **Gratitude.** Try to realize how much God gave you, how much people helped you, how many beautiful things you have in life. Try to condense them and do something beautiful for someone else. This is gratitude.

Gratitude is the manifestation of your understanding of how much God gave you, of how much life gave you. You see a beautiful tree and feel grateful for it. That beauty creates a joy in you, and with that joy you go to someone else, hug him, and say beautiful things. Gratitude is giving and taking. If there is only taking, collecting, eating, "me, me, me," your actions lead you to sickness — social sickness, international sickness, wars, famines, earthquakes, and disasters.

9. **Inclusiveness.** People came 10,000 years ago and taught these things, but we never heard them. Now these ideas are becoming imperative in our lives. Unless we understand each other and include each

other, this planet is going to destroy itself. There is no other way.

You throw a rock in the lake and you see waves forming in concentric circles around it. The circles get bigger and bigger until the whole lake is included in the circle. Try to be inclusive. Don't reject people because they believe something different than you do. This is very difficult advice because from childhood we are taught to "hate that man....This is different. It is square instead of triangular...." When you lack inclusiveness, you are sick.

10. **Courage.** Courage is one of the fundamental qualities of the heart. If you do not have courage, you can never improve. You must have the courage to stand against crystallized ideas and say, "I know you are teaching these things, but I don't think they are right." It takes courage to stand on your feet and say, "My heart says that I must not hate. Well, I don't want to hate." Can you say that? If you can't, be my guest; hate more and more. Let him kill you. You will kill him in the next life; then he will kill you again...like a seesaw... and the world will become the battlefield for blood and suffering. There is no end to this, and it can never take you to perfection.

"...the cure through the heart [is] especially potent. At present, this remedy is almost forgotten, but it is no less powerful than a blood transfusion, for through the reaction of the heart the finest energy is transmitted without the unpleasant low admixture of blood...." The real blood of your heart — sacrificial love, beauty, goodness, truth, psychic energy — is more powerful than the transfusion of blood. Try it. Give your heart to someone. Hug him and give him your heart energy. The heart is a great healer.

The path and the process of perfection must start with the heart, not with the brain. Everything you build without the heart eventually is going to fall on your head. The foundation is the heart. If the heart is beautiful, strong, and cultivated, then whatever you build will perpetuate your love, beauty, goodness, and truth. But if there is no foundation and you are trying to build something great, it is going to fall on your head.

We can see this in contemporary history. We build tremendous things, but the next day we can push buttons and destroy the whole world. Why? Because the heart is lacking. The heart must be developed first; then science; then everything else upon that. Only the heart will use all these things with right direction.

If you don't have right direction, everything that you have and do will be used against your own interests. If you don't have the foundation of the heart, whatever you have is going to work against you. Even your beauty will work against you.

---

1. Agni Yoga Society, *Heart,* para. 96.

CHAPTER 22

MESSENGERS IN SPACE

In the esoteric Teaching, we are told that this planet is one of the "states" or globes in Cosmos where sometimes other people visit. All stars, all galaxies, and all globes in the universe are like other states in the United States. Sometimes we visit other states, and we live there for billions and billions of years in the history of human existence.

We are not stuck only on this planet. The false Teaching says that we are inhabitants of this planet. We are not. We visit here according to the laws and principles and secret karma, but this planet is one of our motels. We come here for 60 years or 60 days or 60 minutes, and then go to other planets in other solar systems and galaxies.

Sometimes we visit these other "states" not with our physical bodies but with our etheric bodies, astral bodies, mental bodies, or higher bodies. We are travelers of the universe, and there is no end to our travel. Every time we go to another state or globe, we increase our experiences; we use our knowledge and intuition there to create results for our future journey. The way that we live here physically, emotionally, and mentally conditions and appoints the planet we will go to physically, emotionally, and mentally.

Actually, we were dropped on this planet when our physical wings were cut. But our emotional and mental wings are not cut, and it is possible to develop them and fly away during sleep, contemplation, or meditation. This may seem like an hallucination for some, but for others it is very real. Many people feel that they are not the slaves of this planet.

> *It was said in antiquity, "All people are angels."*
> *Verily, people are the messengers of the far-off*
> *worlds. Hence great is their responsibility. They*
> *rarely take the responsibility of carrying that*
> *which is entrusted to them and are not even dis-*
> *tressed at losing the treasure. Only a few individ-*
> *uals may sorrow that they have forgotten some-*
> *thing they have heard. Let people not forget that*
> *they are messengers and a bond with the distant*
> *worlds. Such a consciousness in itself beautifies*
> *everyday life.*[1]

An angel means a messenger in Space, a messenger from one star to another star, from one planet to another planet, or from one plane of existence to another plane of existence. You must fix in your mind that you came to this Earth with certain responsibilities. You have special responsibilities, and when you go to another planet you will have other responsibilities there. Do not think that when you leave your body, everything is ended.

Because you are a messenger, your responsibility is great. Suppose you suddenly went to Venus or another globe in the galaxy. What message are you going to take from here? And with what accuracy?

Messengers are like links in the chain. The responsibility of the link is to bring unity and continuity, to keep the flow of energy and integrity between the places he is relating. The responsibility of the messenger is to weave the network of unity in everything. Wherever he goes, he must weave the carpet, the handwork, the network of unity through his messages.

When you go from one world to another, you weave the threads of unity between the worlds through your emotions, actions, and thoughts. This is the greater responsibility of a messenger. If you don't learn the responsibility of your mission, then instead of creating unity in all systems of the universe you will become a disturbing factor in the universe — which means that you will work against the law of unification in the universe.

You are not this nose, this hair, this body, this ear. You are an angel, and because you are an angel you have a mission beyond the earthly troubles and disturbances. You must feel that beyond your daily labor you are living in the *universe* and you have a great responsibility and mission. This kind of expansion of consciousness makes your daily life more beautiful because you contemplate the infinite mission that you have within yourself.

> *It has been said that each man carries his particular mission. Actually, each one who has taken on an earthly body is already a messenger. Is it not wondrous? It changes nothing that most people have no conception of their destination. This forgetfulness is due to a lack of realization of the three worlds. One may imagine the transformation of a man who recognizes the usefulness of his earthly path. Brotherhood furthers such realization.*[2]

For example, in the mountains each different flower is a messenger. One flower's message is to be, for example, blue. Another's is to be this shape. Another's is to have that fragrance. These are the messages that the flowers are bringing from the Far-Off Worlds. Don't forget that they also travel as you travel. The universe is not stationary. It is always bubbling, going and coming, flowing. There is nothing that is stable; everything flows, changes, and revolves. There is a great beauty in this concept.

What is your mission for this planet? Did you come here to bring hatred, malice, slander, crimes, war, destruction? Or is your mission something different? You must find that difference. The strongest note that you are going to sound in this life through everything you are doing is the keynote of your life. What is your keynote? What message are you going to give to this world from Far-Off Worlds? That message is found when you go deeper and deeper into your Self and touch the layers that were formed when you were passing through spheres in the Far-Off Worlds. You are going to go deep into the layers of your consciousness so that you find what impressions you have from Higher Worlds and what you can bring here. This will be your mission.

If you don't have this inner contact, you don't have a mission; you reflect everything around you and you think that is your mission. This is why you are not stable in your life — because you are continuously affected by the surrounding conditions in your life.

If you have an earthly body, you are already a messenger because the life of the universe appropriated you to slowly come and live in physical existence. If you didn't have a physical body, you could not function in the physical layers; you couldn't register physical experiences and impressions and react to them. You are going to bring your message to the earthly life because that instrument is given to you to communicate with the earthly life. This is how the highest concepts and visions can materialize on the physical plane.

You must find out whether you are a messenger of goodness or evil, a messenger of light or darkness, a messenger of illumination or ignorance. But when you go deep into yourself, you will see that you are a messenger of light because "angel" means a lighted, illuminated, radioactive body. Angels are always the messengers of light. In your Inner Core, you are the messenger of Light, Beauty, Goodness and Truth.

> *Some appear as messengers, who have consciously and selflessly accepted the responsibility; others bear tidings without knowing it; a third group partially affirms a useful word; a fourth displays useful actions by the examples of their lives. There are many kinds of offerings and affirmations. Let us not designate which can be especially useful. Each one within his own horizon can direct people to good. Let us welcome each*

good offering. Courage enables one to array one-
self in impenetrable armor.[3]

If you are really fixed in your intention, in your direction, and in your devotion to bring that message into the world, you are a conscious messenger. When you are a conscious messenger, you carry a tremendous voltage of energy from the sources from which you are bringing the message to Earth, because you have continuity of contact. For example, an electrical wire that is cut in many places has no continuity of contact. If you are cut, which means you don't remember and you have no vision or reflection from Higher Worlds, then you don't have that energy flow. When you are not cut, the flow is continuous. All Great Ones carry a tremendous energy within Themselves because Their line with the source from which They are bringing the message is continuous.

When I was 15 years old, I said to my mother, "Why do some Great Ones always have people around Them who sacrifice their lives for Them?"

My mother replied, "They are charged from Their Home, from which They take Their wings and fly to Earth."

Because the message of Great Ones is charged with heavenly fire, Their message is truly fiery.

"*...others bear tidings without knowing it....*" There are other messengers who bring beauty, goodness, and truth, but they don't yet have the awareness of where they came from. They simply have some impression that they are going to do something good. Many of us are like this. We have an urge to be beautiful, to be good, to bring unity and peace; an urge for understanding, an urge to uplift human life, economic life, political life, and educational life. But we don't know from what fountain we are bringing this message to Earth.

The third group is those who "partially affirm a useful word." This group sees part of the Teaching and appreciates it, and often the appreciated part of the Teaching becomes a link which helps people to be involved with the greater part of the Teaching.

The "fourth group" doesn't know about these ideas; about missions and messages; but they exemplify a beautiful life. For example, they didn't have to learn to love, but they love because they have that ability in their systems from different experiences gathered in their past, throughout ages. They are already beautiful and good, and their lives are an example.

Once I knew a tailor, a very simple, illiterate man. He used to make very beautiful clothes. Many times I used to visit his shop and listen to the conversations there. Not once in my presence did he ever speak anything bad about anybody. People came and gossiped and used malice and slander, and he would just look at them and say something humorous or change the subject. I remember saying to myself, "My gosh, I am learning not to gossip, not to misuse my words, and here every day I am making hundreds of mistakes. But this man already knows." With their example, such people bring the message.

"Each one with his own horizon can direct people to good." As your horizon becomes broader, your expression and leadership for the cause of goodness become stronger and more impressive. Your horizon is built by your experiences and your travels to the Far-Off Worlds. If you traveled only between two planets, your horizon is two planets. If you traveled ten light-years away from the planet, your horizon is totally different, and your accumulation of experiences is totally different from the person who travels between two cities.

In your travel, you have four mechanisms for registration of Space. You register the distance of Space with your eyes. There is another registration of Space through your astral eyes, then through your mental eyes, and then your spiritual eyes. When you are traveling in Space with these four eyes, your horizon is really limitless.

*If a very simple man should ask you what is
the purpose of the Teaching, say, "That you should
live happily." Let him not be overwhelmed by too-
complicated considerations. Let his entire being
be filled with the realization that the whole Teaching is concerned with improving his life. The
understanding of responsibility may come later.
First — proclaim the joy and betterment of life.*[4]

The Teaching is given to humanity to alleviate
their pains and sufferings. Wherever there is no Teaching, there are heavy pains and sufferings, because to
live without the Teaching is to live against the laws
and principles of the universe.

If people come to your group and say, "What is this
group," say, "This is a happy group." Three years later
you can say to them, "You are going to work hard, do
meditation, be nice to each other, sometimes sacrifice,
try to overcome your vanities and ego, sometimes work
against your personality...." If you say to newcomers
that they are going to become responsible through this
Teaching, they may escape immediately. Responsibility comes through the development and unfoldment of
your consciousness. If the consciousness is not developed, you are putting water into a bucket that has no
bottom.

*...Affirm success; affirm joy; affirm under-
standing of action. Cast away the thoughts of the
old world.....*[5]

You must emphasize to the newcomer, joy and betterment of life. As his consciousness or his wings
develop, you will take him to higher places to fly. The
first stage is happiness. Second, if the Teaching is
assimilated and really understood, it brings greater
and greater joy. The third stage is to eliminate those
thoughts from your mind that do not fit the expectation of the new life. The new life does not need old-
fashioned thoughts, so you must eliminate them.

We say new life, but is life really new? The new life
is really the old life that you have within your Infinity.

But because many millions of layers of trash are accumulated upon the old life, when you remove them your life becomes a new life.

> ...*When there is talk about raising the people's level, precisely simplicity is required in all its convincingness. This quality must not only be accepted with one's mind but loved with one's heart; from it emanate both cooperation and Brotherhood.*[6]

Simplicity is frankness, straightforwardness, and directness. These things come when you are really informed and aware, and when you have digested whatever you are going to give to others. The best way to lead people away from the Teaching is to talk about the Teaching in a way they cannot understand. Immediately when they don't understand, they hate the Teaching. This is what has been done for centuries.

Simplicity is needed because it convinces people. This is because simplicity is an electrical current that bypasses the intellect and the emotions and touches your core. You don't need to complicate things. Complication comes from the guilt that you are not worthy of the things you are teaching; so you artificially cover yourself, making things complicated so that you give the impression that you know better than they do.

Simplicity creates brotherly feelings because you know that someone is not a hypocrite; you know he is not hiding behind glamors, thoughtforms, and fabrications. He is as he is, and he is direct with you.

To be simple does not mean to be commonplace, meaningless or shallow. Simplicity can compress tons of meaning and ideas in an expression from which all levels of people, according to their level, receive a message. This message deepens as their consciousness expands.

The Teaching of Christ and Buddha are examples of pure simplicity; but behind the simple expressions are many treasures which you can enjoy by going more deeply into Their expressions.

The spark of Infinity must be expressed in everything....[7]

The Spark of Infinity is *you*. Because you are a Spark of Infinity living in all Cosmic Existence, you are going to bring this consciousness, feeling, and experience of Infinity into your daily life. You are not going to live the life of an elephant, putting your nose in the mud and sucking the mud. You are going to look to the stars and bring Infinity into your daily action. In everything you do, say, and feel you must express the Infinity that is within you. The One Who is Infinity and the one who experiences Infinity are both within you.

When you start looking to Infinity, you are no longer limited with finite things. Finite things do not bother you. The greatest pain of the human being is to have an ego. The ego is the pure self identified with the body, emotions, and mind; it is the blinded self. Your ego is an open wound, and whoever touches it or squeezes it hurts you. But if you don't have ego, you have Infinity within you. Ego is separatism; Infinity is oneness and freedom from your ego.

---

1. Agni Yoga Society, *Brotherhood,* para. 278.
2. *Ibid.,* para. 568.
3. *Ibid.,* para. 403.
4. Agni Yoga Society, *Agni Yoga,* para. 65.
5. *Ibid.,* para. 76.
6. Agni Yoga Society, *Brotherhood,* para. 479.
7. *Ibid.,* para. 8.

CHAPTER 23

SIGNS OF THE TEACHING

The Teaching of M.M. is so great that the mind cannot totally grasp it. He writes from His own level, the level of a Master. This is the level of intuitional awareness. In order to understand Him, you must expand your consciousness by reflecting and meditating upon the ideas that He gave. Understanding is similar to the digestion of food. Our bodies grow and improve through digestion. Without proper digestion, the food causes trouble in our system. We must meditate and think about M.M.'s great ideas in order to really digest them.

It is good to take small parts of this Teaching — a few sentences, an idea — and carry it with you in your pocket during the day. When you find a quiet moment, take it out and think about the message. This will refresh you greatly.

> *First of all, the Teaching requires independence of action from the disciple. The Teaching gives direction, generously giving the precious hints, but the disciple must himself "with his own hands and feet" build his path. Therefore, do not expect ready-made formulae. From small hints build the great structure.*[1]

Such is the life of a disciple. In most cases, the Masters do not tell him where and when to go. They do not tell him what to do. They give hints, but by his own efforts he must adapt his life to the Teaching. Each

260

individual must make his own efforts. The Teaching gives the direction; it is up to the disciple to carve the path.

"With his own hands and feet" means by the individual's own labor. Do not depend on someone else to chew the Teaching for you and put it in your mouth for you to swallow. You must chew it with serious meditation and clear thinking. You must find your own path with sincere striving for the good of all humanity. Striving is what makes you really great. Depend upon the Divinity within you and strive toward the future. Only striving will help you change your level.

Striving is the effort to surpass yourself. You must always try to be more and do better. You must always try to raise your level.

By your "own hands and feet" means that you must work to raise your level of beingness. You must use your own energies to lift yourself into greater joy, beauty, and usefulness. Other people may encourage you, but you must do it for yourself with your own efforts.

> *...Therefore, ring the bell only at the right time. Thus you will avoid coercion.*[2]

The Teaching warns against anything forced. When you force someone, you prematurely crack him. You must create the right conditions, and then he will grow. For example, if you want a little boy to learn geometry so that he may someday graduate from college as an engineer, you do not start with complex theorems. If you do that, he will not understand what you are talking about and he will hate geometry from that moment on.

It is human nature to have a negative reaction to whatever you don't understand. But if you start at the beginning with the boy, he will slowly start to see the beauty of geometry.

When you have a teacher who presents material which is too difficult for you, you hate the material and the teacher. But you really love the teacher who teaches you something and helps you to understand it well. A good teacher gives you just a little water so that he creates a thirst in you. Later you will want more water, and he will be able to give you a cup of water and eventually even take you to rivers and oceans of wisdom.

It takes time to prepare the right conditions for something to grow. This is a law of Nature. Give yourself time and try to assimilate the Teaching, and you will see that you are growing. Likewise, you must never force people to study the Teaching, but you must radiate the Teaching to others through the example of your life.

We are also told that the Teaching must not be sold in the bazaars. The Teaching is only for those who search for it; it is for those who are purifying their natures and striving toward Cosmos. This practice will keep the Teaching from degenerating. If you present the Teaching to people who are not ready for it, they will change it to suit their own personality weaknesses or interests. This is what happened to Buddhism, Christianity, and many other beautiful religions. People started to become separative, superstitious and dogmatic, and the real Teaching was lost.

The ultimate goal of the Teaching is complete self-denial. Never forget this. Complete self-denial is the aim for which you are striving.

In a certain monastery, the Teachers would give certain rules to the new members. The first rule was to cut all ties with the world. Whatever possessions they had were to be distributed to the poor and they should come only with a shirt.

One day a young man wanted to become a monk and renounce the world. He went to the door of the monastery and said that he wanted to become a monk. The doorkeeper asked him, "Did you cut your ties with the world?"

The boy answered, "Yes."

But another Teacher who was standing by the doorkeeper asked, "What is that string around your neck?"

"Oh, it is nothing."
The Teacher came and pulled the string. He found at the other end a bag containing a lot of money. He said to the boy, "Unless you renounce this bag of money also, you cannot come to the monastery." The boy immediately threw the bag into the lake.

The time comes in the life of every disciple when he has a major shock. He faces a drastic decision. Does he pass, or does he go back another 10,000 years in his evolution? Does his love for the Teaching motivate him, or do his attachments to money, sex, or separative interests control him? This is the turning point in every disciple's life.

We are dissipating superstition, ignorance and fear. We are forging courage, will and knowledge.

Every striving toward enlightenment is welcome. Every prejudice, caused by ignorance, is exposed.

Thou who dost toil, are not alive in thy consciousness the roots of cooperation and Community?

If this flame has already illumined thy brain, adopt the signs of the Teaching of Our mountains.

Thou who dost labor, do not become wearied puzzling over certain expressions. Every line is the highest measure of simplicity.

Greetings to workers and seekers.[3]

Superstition has to do with the beliefs that originate in the emotional nature and are handed down without any mental analysis. Fear is an identification with the not-self. It is a reaction to eyes which are not there. Fear is like a knot in a person's consciousness which constricts its natural flow. When you untie this knot, the consciousness becomes like a river again.

The true Teaching is a focused effort to dissipate the three monsters of superstition, ignorance and fear. This is accomplished in proportion to the effort and striving which a person puts into his study of the Teaching.

A great Sage says that the fear of death will soon
be erased. Many disciples have already conquered this
fear. They were able to see themselves as separate
from their bodies, and this helped them lose their fear
of death. They had a change of attitude when they saw
that it was possible to leave the body and enter a new
one just as easily as changing one's jacket. Unfortunately, most of us have not yet learned this lesson.

Courage is not to be confused with recklessness.
Courage is self-forgetfulness with clear reason and
logic. Courage requires a clear mind and daring.

M.M. says in this verse that those who are active
in the work of spreading light have the roots of their
consciousness in cooperation with the "Community."
The Community refers to the Hierarchy. One of the
Agni Yoga books called *Community* explains this way
of living. The members of the Hierarchy have a super-
state of communal life which is not to be confused with
average communes. The members of the Hierarchy
share everything communally in the light of pure
striving toward spiritual victory.

Cooperation means that people see the same vision
and coordinate all their activities to reach this goal.
They may use different means of achievement, but
their efforts are aligned and balanced so that the
vision is realized. To build a building an architect, a
foreman, carpenters, and painters are needed. Each
must do his own job so that a beautiful building can be
constructed. The Hierarchy operates in the same
manner. They all have the same purpose, but Their
individual parts in the Plan vary according to Their
area of activity.

A person who really labors for the Teaching deepens his cooperation with *the* Community — the Hierarchy. He takes all his nourishment and energy from
the concept of cooperation and community.

The "signs of the Teaching" are discipline, courage, striving, fearlessness, and labor. You cannot
climb the mountain without letting go of the burdens
which hinder your progress. As you climb, you slowly
understand that you cannot carry your old clothes to

the mountaintop. You must drop them one by one because they are not needed.

As the striver grows, he becomes the mountain itself. The inner, esoteric meaning of a mountain relates it to being close to the sky and close to Infinity. Mountains are a sign of initiation. One who climbs the mountain of striving and self-denial is one who is on the path of initiation.

Great artists are those who are able to deny themselves. When we speak of self-denial, we are not referring to your real Self. We are referring to the little selves, which are identified with the physical, emotional, and mental bodies. These include all hatreds, jealousies, angers, and fears which manipulate you for their own satisfaction. A great artist knows how to deny these and find his real Self, his true inner Essence. As he comes closer to his real Self, he comes closer to the fountain of all creative energy.

When you make a list of the greatest people who have lived in the world, you think about those who gave everything they had for humanity. They were great because they had great love for humanity. The measure of their greatness is determined by the extent of their giving. The more they gave, the greater they became. Greatness is found in giving and in loving.

When one speaks of someone's usefulness it is not meant to call him the pillar of the Teaching. One must needs take things in their reality, because exaggeration is equal in nature to minimizing. One must not drag anyone forcibly to heaven. At the hour appointed, the blind regain sight. It is useful to point out the measure of the order of life, so that the humblest may see the logic of technical applications, avoiding superfluous dross. But it is not necessary forcibly to wash people. Mark the usefulness of each messenger and do not place the load of a camel upon a donkey.[4]

Man is the victim of his own imagination. He builds exaggerated thoughtforms, and they press on his brain so much that he falls into dreams, hallucinations, and nightmares. Depression is the result of the exaggeration of negative thoughtforms. Depression starts from the mind, not from reality. If you have a little pain somewhere, you think you have cancer, a tumor, or heart problems...when in reality, you don't have anything.

People think that exaggeration is a moral defect. It isn't. Exaggeration is a crime — a crime against yourself and a crime against others. Exaggeration is going on all over the world through television, radio, newspapers, daily conversations....Everything is blown out of proportion, and you lose your direction. Once you lose your direction, you become confused; you become a slave in the hands of those who want to control you.

Exaggeration brings confusion, and confusion takes away your will, your observation, and your discrimination. In order not to be controlled by exaggeration, you must develop your discrimination, sound judgment, and peace of mind. You must develop your sanity and your down-to-earthness. Prejudice means to develop some kind of thoughtform that is not based on reality. Prejudice and exaggeration are methods to achieve self-interest.

Remember that whenever you exaggerate something, you destroy its own value.

"At the hour appointed, the blind regain sight." When your Soul kicks, suddenly you start seeing that you are living in illusion. Every time you exaggerate, something becomes less in your aura. You lose your aura and your energy. You create contraction within yourself; you create battle within yourself.

Your Soul has a cycle. Maybe every month, or every full moon, or every seven months, It hits you, and you come to your senses. In such moments you have unification with your inner fire. A window opens and you start to become yourself; you see that the path you are going on is the wrong path.

You must have the inner capital to do something or to be something. If you tell your son he is going to be a great inventor and he doesn't have that capital, he starts to visualize himself becoming something he can never be. He slowly becomes beaten by his own visualization, and he shifts to depressions, to sickness, to mental insanity and disorder — all because of exaggeration of his capabilities by his parents.

The inner capital means the preparation of ages of incarnations, which must be developed for years and years and years. If you speak the truth, you awaken the fire in someone. If you exaggerate, you lead him to eventual disillusionment and failure.

You are not going to believe your own lies. When you tell a lie and repeat it several times, you build a thoughtform and it becomes a reality. Later you must break that thoughtform.

Once there was a girl who suddenly became paralyzed and couldn't walk. No doctor or psychiatrist could help her. I went to see her. She was hypnotized; she had hypnotized herself into playing a drama about a paralyzed girl.

I sat and talked with her and her parents for a while. Then I started to play the piano for her. Suddenly I shouted at her, "There is a rattlesnake under your feet!" She jumped up and ran away.

I said, "You silly girl, come on now, walk."

She could not believe she was really walking.

It is very important to know what charge of energies you can carry within your system and what charge of energy an individual or a group who are under your supervision can carry. We talk about things to children that would be confusing even for adults, and we say things to adults that children would be bored hearing. Similarly, we load people with more responsibilities and duties than they can carry. Such behavior creates rejection and eventually hatred.

Real Teachers or Leaders have a very precious sense by which they can determine the spiritual, mental, emotional, and physical capacities of people and deal with them accordingly. The most successful leaders are those who do not overload, but challenge. To challenge means to create striving in others, to make efforts to expand their consciousness to receive more, or to expand their consciousness in order to understand and create more.

> *I tell thee, let the flame of thy heart be alight with
>   the fire of compassion.*
> *In compassion is buried the great pearl of Secret
>   Knowledge.*
>
> *All Bodhisattvas, all Holy Ones, all Martyrs,
>   strove along this Path.*
> *Remember the legend of the Seven Gates.*
> *Not for all is the thorny way a hardship.*
> *There are souls to whom the thorny crown is
>   sweeter than a kingly one,*
> *And a coarse garment more precious than the
>   royal purple.*[5]

The Seven Gates refer to Shamballa. There are four gates and three doors to Shamballa.[6]

The Law of the Hierarchy is the Law of Compassion. The members of the Hierarchy are called the Compassionate Ones, and They work under the sublaws of the Law of Compassion.

Compassion is a response to the painful and devastating conditions of humanity. It is an effort to relieve humanity's suffering by meeting its needs. It takes a tremendous amount of strength of spirit to enter the path of compassion. There is much suffering and rejection on this path. This is why the thorny crown is the symbol of the person of compassion: he is always subject to the suffering of the world. He feels the hardship and pain of the world. Because of his compassion, he can do nothing but try to elevate, heal, and ease the suffering, ignorance and limitations of humanity. Every effort he makes adds another thorn to his crown.

Some invisible guides must have been directing the people who placed the crown of thorns on Christ's head. With this act they were symbolically showing that He was the Lord of Compassion.

It is very interesting that M.M. mentions the "royal purple" in this verse. He wants to create an association in people's minds. Purple is the color of royalty because it symbolizes the integration of the soul with the spirit. In royal courts, kings were expected to dress in purple because the king is the glory of the nation. In the Catholic Church, the high-ranking clergy wear purple. It is the same in the churches in the East. They want to show that the auras of the dignitaries radiate purple; they want to show that they are the symbol of the achievement, pride, and glory of the nation.

Solemnity is so important. Solemnity is achievement of inner integration, which results in the radiation of your Divine beauty. You can't teach this to people; it must come from a sense of internal dignity, poise, and sacredness.

When this is developed, you can start to become a creator. The thread of creativity in your personality field connects you with higher sources, and you slowly become a universal and Cosmic creator. Let's say that a great Heavenly Man is creating a solar system. He has a creative thread that extends from the Zodiac to the Greater Zodiac. This thread enables Him to create an entire solar system. It is like an electrical wire connecting Him with higher sources of beauty and knowledge.

Imagine that you are the foreman of a construction crew, but you are not in contact with the architect and engineer. What kind of a house are you going to create? You may be extremely intelligent, but you need a plan to build upon. The architect is your source, and you need to be in contact with him.

The level of the architect will determine how great your construction is. If you are in contact with an architect who has graduated from high school, you will have one level of a building. But if your architect has graduated from a college with great honors, you are going to build a magnificent building which will last for many years.

This is why a great Sage says that a Master strives toward the Planetary Logos and the Planetary Logos strives toward the Solar Logos....Each is trying to construct a channel of greater creativity.

It is so important not to waste our energy, in particular our sexual energy. When we waste ourselves, the chemistry of our bodies is altered and the pranic currents cannot reach our brain and nervous system. They either cannot make the connections, or they become distorted by wrong or partial connections. This is why people become senile. In old age, many needed chemicals are used up or not produced any longer.

When a teenager wastes his sexual energy, he is using precious reservoirs of energy which he will need in his fifties and sixties to maintain an active mind. People have the potential of functioning at top capacity until they are ninety, but if they waste themselves when they are young, they will have problems later on in life.

In the West there have appeared many yogis, prestidigitators, teachers, hypnotists, occultists, who are dealing with the effects of will. Brilliantly multiplying their coins, they teach anyone, for a fair fee, how to improve his material conditions; how to gain people's confidence; how to win influence in society; how to conduct business; how to dictate numerous orders; how to make a roseate garden of life. In developing the will, some of these teachers are seemingly following the right path, but they do not indicate any goal in this wandering, and thereby they only serve to worsen the ugly conditions of life.

Is not the powerful will that works for the increase of antiquated prejudices a true horror? How much energy will have to be expended on these neo-occultists in order to annihilate the harm of their spiritual viciousness!...

First of all, the Teaching is not sold; that is a most ancient law. The Teaching gives perfection as its goal; otherwise it would be bereft of a future. The Teaching overlooks personal comfort; otherwise it would be egoism. The Teaching previsions the beautifying of existence; otherwise it would be submerged in ugliness. The Teaching is always self-denying, because it knows what is the Common Good. The Teaching reveres knowledge; otherwise it would be darkness....[7]

We have millions of colleges and universities, and still crime is continuing to increase. Why? Because these educational institutions are not teaching people how to perfect life and perfect themselves.

"The Teaching gives perfection as its goal." The only Teaching that is worthy to be called a Teaching is the one that improves your life instead of deteriorating or degenerating it. This perfection starts on the simplest levels: make your body healthy; make your emotions pure and positive; make your thinking clear and benevolent; make your motives right and clean; make your relationships with others beautiful. If you cannot do these things, whatever else you are accumulating in life eventually is going to work against your survival.

"The Teaching previsions the beautifying of existence; otherwise it would be submerged in ugliness." The Teaching is given to beautify all existence. Make your life more beautiful in any way you can; this is the meaning of the Teaching. But the Teaching also presents the difficult path. It is easy to be ugly, but it is difficult to be beautiful.

Once I saw a little boy playing with a wooden cane. He started knocking down flowers; then he broke the branches on two little trees. I became very upset and I asked him, "What do you think you are doing?"

He said, "Leave me alone. I am just having fun."

Whoever taught this little boy — his teachers, parents, friends — created a great failure by teaching this little boy to work for ugliness. This little boy was so different than an old neighbor of mine. One day I saw him planting little trees next to the road. His grandson asked him, "Grandpa, why are you planting all these trees now? You are 90 years old."

He answered, "So that people enjoy the beauty of the trees for many generations."

1. Agni Yoga Society, *Letters of Helena Roerich,* Volume I, page 144.
2. Agni Yoga Society, *Community,* para. 129.
3. *Ibid.,* preface.
4. Agni Yoga Society, *Agni Yoga,* para. 35.
5. Agni Yoga Society, *Leaves of Morya's Garden,* Volume I, para. 324.
6. See *The Legend of Shamballa,* pp. 57-67, by T. Saraydarian.
7. Agni Yoga Society, *Agni Yoga,* para. 404.

CHAPTER 24

HOW TO COMMUNICATE THE TEACHING

People try to talk about a subject which they themselves do not know and which they are not prepared to talk about. Or they try to talk according to the need of their audience about a subject they really know. Or they talk about all that they know to the audience, who will understand only half of it, or if they do understand, they will not apply it. This is why the Teaching needs those who do it justice in their teaching of it, without the interference of their vanity and self-interest.

One of the most difficult conditions of the Teaching will be the ability to speak proportionately: to speak so as to give the correct direction of thought, not intruding upon the karma. To tell all means to put on chains. But to awaken the striving and to indicate a direction will be the task of the Teaching. The protective care will watch invisibly after the growth of consciousness. As a hand leads in the dark along winding streets, so the Teacher lays a Hand upon the shoulder of the disciple. Not vacuum but vigilance corresponds to the leadership. The Command fills the space but does not strike the crown of the head. Not for a single personality but for the general evolution is the Teaching given. It is a ray of the sun. Blessed is he who resembles a hunter of light![1]

You must be a balanced and proportionate speaker or transmitter of the Teaching. Some people may go to a lecture and be able to absorb 90 percent of what is being said. But others can take only 10 percent; so you give only as much as they can take. Once you know what the real Teaching is, you will be really careful about passing it to others. You will be especially careful not to pass it to people who are not ready for it.

You must use co-measurement to measure your audience before you start to speak, and you must use it when you speak. You may have prepared a beautiful lecture, but when you stand up to speak you see two new people, so you change your lecture on the spot to meet their needs. It is very important to know the level of the people present whenever you are talking about the Teaching.

Sometimes a person reads the Teaching for a few years, and in his vanity and hypocrisy he thinks he is now a master. That vanity must be broken. Once the wind of vanity catches your sails, you will sink to the bottom of the ocean. You will not have control upon yourself because the wind of your vanity is so strong.

The Teaching must be given in such a way that people see a direction and strive for it. You must not limit people or give them orders and advice when you speak. "To give the correct direction of thought" means to inspire people to try to be perfect. How to be perfect is each individual's business.

You will tell people, "Your direction is from here to the mountaintop." But you will not tell them, "In one month's time you must be there." Show the mountain-top, which is Beauty, Goodness, and Truth, and let people go there if they want to. If they don't want to go, don't push them. When you push people, you often lead them in the wrong direction. They must make their own choices and fail if they have to; then they are ready for the Teaching.

To "awaken the striving" in others is the most important thing. Striving is even more important than their knowledge and their achievements because if they achieve something and stop striving, they are dead. Lot's wife became a pillar of salt because she turned and looked back; she looked to the past. When people are stuck with the past, they let their striving die. They no longer strive to go forward, and they crystallize, like pillars of salt.

Your so-called holiness is not determined by what you are; your holiness is determined by how you strive. Your striving must never stop. When you look at the stars and think about Cosmos, you must feel your nothingness and wonder how far you must still strive to be like those stars.

You went to college and earned your bachelor's degree. That's wonderful, but can you strive beyond that? You must never forget that no matter how much knowledge you have, there are still so many things for you to learn. This is what Socrates meant when he said, "I know one thing: that I know nothing."

The next verse is especially important for students of wisdom:

> ...Waste is condemned by Us. Each accumulation is a step toward freedom. Where shall we set the boundaries of permitted acquisitions? By straight-knowledge and experience the Teacher will sanction all that is permitted. A Yogi can do everything. Yet all is not permitted the Yogi. Then where are the borders of limitation? Responsibility, through spiritual possession. Only that possession is worthy of a Yogi. The rest is nothing more than the arms of the warrior, returned to his commander after the battle. Here can be no hesitation....[2]

Whenever you waste anything, you are exploiting and hurting Nature, Who is your mother. If you need only one hair from the head of your mother, don't take a bunch of hair. Then your mother will become bald!

It is very interesting to note that people only waste things when their greed increases. Don't be greedy, and you will not be wasteful.

Whenever you are wasting anything, you are becoming a slave. When you accumulate only the things — energy and money — you need, you become more free. M.M. says that only your intuition, your straight-knowledge, will tell you how much you really need.

> *...people come to you with the question, "How to think?" Reply briefly, "With the New World; cast out all limited opinions." Reflect how it is possible to depart from old habits. Exert yourselves to accept the full chalice.*
>
> *Not words, but the filling of space impels you in an immutable command. The abolishment of fear will help you in a difficult hour....*[3]

The new world is the vision that you have about the future of the world. You must let go of all limited, crystallized, or old-fashioned thoughts. You must get rid of superstition, prejudices, and fanaticism because you cannot think until old thoughts are left behind. If old thoughts are in your mind, the new thoughts will be eaten by them and used by them. Your new thoughts will create energy for them, and your future will be worse than the past.

Think about the future of humanity. Think about the perfection of human beings. Think about the planet as being one world. Think about humanity as one brotherhood. And when you are thinking about the new world, think about yourself, too. People eat themselves with their thoughts. One day when I was a young boy living in the monastery I was sitting alone feeling sorry for myself, thinking about how much I missed my parents, my dog, my goat....My Teacher came and said to me, "The past is eating you."

Whenever you think about your past memories, your weaknesses, and your failures, you let the past eat you. Think in terms of the future. There is an important law in the universe which cannot be repeated enough: Whatever you think about yourself, that is what you are going to become. If you think about yourself as a monkey, I guarantee you that you are going to be a monkey. Think instead that you are a victorious human being. Even while in the depth of the ocean you must say, "I am going to do it — because God is within me." Remember, you are "more radiant than the Sun, purer than the snow...."

To "accept the full chalice" means to accept all the consequences of your striving. When Christ was praying in the garden at Gethsemane He accepted the full chalice. With this act, Christ took on the blood, suffering, hatred, refusal, denial, and crucifixion and said to His Father, "Thy will be done."

Sometimes you may feel an inner command to do something. There is no reason or logic behind it; it is not expressible in words. It is rather an energy that saturates or fills that space and impels you to do something. This energy is psychic energy, and psychic energy comes only from your *striving*. With striving, you create psychic energy. And it is only with your steady striving and your image of the future that you can conquer fear.

> *The New Era can be built only by means of culture. Therefore, culture will be proclaimed as the one defense against disintegration. Nowadays one should strive only in this direction. Our command is to miss no opportunity of reminding people about culture. Though We be regarded as fanatics on the subject, people will nevertheless harken and become accustomed to it. Thus We introduce brain patterns.[4]*

Culture is the manifestation of Beauty. Culture makes you beautiful because culture brings out the Divinity in you. N. Roerich emphasized continually that the world will be saved only through culture. When a person is cultured, he is integrated. Look at the life of a criminal, and you will find that he has no culture in his life; he has no nobility.

You do not become cultured by going to college and earning a degree. To become cultured means to live in the light of your Soul and become beautiful.

Our minds are so brainwashed by the past ugliness and trash to which we have exposed ourselves to.

Culture and beauty introduce new patterns into our
brain, patterns based on harmony, order, and synthesis.

1. Agni Yoga Society, *Agni Yoga,* para. 642.
2. *Ibid.,* para. 223.
3. Agni Yoga Society, *Community,* para. 234.
4. Agni Yoga Society, *Fiery World,* Volume I, para. 190.

CHAPTER 25

PARABLES FROM AGNI YOGA

When I was in a monastery, one of my Teachers was a very handsome Mongolian man. He had an iron face with a long beard. He stood like a graceful statue. One day I asked him what I could do in order to progress. He said, "Observe. Observe everything. Observe carefully." I thought that observation was really going to be an easy thing, but I soon learned what a difficult task it really is.

To start with, I decided to pick one thing and observe it from a to z. I picked one of my favorite things, which was listening to parables. Sometimes at night, the Teachers would build a nice fire in the temple or in a nearby cave. There would be deodar branches and leaves on it so that the air would smell fresh and clean. Then when everyone was settled, they would tell us parables. I loved to listen to the parables, and I decided to observe myself while I listened.

After doing this over a period of time, I noticed that three gears were working in me simultaneously. The first gear was imagination. The second was creative imagination, and the third was intuition. I noticed that the imagination I was experiencing was not daydreaming. (Imagination is actually a higher emotional activity. Creative imagination is carried on in the mental centers corresponding to higher centers of the astral body. Intuition is beyond the mental plane.)

When the three gears meshed, I felt a tremendous wealth of inspiration. I intuitively felt what stood behind

279

the parable. Though the meaning of the parable was not expressly given, it gradually emerged from the mist.

After reading each parable, my emotional centers were so energized that I was almost ready to burst into a joyful song. When the three gears work together, there is a great energy surplus, and you are really charged. This is one reason why eastern Teachers always speak in parables. Each Teacher creates his own parables from his own experiences.

Christ taught many beautiful things in His parables. His parables were really ingenious because they were very deep and had many levels of meaning. He was not like Aesop, who told one- or two-dimensional stories; Christ's parables had four or five dimensions. The disciples listening to Christ's parables learned more from them than the average people who were listening, and the twelve Apostles penetrated even deeper into their inner meaning.

The great Teachers who taught through parables were able to create a powerful dedication to a vision in their students and, at the same time, show them practical things about life.

Parables work in such a way that imagination, logic, and inspiration are balanced, and harmony in the centers results. The student of parables will become physically, emotionally, and mentally harmonized.

Fairy tales are much like parables. Many people think they are just for silly entertainment, but genuine fairy tales were given by great Masters. If you read a fairy tale with an open mind, you will find an esoteric sense in it; great images of beauty and heroism are presented there.

Read the newspapers today and you will read about all the crime that is happening. The crime rate is becoming higher and higher. If you turn on your television, you will see so many programs with fighting and shooting. Or you will see police stories with crime as the central issue. It is all the same story of fighting and killing. What kind of values do these movies develop in our children? Why are we not presenting them with examples of nobility and right human relations?

When you present children with beautiful fairy tales and parables, they learn how to live as noble people. They develop virtues to meet the world with a spirit of sacrifice and kindness. Children who are filled with heroic images grow up to be courageous men and women who care more about their worth as human beings than about the size of their bank accounts.

We need new-age teachers to establish high standards in our youth. We need teachers who feel a strong sense of responsibility to their students and to their nation. For example, when I was in college in the old country, one of the students beat his mother. Several of the teachers burst into tears when they heard the news. They were so ashamed that any student of theirs would do such an awful thing to his mother. They wondered what their part in the act had been and what they could have done to prevent it. They took their jobs very seriously and felt a moral obligation to shape their students into noble people. Do we have such teachers? If we don't teach heroism and nobility, we can't expect heroes in our society.

In order to be a balanced person, you must eat a balanced diet. In a similar way, you must try to achieve spiritual balance through your spiritual diet. You must try to achieve balance between your physical, emotional, and mental bodies. If one body is developed and the others are neglected, you are out of balance and you become spiritually sick. You may become the slave of your habits; you may become controlled by your desires; or you may become a fanatic.

Sometimes we go too far in one direction when we try to balance ourselves. We may actually charge what we are working against in our nature and make it become stronger. The best way to weaken or balance anything in our nature is to proceed in the opposite direction. If one aspect of your nature is too active, simply work on the opposite aspect without giving any attention to the first aspect. When attention is withdrawn, that aspect will balance itself.

It is your attention that fortifies and energizes any center. It is natural that when the energy is withdrawn, the center will balance itself. Stop the excessive flow of energy, and the center or system will adjust itself.

Anything which is done to an extreme becomes a vice. This is why Buddha taught the Noble Middle Path. When you are balanced, your Inner Reality, the true Self, is able to manifest. This is what the Teaching stands for: the emergence of the real You from the fog of inertia, glamor, and illusion.

Most of humanity is living in dreams. People are either comic or tragic figures. They play out their roles with heavy masks on, and it never occurs to them that they are just actors on the stage of life. But the Teaching asks, "When are you going to take your masks off and stand as you are?"

Balance is the first key to destroying your masks. Balance creates the right conditions so that the Self may emerge. Emergence means that you are going to make a breakthrough and come out of the fog and mist which clouds your vision. You will be able to find your true identity when you come out of the dark mess that you have been living in.

If you boil all the great Teachings of the ages down to their essence, this is the basic thing that they all teach. They teach moderation in all things and how to manifest the Divinity within.

Emergence also means that our greatest dreams are going to be actualized. In our imaginations, we all have humanitarian visions; we have great beauties in our hearts and minds. Through our efforts of trying to manifest these beauties, the Real within us slowly emerges. In manifesting beauty, we are manifesting our Divine nature.

We must remember that light does not shine alone by itself. As the light emerges, the darkness also tries to emerge. When you build something for light, darkness is immediately attracted there. This means there will always be a battle between your light and dark sides.

In order to begin the process of emergence, try to find out what you are not. Start by detaching yourself from those things which do not relate to your essence, and then you will come closer to that which you really are. M.M. has given many parables to help us find our essence. As you read these parables, observe yourself. Observe the gears that are working in you, and see if they are meshing together.

> *A known Rishi sat in silence and his face expressed striving.*
> *He was asked with what his mind was preoccupied. The Rishi answered: "I am building at this moment a temple."*
> *"And where is thy temple?"*
> *"Twenty marches from here, and the builders are in great need."*
> *"So even in inactivity thou buildest?"*
> *The Rishi smiled: "Is action only in the hands and in the feet?"[1]*

In this parable, M.M. is impressing us with the idea that we can build without physical exertion. He is emphasizing the power of thought and inspiring in us the urge to develop it.

> *In the Mysteries of Egypt there was a proceeding called "The Sharpening of the Sword." The neophyte was placed in deep darkness. He was approached by the Great Hierophant, who disclosed to him some of the Mysteries; and light illumined the Hierophant. Then again everything sank into darkness. Then approached the priest designated as the Tempter. Out of the darkness, the voice of the tempter asked: "Brother, what hast thou seen and heard?" The tested one answered: "I was honored by the presence of the Great Hierophant."*
> *"Brother, art thou convinced that this was the Great One Himself?"*
> *"My eyes have seen and my ears have heard."*
> *"But the image could be deceptive and the*

voice could be false."

Then the tested one either was confused and was rejected, or he was filled with firmness and spoke: "One can deceive the eyes and ears, but nothing can drag the heart into delusion. I see with the heart, I hear with the heart, and nothing impure will touch the heart. Sharpened is the sword entrusted to me."

Then again the Great Hierophant approached and, pointing out a chalice filled with a red beverage, said: "Receive and drink of thy chalice; empty it to see the mystery on the bottom."

On the bottom was an image of a supine man enclosed by a serpent curled in a circle, with the inscription: "Thou art thyself the all-giving and all-accepting." Thus reads the same Teaching at all times, but the darkness of ignorance causes one to forget its meaning.[2]

In this parable, the intuition of the man is being tested. They want to see if he can recognize reality. If he cannot, it will be dangerous for him to proceed. If he can recognize reality, he will be initiated.

The neophyte who passes the test is left in the King's Chamber of the Great Pyramid for three nights. He sleeps in a trance, and early in the morning of the third day he is carried to the top of the Great Pyramid. When the Sun hits the top of the pyramid, the neophyte awakens. He has taken his first initiation. When the Hierarchy reappears, They will slowly introduce such mysteries to those who are striving on the path.

The court historian of Akbar once said to the ruler, "Among potentates I observe an insoluble problem. Certain rulers held themselves unapproachable, aloof from the people. These were deposed because of their futility. Others entered into the daily lives. People became used to them and deposed them for being commonplace."

Akbar smiled, "That means that a ruler must remain unseen, while entering and directing all actions."

Thus spoke the wise ruler, foretelling thereby

the future.
Invisibly visible![3]

If they will ask about reward, tell them this parable:

"A man gave much gold for good works. But he awaited reward. Once his Teacher sent him a stone with the note: 'Accept the reward, the treasure of the far-off star.'

"The man became indignant. 'Instead of my gold a stone is given me! What is a far-off star to me?'

"And in dejection he cast the stone into a mountain stream.

"But the Teacher came and said, 'How did you find the treasure? In the stone was contained the most precious diamond, sparkling beyond all earthly gems.'

"In despair the man rushed to the stream. And following the current, he descended lower and lower.

"But the ripples of the waves forever hid the treasure."[4]

Once a French nobleman said to St. Germain, "I cannot grasp the nonsense going on around you."

St. Germain answered, "It is not difficult to understand my nonsense if you will give it the same attention you give your own, if you will read my reports with the same attention as the list of dancers at the court. But the trouble is that the order of a minuet is of more importance to you than the safety of the Earth."

Just in these words is contained also the calamity of our times. We have an unlimited time for all kinds of degrading occupations, but we do not find an hour for the most vital.[5]

The Blessed Buddha once said to his pupils, "Let us sit in silence and let our eyes behold."

After a while the Teacher asked, "How many times did I change my position?"

Someone noticed ten changes, one only three, and one insisted that the Teacher had remained immovable.

The Lord of Wisdom smiled: "I changed my position and the folds of my garment seventy-seven times. As long as we do not learn to discern reality, we shall not become Arhats."

Before the realization of psychic energy one has to acquire attentiveness. Therefore unexpected questions are useful, as well as descriptions of occurrences; and very useful are daily notes. It is known that even a very slumbering attentiveness awakens from such exercising. The inattentive, the unobservant, cannot pursue the development of psychic energy. The advice to observe is the advice of a friend, as the future demands attention.[6]

1. Agni Yoga Society, *Agni Yoga*, para. 489.
2. *Ibid.*, para. 520.
3. *Ibid.*, para. 274.
4. *Ibid.*, para. 353.
5. *Ibid.*, para. 451.
6. *Ibid.*, para. 551.

CHAPTER 26

HIERARCHY

The Hierarchy is the group of all those great heroes who have dedicated their lives for humanity, to improve humanity and lead it on the path of perfection. A hero is a person who is not selfish. A hero is a person who is really intellectual. A hero is a person who is all dedication and all heart. Heart, intellect, and dedication make a hero.

The Hierarchy is formed by those human beings who throughout ages in every religion, race, and nationality perfected themselves physically, emotionally, and mentally and dedicated themselves for the upliftment of humanity. If you want to become a part of the Hierarchy, you must rise above your little self. You must forget all those activities that turn on the axis of your self-interest. You must stop cheating people. You must stop slandering people. You must stop harming people. You must be pure physically, emotionally, and mentally. And you must have only one aim in your life: to live a life that makes the lives of others more beautiful.

The Hierarchy is formed by those individuals who have principles. According to esoteric sciences, a principle is a divine law which you cannot change and which stands for the perfection of humanity. For example, Righteousness is a principle. Harmlessness, Nobility and Beauty are principles. Members of the Hierarchy live according to these principles.

We are told that members of the Hierarchy have

287

achieved purity of body, emotions, and mind. Every member of the Hierarchy has an outstanding mental quality: They always think in terms of inclusiveness and synthesis. They are not separative in any way because They know that separatism takes one away from God and inclusiveness brings one closer to God. If in your daily thinking you are separative instead of inclusive and synthesizing, you are not on the road to the Hierarchy.

It is important for us to know about the Hierarchy because the Hierarchy is our future. We are going to eventually be part of the Hierarchy. Hierarchy means the maturity of the human being, the future of the human being. We are going to be like the Hierarchy, whether we like it or not. If not, the universe is going to annihilate us.

Every human being has one dream, whether he is conscious of it or not. That dream is immortality. Every human being has a craving in his heart not to die. Man wants to live forever because he knows that within his Innermost Self he is an immortal Spark of God. The members of the Hierarchy achieved this dream: They became immortal.

References to the Hierarchy can be found in many world traditions. In Egyptian tradition, members of the Hierarchy are called immortals, full of wisdom and knowledge. In Chaldean tradition, They were those Great Ones Who knew the science of the stars; They gave the science of astrology to humanity. In Persian tradition, They are called Magis, such as the Magis who came to visit the Baby Jesus bringing gifts.

The Hierarchy is called by different names throughout history:

1. The Kingdom of God
2. Christ and His disciples, or servants of God
3. The Community of Arhats
4. Enlightened Ones
5. The Link between Infinity and humanity
6. The Masters of Wisdom, or men made perfect
7. The Invisible Church

8. The Center of Love Wisdom
9. The Inner School
10. The Brothers of humanity
11. Victors — over Their bodies, urges, drives, negative emotions, limiting thoughts, aggressiveness, hatred...
12. Warriors — Who fought against Their own egotism and vanity and eventually won
13. Silent Watchers — Who watch the progress of each human being from the cradle until death
14. The Custodians of the Plan

The Plan for humanity is for One Humanity; for forgiveness, gratitude, responsibility, and cleaning the planet of all pollution. The Plan is like a blueprint upon which a structure is built in the best way possible. The Plan is to make all possible arrangements so that the seed called humanity may flower and reach its destined glory.

We look to the Hierarchy as those human beings who conquered human evolution; who conquered human pain and suffering; who conquered their emotional and mental problems. Hierarchy stands for *direction* for humanity. Direction is a link between what you are now and what you can become in the future. For example, direction is like the link between the seed and the flower.

Hierarchy gives *inspiration* to humanity. Inspiration is the reception of those ideas and visions which make you surpass or transcend yourself. Hierarchy also gives *comfort*. If in your own time of suffering you remember the suffering of Great Ones, your suffering becomes so small and insignificant and you find the courage to overcome your problems and sorrows.

The Hierarchy inspires humanity with the vision of the *future*. They lift humanity up from their sorrows and depressions. When you are depressed or lonely, try thinking about the Hierarchy and Their victories over life, and you will see that immediately your depression is going away. Loneliness is a sign that you do not have Hierarchy in your mind and heart. When Hierarchy is with you, you are never alone.

Many people ask, if the Hierarchy is so great, why are They not changing the terrible conditions of the world? The answer is that Hierarchy does not violate human free-will. You can build yourself or you can destroy yourself; but Hierarchy will continue to stand as an example of purity and immortality. The members of the Hierarchy give the Teaching, but They never force Their will upon people. If you hear or read that a "master" forced his will upon someone, he is not a master; he is a human being. The greatest characteristic of a Master is that He never imposes His will.

The second characteristic of the members of the Hierarchy is that they never violate karma. If you do something wrong or you break a law in the universe, They let you face your karma, understand your lesson, and pay for it so that by your own hands and feet you climb the ladder of evolution. But if you ask for help, They help you, if your karma tolerates that help.

The third characteristic of the members of the Hierarchy is that They have tremendous wisdom because throughout the ages They gathered knowledge and experience in Their souls; and through experience They know what is right and what is wrong, what is in harmony with the Divine Will and what is against the Divine Will. The members of the Hierarchy are sources of wisdom; this is why the Masters are sometimes referred to as the "Masters of Wisdom."

People may wonder, is it good to believe in the Hierarchy? What if the Hierarchy is just a fairy tale? The answer is that it doesn't really matter whether They are a fairy tale or not because fairy tales are the prototypes of our achievements. The greatest reality that exists is our vision. We can create reality with our visions because we are each potential Gods.

Merging into the waves of the Infinite, we may be compared to flowers torn away by a storm. How shall we find ourselves transfigured in the ocean of the Infinite? It would be unwise to send out a boat without a rudder. But the Pilot is predestined and the creation of the heart will not

be precipitated into the abyss. Like milestones on
a luminous path, the Brothers of Humanity, ever-
alert, are standing on guard, ready to lead the
traveler into the chain of ascent.

Hierarchy is not coercion — it is the law of the
world-structures. It is not a threat — but the call of
the heart and a fiery admonition directing towards
the General Good.

Thus let us cognize the Hierarchy of Light.[1]

The rudder of your boat is the Hierarchy. The only real direction humanity has comes from the Hierarchy. The only authority is the person who knows how. Without direction, you are lost in the infinite universe, like a bubble on the surface of the ocean.

How can we be led "into the chain of ascent"? Only by creating striving in ourselves and living according to Their laws and principles. For example, Christ said, "Love your brother as yourself." Have we really learned this? The fact is that only those who have learned to love their brothers as themselves have become Masters.

...Only when Our Covenant is adopted in life,
can the higher step be affirmed....[2]

The Covenant is, simply put, selflessness, sacrificial service, purity of mind, inclusiveness, and dedication to higher ideals. If you examine the *New Testament,* the *Bhagavad Gita,* Zoroastrian literature, and the literature of other world religions, you will find the same convenant because all the covenants are coming from the same Hierarchical source. Throughout the ages, Great Ones have appeared and taught the same wisdom through different languages and different symbols, but the reality behind them all is the same: transcend yourself, find your Divinity, and become immortal.

...It is wise to become accustomed to there
being no rest nor end. But the sole realization of
Our Brotherhood and Hierarchy already directs

the traveler along the shortest path to Infinity.[3]

Those who really believe in the Hierarchy know that there is no end to their development, perfection, service, and dedication. If you start learning this, you will begin to enter the ranks of the Hierarchy. Many people finish their formal education with high school or college and then decide that they have learned all they need to know. In doing this, they put themselves on the path of death.

You can remain alive, progressive, and vital only through one thing: steady, endless, and progressive development and improvement in your life. You must never be satisfied with what you are, with what you know, and with what you did for others. In your service, you must create progressively greater fields of service. You can be a real server only if the field of your service is continuously expanding. If the field of your service is not continuously expanding, you are becoming a selfish person; you are exploiting other people; you are working for your own vanities, urges and drives.

This is one of the secrets of the Hierarchy: that Their service never ends.

The Hierarchy is an organized system with specific duties and offices. Our governments are nothing else but distorted reflections of the Hierarchical government. Sometimes the members of the Hierarchy are called warriors. But this does not necessarily mean warriors who fight with guns and weapons on Earth. There is also battle in the emotional plane and the mental plane. Christ is often called the Commander of the Forces of Light, and M.M. says, "My disciples must be warriors."

What are the weapons of the Hierarchical soldiers in the emotional and mental planes? One of their ammunitions is truth. Their shield is beauty. Their sword is honesty. Their guns are courage, daring, and striving. When you pass away, you are going to fight against the darkness with the weapons of the virtues you have. If you don't have virtues, you are going to be imprisoned by the camp of darkness.

Everything you do, say, think, and feel on this Earth is recorded in space in a great "computer" or in the "book of God." On the day of judgment it will be known what you are. So try to write your life in a better way. This is what the Hierarchy is doing: trying to write Their lives in the best way possible.

One day a teacher gave a little chick to ten different children and told them, "Go and kill the bird, but no one must see you kill it." Everyone went and killed his bird and returned to the Teacher except for one little boy. When they finally found the little boy, he still had his chick in his hand. The teacher said, "Why didn't you kill the chick?" The boy replied, "I couldn't find any place to kill it where God would not see."

This boy was a seed of the Hierarchy. What will happen in your life if you suddenly realize that the Hierarchy is watching your thoughts, words and actions?

> *Certainly one can attain only through adherence to the Hierarchy. Only the understanding of the great law will open the eyes of humanity....*[4]

Adherence to the Hierarchy means to understand Their laws and try to live according to Their laws. The first law of the Hierarchy is **inclusiveness.** Any time you work for separatism with your thoughts, emotions, or actions, you are working against the Law of the Hierarchy.

The second law of the Hierarchy is **harmlessness.** One of the ways we do the most harm is with our tongue. A great Saint once said, "Whoever cannot control his tongue, cannot reach perfection."

There is a story in Aesop's fables about the tongue. One day a king called his servant and said to him, "I want you to cook the best dinner today."

"Yes, sir," said the servant.

When dinnertime came, the king found that every dish the servant had cooked was of tongue. "What is this?" he asked the servant.

"But Master, there is nothing better than the tongue. With the tongue you can praise God; you can sing; you can recite poetry; you can speak beautiful things."

"All right," said the king. "But tomorrow night I want you to cook the worst dish."

The following night the king found that his dinner contained, again, nothing but dishes of tongue! "What is the matter with you?" asked the king.

"Master, everything that is destructive, corruptive, degenerate, and poisonous comes from the tongue. You wanted the worst dish, and this is what I cooked."

The third law of the Hierarchy is endless **service.** Your service will start with your own interest, but it must gradually become free of self-interest. Eventually, you must come to the conclusion that you are here only to serve and not to exploit or cheat others.

The fourth law of the Hierarchy is **selflessness.** Selflessness means to love others more than you love yourself. Like all the other laws of the Hierarchy, there must be no end to your selflessness. Your selflessness must start with little things and grow and grow.

> ...I advise to realize Hierarchy from the highest spiritual striving to even the smallest bodily requirements....[5]

The fifth law of the Hierarchy is **righteousness.** Your measure or principle for righteousness will be the Laws of the Hierarchy. According to Their Laws, you will make yourself righteous.

> Reverence of Hierarchy will affirm the closeness of the Higher World. In cooperation with Hierarchy do you find firm bridges to that shore. Every belief reveals the Guardian Angels, Guides, and Comforters; under the various names lies the same concept of Hierarchy. Verily, let each one understand in his own way, but let each heart strive upwards. In this alone is the path to perfection....[6]

1. Agni Yoga Society, *Hierarchy*, preface.
2. *Ibid.*, para. 42.
3. *Ibid.*, para. 50.
4. *Ibid.*, para. 73.
5. *Ibid.*, para. 126.
6. Agni Yoga Society, *Aum*, para. 60.

CHAPTER 27

VIRTUES

There are three main virtues which are often emphasized in the Agni Yoga literature. These virtues are striving, daring, and gratitude.

Striving is not an activity of the vehicles to reach something or be something or do something. Striving is the activity of the spirit or the Self to manifest itself in Beauty, Goodness and Truth. As striving manifests, the vehicles of the person appropriate themselves to the new rhythm. All discipline is the response of the bodies to the striving spirit.

Striving is a result of the pressure of the Self hitting the rocks and obstacles of life and slowly purifying them from His path. Through striving, the Self purifies first physical obstacles, such as too much eating, too much sleeping, drugs, alcohol, tobacco, excessive sex, etc. On the emotional plane, striving purifies separative and negative emotions, glamors, and attachments and makes the emotional vehicle a pure channel for the activities of the spirit.

Then striving reaches the mental plane, to purify the mental body from illusions, superiority complexes, vanities, pride, and memories of past unhappy or happy events.

Unless we strive, we will always be satisfied with our individual or group achievements.

On Our scales the striving of the spirit is weightier than aught else. The success in life is strengthened only by the electricity of the prayer of achievement....[1]

Striving is the boat of the Arhat. Striving is the manifested unicorn. Striving is the key to all caves. Striving is the wing of the eagle. Striving is the ray of the sun. Striving is the armor of the heart. Striving is the lotus blossom. Striving is the book of the future. Striving is the world manifest. Striving is the multitude of stars.[2]

One should firmly understand the difference between expectation and striving. In expectation there will always be an hour of motionlessness. But in striving there is always a flight into the future. Such difference may be understood only by him who is not satisfied with the flow of his present life and thinks of the incessant flow of existences on other planets.[3]

The quality of action is affirmed in striving. When words are transmuted into action, the higher energy is affirmed. Hence, only in life can one manifest the higher energies. Not words but actions are considered to be the affirmation of higher energies. Only when the potentiality of the spirit is manifested in action is the higher concordance affirmed.[4]

There are two kinds of **daring** — personality daring and spiritual daring. In personality daring, you do every kind of crazy thing to reach your physical and emotional goals and satisfy the interests of your mind. In physical daring:

you wrestle with someone bigger than you.

you lift something very heavy.

you drink two bottles of wine.

you jump on a moving truck.

Examples of emotional daring are:

you walk on a lonely beach or in a forest.

you dare not to attach to a girl or boy for

emotional reasons.

you dare to talk about things that are risky.

you ask questions that are dangerous or out of place.

Examples of mental daring are:

you read books beyond your capacity.

you study subjects beyond your level.

you plan things which are considered dangerous by others.

you write letters on subjects which you have not yet mastered.

The other kind of daring is spiritual daring. In spiritual daring, you make an effort to break the limitations presented by your personality through its maya, glamors, illusions, and limitations of energy and creativity, and you stand in the light of your Soul and live according to the implications of that achievement. Real, spiritual daring is the ability to stand in the light of your Soul and live a life *conceived in the light of the Soul.* Unless you stand in the light of the Soul and see the true standards and principles of the Soul, you have no chance to dare.

Once you enter the light of the Soul, you have the challenge to dare, or to try to stand in the outer life as you feel you are in the presence of the Soul — as the Self. Daring is the effort of the human soul to awake and master. Daring is the ability to stand and live in your daily life by the standards you perceived while you were in the presence of the Higher Self, and according to these standards, to *serve.*

There is a higher stage of daring. In this stage, you perceive and realize yourself as the Self and try to live as the Self in your daily life. This effort to live as the Self in your daily life is called daring.

The same thing applies when you have a contact with Christ, the Hierarchy, or Shamballa: all your life turns into a demonstration of daring because you try to live by the principles and standards you have seen in the subjective realms and to break the limitations in which humanity lives.

When some people hear the word, Shamballa, they

turn into bulls facing a red flag. They turn off and become angry. But if you tell them that Shamballa is the Sanskrit name for the Father's Home, they feel stupid. "There are many mansions in My Father's Home," said Christ, and no theologian dared to give us more information about this because they thought that Christ was making up a story.

If one wants to know about the Father's Home, he must search in esoteric literature, especially Sanskrit esoteric literature, because the writers of these treatises knew what they were writing. In the New Testament, Shamballa is referred to as "the New Jerusalem."

Daring comes into being through the interaction of two elements: an expanding spirit and the opposing agents. Daring spreads great energy of the spirit; joy, courage, and decisiveness.

> ...Darkness cannot withstand the daring of light.... We shall select that which is most daring, in order that these seeds should weigh down the balance.
> Lord, grant me to cast into the flames the deceptive rags of the customary. I shall not err in realizing that winged daring has Thy blessing.[5]

> They will ask, "Who gave you the right to dare?" Say, "We dare by the right of evolution. The right of evolution is inscribed in flame in our hearts...."
> Daring! Should one understand it as an unheard-of achievement? Shall not daring be the daily repast and the garment of every thought? Will not the prison walls become transparent? And will not the seal of the secret scroll melt for the one who dares?[6]

> Only the Fire of the Lords will kindle daring.[7]

> The evidence of daring yearning for the future indicates that the spirit is ready for fiery cognitions....[8]

Gratitude opens the channels of reception of Higher Forces. Through gratitude one comes in contact with the principle of the One Life, and that Life passes through him, giving him Joy, Health, Beauty, Solemnity and Magnanimity. Gratitude is acceptance of all the beauty of life and all the lessons of life. A great Apostle says, "Give thanks always, for everything."

One cannot give thanks to God if he gains something at the expense of others. A thief cannot really be grateful because he robbed another human being. There is a great morality in the idea of gratitude. One must be totally righteous and honest in relation to the things he has in order to be able to make the spiritual laws record his gratitude.

> *Gratitude is one of the main qualities of justice. Without justice one cannot reach the path of the Great Service. Therefore, pointing out the necessity of the realization of gratitude, We only assist the Great Service....*[9]

Real gratitude is not expressed in words, but through sharing. You can prove your gratitude only by giving or serving. One must be grateful not only to God, but also to those who sacrificed their lives to show us the right way of living and progressing on the path of our evolution.

In order to express gratitude, you must also be sorry for the harm which you did to others through your thoughts, words, and actions. Christ once said that if you are taking a gift to the altar, you must pause a moment and remember if you hindered the path of someone else. If you did, you must first go and ask his forgiveness. Then you can offer your prayer or gift.

> *We have spoken about solemnity, friendliness, magnanimity — let us complete the square with gratitude. From the most minute through the entire line of Hierarchy, shine the sparks of gratitude. Precious are these fires!*[10]

*...Know to regard gratitude as the union of joy
and beauty....[11]*

*...The quality of gratitude is likewise the
finest purification of the organism....Great is the
healing power of the emission of gratitude....* [12]

1. Agni Yoga Society, *Leaves of Morya's Garden,* Volume II, page 12.
2. Agni Yoga Society, *Community,* para. 55.
3. Agni Yoga Society, *Agni Yoga,* para. 147.
4. *Ibid.,* para. 658.
5. *Ibid.,* para.11.
6. *Ibid.,* para. 49.
7. Agni Yoga Society, *Fiery World,* Volume I, para. 10.
8. *Ibid.,* para. 425.
9. Agni Yoga Society, *Hierarchy,* para. 182.
10. Agni Yoga Society, *Fiery World,* Volume I, para. 191.
11. Agni Yoga Society, *Agni Yoga,* para. 98.
12. *Ibid.,* para. 31.

CHAPTER 28

IRRITATION

According to advanced esoteric psychology, irritation is caused by negative selfish thinking and negative emotions. If we have negative emotions, our tranquility is distorted and some movement appears in our aura, or our electromagnetic field, which is not in harmony with the other atoms of our bodies. This movement is called irritation.

Irritation also causes distortion in the nervous system. Irritation causes a certain kind of substance called imperil to settle on the nerve channels. Wherever it settles, the corresponding organ cannot function properly. That organ cannot be healed unless the imperil is eliminated.

Different emotions affect different parts of the body. For example, if you have fear, your heart and lungs are affected. If you have anger and hatred, your kidneys are affected. If you are in depression, your liver is affected. If you are in grief, your sexual organs are affected. If you are in worry, your brain, eyes, and ears are affected. Every emotion has a special frequency, and this frequency affects the electromagnetic body or the aura in various places, and then the corresponding organ suffers.

M.M. says that irritation must be eliminated from our daily life so that tranquility and serenity settle in our hearts. Only in a calm, serene heart do the Cosmic beauties reflect themselves and can right human relations be expressed.

Through joy, purify the path.
While thou art pupils, learn to overcome irritability.
My pupils must have a sympathetic eye.
As through a magnifying glass behold the good,
    and belittle tenfold the signs of evil, lest thou
    remain as before.[1]

The path is our life and all our relationships; it is the path to eternity. This path can be purified with joy, and whenever we have joy, we do not have irritation. One of the greatest qualities of discipleship is to be in joy and express joy.

A joyful person is not selfish; he does not hurt people. Joyfulness means to be in harmony with your Higher Self; to be in harmony with the greatest Beauty within you. In joy there is no fear, no hatred, no jealousy, no exploitation, no "mine and yours." There is only radioactive serenity.

"My pupils must have a sympathetic eye." When you have a sympathetic eye, whomever your eye falls upon, you love. This attitude is an antibiotic to irritability. If you love, you cannot be irritated. If you don't love someone, whatever he does irritates you. Whenever you deal with others, try to use a "magnifying glass" to see something good in them. There is a great secret in this technique: only in seeing good in others do you progress, because when you see good, you become good.

One of the problems with television is that it is presenting so many ugly pictures of the way the world is. When we create ugly pictures for our children, we increase the ugliness in them because those ugly pictures are impressed in their minds and slowly condition their attitudes and behavior.

...The flame of the candle spreads light to all, but
    smothered under an irritant drop it flickers
    and must be set aright.
Let thy flame be steady — M. is ever with thee.[2]

The flame which we must keep steady is the light of our Soul and our vision of the future. Keeping this

flame steady is an exercise in self-mastery. A great
Sage says that it is according to the intensity of the
flame that radiates from our head that we are taken
into initiation. That flame is our head center, the
thousand-petaled Lotus. This is the same flame that
burst from the heads of the disciples at Pentecost.
Whenever we have contact with the Divine side of our
being, we radiate a flame. A flame is also a great
vision, idea, or inspiration.

> *Messages come more readily through dry chan-*
> *nels.*
> *Smile — tears interrupt the current.*
> *Only certain glands may be used, and these as*
> *long as they are not irritated.*
> *With clouds of tears does the world obstruct the*
> *beneficial currents.*[3]

To have dry channels means to be non-emotional.
If you have negative emotions in your heart or system,
no message or inspiration can come to you; or if it
comes, it is distorted. Self-pity and touchiness, in
which you think that you are the center of the universe,
are two emotions of epidemic proportion at this time.
These two emotions must be eliminated if you want to
eliminate the causes of irritation.

> *Let Us speak kindly and scientifically.*
> *Not for Ourselves but for thee, do I speak of trust.*
> *The messages shatter themselves against the*
> *barricaded heart.*
> *When needless words are uttered, the currents are*
> *mixed.*
> *The emanations of irritation not only deny entrance*
> *to the thoughts We send, but even a touch is*
> *not to be sensed by the hedgehog.*
> *In this, discern the difference between the quills of*
> *a hedgehog and Our feathered Shield.*
> *The benign arrows, like feathers, outline, the circle*
> *of salvation;*
> *But if the needles of doubt forbid the entrance of*
> *Our Message, special difficulties arise....*[4]

In all esoteric Teaching, there is great emphasis

placed on speech — right speech without exaggeration. Even one word used unrighteously or improperly creates an effect on your consciousness. You must learn to be silent in many, many instances. You must learn to speak only what needs to be said. Your level of achievement or whatever you are is the result of your speech. Even your sicknesses are related to your speech.

Speech creates a tremendous vibration in your electromagnetic field. Wrong speech — criticism, lies, hatred — creates stones in your electromagnetic field. This is also the reason why great Teachers advise us to be silent when we are sick so that we heal ourselves more quickly. Whenever you speak about wrong things, you disturb and distort the symphony of your being, just like a man who enters a symphony hall and starts to bang on a barrel while the orchestra is playing. Whenever you distort your being, you cannot have health.

> *One should not consider as a loss a concession to cunningly scheming hands.*
> *The follower of wisdom likes to look far ahead. Stay the vile slanders by a smile bereft of irritation. The success of lightminded people is like the trickle of a small fountain, but a wise householder will labor to bring the water from the ocean and will then enjoy the eternal coolness of his fountain.*[5]

Sometimes an apparent loss is really a gain. When you lose, you experience a valuable lesson. We are not talking about wasting yourself, such as losing yourself in a life of drugs, but about gaining wisdom from the experiences of apparent failures in life.

> *I say irrevocably: While with Me, while without irritation, while without doubt, the streams of possibilities are incalculable....*[6]

A great Sage, writing about the stages of discipleship, says that a Master does not accept any disciple who has irritation because it distorts His aura and creates agitation and static. Irritability must be avoided by all possible means.

One of the ways irritation can be lessened is through meditation. Through meditation you raise your consciousness to progressively higher levels — from the physical level to the emotional level to the mental level — in the same way that an airplane climbs to higher altitudes and can fly faster where there are fewer crosscurrents. If you can raise your consciousness above the personality realms, everything in the world falls into right perspective.

This is why Christ said that when you seek the kingdom of God first, everything else will be given to you. When you raise your consciousness to the realm of Harmony, Beauty, Goodness, Peace and Love and try to live these things, other things will not bother you so much and your problems will slowly disappear.[7]

> *The poison resulting from irritability is called "imperil" — a commanding danger. This poison, a quite substantial one, is precipitated against the walls of the nerve channels and thus spreads through the entire organism.*
>
> *If modern science would try impartially to examine the nerve channels, giving heed to the astral currents, it would encounter a strange decomposition of the astral substance during its passage through the nerve channels — this is the reaction to imperil. Only rest can help the nervous system to overcome the dangerous enemy which can call forth the most diverse irritations and painful contractions of the organism.*
>
> *He who is afflicted with imperil must repeat: "How beautiful is everything!" And he will be right; because the flow of evolution is rational, in other words, beautiful. The more subtle is the nervous system, the more painful is the precipitation of imperil. This same poison, by the addition of one ingredient, may contribute to the dissolution of matter.[8]*
>
> *For the last time I shall speak of irritation.*

Discern its harm — not only personal, but also for space. This worm, concealed by a smile and politeness, does not cease to devour the aura. Its harm creeps beneath all works.

For the sake of creation, be permeated with the conviction against irritation. When, as a bloody clot, it closes the ear, can a man hear? When the eye is clouded, can the man see? When the curtain falls on the consciousness, where then is acquisition?

But one should guard the fire as a treasure. The phosphorus of the nerves is being consumed as a wick; and is the lamp fit without it? One can add the oil of ozone, but without the wick the nerves will not kindle the fire.

The symbol of fire recalls the most sacred substance, which is accumulated with such difficulty but which is instantaneously erased. How can we expect results in the photographs of the physical emanations if we begin to merge ourselves into darkness?

Untiringly warn the friends.[9]

---

1. Agni Yoga Society, *Leaves of Morya's Garden,* Volume I, para. 32.
2. *Ibid.,* para. 97.
3. *Ibid.,* para. 151.
4. *Ibid.,* para. 249.
5. *Ibid.,* Volume II, page 16.
6. *Ibid.,* page 22.
7. For more information about irritation, read *Irritation — the Destructive Fire,* by T. Saraydarian.
8. Agni Yoga Society, *Agni Yoga,* para. 15.
9. *Ibid.,* para. 369.

CHAPTER 29

DANGER AND DISCIPLESHIP

Danger is a concentration of the vibrations of tension. A great number of perils surround people, but only a few of them are noticed. When the Leader says, "live in danger," he might well say instead, "observe the dangers and thus succeed." One cannot live outside of dangers, but it is beautiful to make out of dangers a carpet of achievement. The Leader knows that he bears a mission, and dangers are only propelling forces; therefore the Leader does not even think about dangers. The very thought of peril is harmful. Thinking about dangers, we strengthen their vibrations, and thus disturb our equilibrium. Conservation of forces must not be disrupted by fear and confusion. We are watchful and careful for the best execution of the commission. But dangers cannot overburden our attention. The Teacher should, first of all, insist upon the disciple's liberation from the phantom of perils. The disciple should always remember not to expend a drop of the higher energy uselessly. Thought of danger agitates many of our centers and in disorderly fashion consumes the precious energy. Thought of danger reflects even upon the pulse; but the heart is strengthened by the desire to carry out well the mission. Thus, let us act in the most efficient manner.[1]

The Teaching of Christ strongly emphasized extreme fearlessness, endurance, suffering, and also living a

308

dangerous life. It is very interesting that whoever wants to be an apostle of Beauty, Goodness, Truth and Love must be prepared to pass through dangerous paths. If a person is not used to playing with dangers and living in dangers, he cannot be an apostle or a disciple.

One of the characteristics of a true disciple is that you can beat him and kick him, but he always stands up again and keeps on going. Only those disciples who are cooked and baked in the spirit of danger, endurance and suffering can carry the fire. Those who are attached to their personalities, their reputations, their money, their loves and their pleasures are always fearful. They are attached to their skins, and they cannot carry the fire of Christ, the fire of beauty and goodness.

For the sake of the Teaching, the body must be put into danger. The emotional world and the mental world of the disciple must be put in danger, and the disciple's life must be put on the fire. If a disciple is prepared through such a fiery baptism, there is no power in the world that can stop him. This power was seen in the disciples of Christ. Twelve men who didn't even have shoes carried the fire of the message of Christ all over the world.

If people failed to live according to His Teaching, it was not His failure, but the failure of humanity. Christ's disciples gave the example of Beauty, Goodness, and Truth. If we do not live their Teaching, that is our mistake, not theirs. They went all over the world and raised the level of humanity, and many thousands of people took higher initiations because of this Teaching.

This Teaching is not really for the masses. This Teaching is not intended to suddenly bring the kingdom of heaven to earth. This Teaching belongs to a small number of people who are ready to penetrate into it, contact the creative forces within themselves and the universe, and take higher initiations. On the other hand, no single individual can achieve any progress without pulling humanity up with him.

Let us discuss the verse from *Fiery World:*
"Danger is a concentration of the vibrations of

tension." When you read the New Testament and the life of the disciples, you will understand one thing: that to transform the ugly and dirty metal of human character into a golden bowl, a fiery process, tension, or crisis is needed. Unless man passes through crisis, there is no sublimation or transformation.

It is very interesting that immediately when danger comes and you pass through suffering and crisis, you pay your karma, you see your hindrances and obstacles, and you break the limitations of the personality and walk as a soul instead of as a physical body or an animal. This is the Teaching that the disciples of Christ gave to humanity. They didn't teach to escape and hide within your own shell. They said, "Expose yourself, face danger, because you are not worthy for the Teaching if you are not able to face danger and proceed through it." Your worth and your value are demonstrated when you prove that you can face dangers, live through them, and come out of them triumphantly.

M.M. continues, *"A great number of perils surround people, but only a few of them are noticed."* People sit comfortably in their chairs and say, "There is no danger." Who said so? In one minute, an earthquake can wipe away everything, a huge airplane can crash, you can have a heart attack or be robbed. Danger is everywhere.

"One cannot live outside of dangers." Where are you going to escape? As far as you have a human body, interests, attachments, and hangups, you are in danger, from your friends and from your enemies.

"...but it is beautiful to make out of dangers a carpet of achievement." Our challenge is to enter into a danger and, like a craftsman or an artist, change the dangers, agony, suffering, and tribulations into a carpet of achievement and say, "I did it." The coward will run away, but the person who is baptized in fiery danger will stand up, no matter how much he is beaten.

"Dangers are only propelling forces." The most serious crimes and acts of corruptions are committed

by those who are fearful. Fear paralyzes them and obscures their radioactivity. Fear paralyzes their daringness and courage, and they are tied to their skins. They say, "I don't want to do that. I don't want to talk. I don't want to fly. I don't want to organize these things …because I don't want somebody to hurt me." Such people are bound to their skins.

Living a dangerous life is just the opposite of living for one's self-interests. It is a living for the interest of all.

"The Teacher should, first of all, insist upon the disciples' liberation from the phantom of perils." This is what is tying the hands of those who know the truth, who know beauty, and who know what corruption is, but still shut their mouths and sit there because they are paralyzed. A disciple stands up and speaks the truth. He faces dangers, and he is mature and unfolded in dangers. His achievements are gained through facing dangers, meanwhile doing his duty and his service for humanity.

"Thought of danger agitates many of our centers and in disorderly fashion consumes the precious energy." When one breathes in fear of danger, most of his creative centers are paralyzed, his daring and courage disappear, and he slowly withdraws into the skin of the interests of his body.

"…but the heart is strengthened by the desire to carry out well the mission." You can see this in the lives of the disciples of Christ. How many dangers they passed through in order to carry out the mission given to them by their Teacher. For example, we read:

> *Three times I was beaten with rods, once I was stoned, three times I was in shipwreck, a day and a night I have been adrift in the sea in shipwreck. On many journeys, I have been in perils from rivers, in perils of robbers, in perils from my own kinsmen, in perils from the Gentiles, in perils in the city, in perils in the wilderness, in perils in the sea, in perils from false brethren....[2]*

These are the dangers which the average person

tries to escape from. People hate such dangers, but it is
only in such dangers that a person is transformed into
an apostle, into a world disciple.

The Apostles of Christ knew this secret, and they
consciously and voluntarily confronted dangers in
order to proceed on the path of service and the path of
perfection. It is only such people who carry out the
mission given to them. But those who are stuck to their
bodies and pleasures become useless human beings
and eventually lose the treasures given to them by the
Great Life.

> *In toil and weariness, in sleepless nights, in*
> *hunger and thirst, through much fasting, in cold*
> *and nakedness. Besides other things, and the*
> *many calling on me every day, I have also the care*
> *of all the churches. Who is sick that I do not feel the*
> *pain? Who stumbles that does not have my heart-*
> *felt sympathy?*[3]

One can feel what a suffering the Apostle was
passing through, but also what a great joy in realizing
that he was carrying out his mission in spite of all
adverse conditions.

> *If I must needs boast, I will boast of my sufferings.*[4]

People boast about their wealth, their physical
strength, their financial success, their educational
achievements...but there are only a few people who
can boast about their pains and sufferings. Those who
are able to lay down their lives for a great mission are
rare, but they are those who are able to transcend
themselves and stand as great leaders and heroes in
front of humanity.

No person can be great if he is not greater than
himself. A person who wants to be great must demonstrate that he is the person that you know, that he has
surpassed that level, that he is greater than his average self. When the moments of fearlessness start to
increase in your life, you become an arrow flying to the

Sun, carrying the message of Beauty, Goodness, and Truth all over the world.

The danger quoted in this verse refers to the destruction of those hindrances and obstacles that are blocking the path of progress for humanity. A person who faces dangers sacrifices himself in order to redeem and liberate other people. He is totally out of his personality and functioning as a living soul.

> *At Damascus the general of the army of King Aretas placed the city of the Damascenes under guard, in order to seize me: And I was lowered in a basket from a window over the city wall, and thus I escaped from his hands.*[5]

In an unpublished writing, a great Teacher says, "Often we did not know where we could pass our nights." They were completely surrounded by dangers, but they were in communion with the powerhouse — Christ — so they were fearless.

> *...there was delivered to me a thorn in my flesh, the agent of Satan to buffet me, lest I should be exalted. Three times I besought my Lord concerning this thing, that it might depart from me. And he said to me, "My grace is sufficient for you: for my strength is made perfect in weakness...."*[6]

The Apostle is not only under attack by evil ones living on earth, but also by agents of Satan. The strange thing is that the Lord is leaving him alone to fight against them so that in fighting against them he draws himself closer to the Lord.

> *Therefore I am content with infirmities, insults, hardships, persecutions, and imprisonments for Christ's sake: for when I am physically weak, then I am mentally strong.*[7]

If you study the lives of great leaders of humanity, you will see a similar pattern in the way attacks were made against them, in the way they confronted the

attacks, and in the way they unfolded, developed, and
bloomed spiritually because of them. Christ never
promised a life of luxury and comfort to His disciples.
On the contrary, at every moment He spoke about
dangers. He lived in a very dangerous situation and
trained His disciples to love danger, because it is
almost impossible to expand the consciousness of people and destroy their crystallized life-patterns without
endangering their lives.

Great warriors and leaders are tempered in the fire
of dangers, as steel is tempered under hammer and
fire. You can find very interesting stories about how
the disciples of Christ suffered, not only in the Epistles
but also in the life stories about them in many
traditions.

All disciples in all fields of human endeavor are
advised not to be preoccupied with possible dangers.
The human imagination becomes very active creating
images of dangers when the physical, emotional, and
mental bodies are under strain. These images are
sources of discouragement, depression, and inertia.
Great services are postponed, and even the plans and
visions of servers are destroyed by such images.

The images of danger are very contagious. One
fearful person can poison the consciousness of a group
who is ready to fight for beauty, goodness, righteousness, and peace. The Great Ones train Their disciples
to stand above the images of danger and to even risk
their lives if it is worth doing that. This is because
They know that human progress demands a great
price from those who are ready to sacrifice.

It is so important to realize that every moment we
are in a danger. How can we live if we are chained by
fear of danger? If people listened to the prophets of
danger, we would not have any political, educational,
scientific, financial, or religious reform. Every bit of
progress in their fields is the result of fearless action in
the presence of accumulating dangers.

The history of humanity is full of images of those
who risked their lives to bring a new way of thinking,
feeling, and acting to humanity. But not everybody

can stand above the thought of danger. Those who are masters of fearlessness, courage, and daring are special people. Their consciousness has shifted from their lower self and is focused either in their soul or in the Spiritual Triad; or they live a life in the presence of Christ.

It is only through such a shift of consciousness that the lower storms of the personality and its attachments will not disturb such people. Instead of falling into confusion and paralysis in moments of danger, they feel the flame of their hearts and turn into invincible fires. It is the moments of danger that present to them the best opportunities for victory over their lower nature, the best opportunities to prove their devotion to the Cause, and the best opportunities to rise above their present state.

"We are watchful and careful for the best execution of the commission. But dangers cannot overburden our attention."

"One should not think that the expansion of consciousness is achieved without a battle. Everyone who wishes to serve with Us is bound to meet the assaults of darkness. In words, all are ready for battle, but in deed, almost everyone wishes to avoid it. Wouldn't one think that such an evasion prolongs the path?" M.M.

---

1. Agni Yoga Society, *Fiery World*, Volume II, para. 190.
2. II Corinthians 11:25-26.
3. *Ibid.*, 27-29.
4. *Ibid.*, verse 30.
5. *Ibid.*, 11: 32-33.
6. *Ibid.*, 12: 7-9.
7. *Ibid.*, verse 10.

CHAPTER 30

INSIGHT AND WORLD EVENTS

...When humanity will learn to realize and
coordinate world events with the complexities of
Cosmos the progress of insight will be affirmed.
The manifestation of the chain of events, and a
full realization of that which as the heritage of the
ages proceeds from one period to another, can
impel the consciousness toward the understand-
ing of Cosmic Infinity....[1]

World events are the result of the responses of man
to incoming energies. The energies coming to this
world include energies from various stars and constellations, and also energies from the world of ideas,
thoughts, and visions. These energies come to Earth
and stimulate the human brain, mind, and nervous
system, causing them to react. These reactions create
world events.

The various kinds of human reactions and responses
to incoming energies manifest, for example, as ruler-
ship, worship, deep thinking, art, sciences, aspirations, and business; as well as service or crime, love or
hatred, and generosity or greed. The energies evoke
that which you are.

As the human responses differ or change, the
events change, too. For example, one person responds
to the incoming energies as an artist and creates works
of art; another responds as a philosopher and creates
philosophy; another responds as a criminal and com-

mits crimes. The energy is the same, and the source of the impression is the same; but the results are different, according to the various responses of the individual on different dimensions and levels of unfoldment.

On the individual level, this process of reaction and response creates small-scale events. When thousands or millions of people respond to an energy in a certain way, world events are created, whether they are positive or negative. This means that wars and crimes cannot be eliminated by teaching people new things. They can be eliminated by raising the level of people. People must be transformed and transfigured so that instead of responding to incoming energies on levels six and seven, they respond on levels five or four — or higher. This is the key to changing the outcome of world events.

Suppose a beam of light comes and hits a film on the wall. The film is you — the totality of your mind and emotions. If there is a monkey within the film (which is you), no matter what kind of light hits that film, you will always have a picture of a monkey. When light hits your film, all that you are is projected into the arena of life. You are the conditioning factor of what will be expressed on the film.

When new-age energies come to this planet, they can have a very chaotic effect on the world. In the Cosmos, the world of energies has a great harmony of circulation and coordination. But our record player or our speakers are damaged or even broken, and the music we hear in our world is only noise, or chaos. Because our speakers are not in the right condition, we have complexities, complications, and problems in the world.

When you can understand this situation, you have *insight* into the causes of events in the world. Insight means that your eyes see the light, the negative, and the projected picture simultaneously and relate them to time. The negative, which is the main factor for reaction and response (or the effect), is not only a small, personal event, but the culmination of all reactions of humanity to incoming energies.

When you can look at the negative and the energy

current and have a balanced outlook and penetration into the depth of the event and how the energies are expressing themselves, you have insight. Insight means the ability to see the cause and the result together through the process; the ability to see how the cause is changing into results.

Let's say that your mind is not pure. If you are doing meditation and generating lots of energy in your system but meanwhile you are impure physically, emotionally, or mentally, you damage your brain. You create overstimulation in yourself, and you are on the road to becoming one of the millions of "crackpots" in the world.

There are many groups which are trying to make money by teaching things they don't really know about. They are overstimulating the etheric centers in people, causing tension and stress in them, and encouraging them to be "spiritual" and "new-age" by using drugs, doing breathing exercises, chanting, etc. Human development is the most serious science. You cannot unfold the treasures within you with drugs, different spiritual exercises, and psychic hocus-pocus. A close investigation of such groups will reveal that in the years they have been in existence they didn't produce one decent person, only "crackpots."

To have insight means to clean the "film" of your emotional world, removing all negative emotions, so that the energy or light being projected through it causes you to bloom and become more beautiful in every way. Insight means to see three directions at once — past, present, and future — and to understand the process of transfer of energy, transmutation, and the result for the mechanism.

"The manifestation of the chain of events...can impel the consciousness toward the understanding of Cosmic Infinity." When you study the chain of world events from this point of view, you expand your consciousness and begin to see the great Cause of all creation. All that is created is a materialization of ideal types in the world of energy. For example, before you build an airplane, you must have in your mind a

visualization of how that airplane should be built. The same thing happens in the mind of a Great Being. First, all creation is visualized; then that visualization becomes materialized. A great book called *The Secret Doctrine* says that man is the condensation of an *idea*.

> *The renaissance of a country is always created through cosmic influences. The agglomeration of propelled thoughts attracts from space the necessary layers of manifested sendings. Cliches of great discoveries float in space. Those who can intensify their psychic energy with the rhythm of cosmic energies will absorb treasures into their consciousness. The broadening of consciousness will propel toward the chain which connects all creative forces of Cosmos....*[2]

We are told that our solar system is now entering the energy field or influence of the constellation of Aquarius. This is an example of a Cosmic influence. This energy field may either completely destroy us or cause us to bloom, depending upon our responses to it. This Cosmic influence may create great scientists or philosophers; it may give vision to young people; it may create new civilizations and new expressions of culture through art, religion, and education.

This will be the "renaissance." A renaissance means awakening, blooming, unfolding. This is how the new world will be created.

Cosmic energy is transferred into the life of humanity through those disciples and initiates who know how to meditate. Meditation means to build an antenna which is so tall that it can penetrate into the world of archetypes and prototypes, into the world of ideas, into the world of significances.

The Teaching reminds us not to waste our energy because we need energy in order to control energy. When energy comes and we don't have the proper mechanism to control and channel it, it destroys whatever we have. This is why many species disappear from the Earth — because they cannot control and use the new, incoming energy.

We can sustain our life and evolve only by preparing

a more advanced mechanism and the consciousness to
meet the new energy, control it, assimilate it, and use it
creatively.

"*The agglomeration of propelled thoughts attracts
from space the necessary layers of manifested send-
ings.*" The world agglomeration means bringing together, grouping together. In your mind, you have lots
of thoughts. At the time of meditation, you align these
thoughts. Meditation puts your thoughts in order, in
line with the vision of your goal. Once the thoughts in
your mind are put in order and gathered together in a
focus, they attract energy from Space. The beautiful
arrangement of your thoughts creates a magnet in
your mind, which draws energies into your mind.
Through meditation, you create a focused mental
mechanism which attracts, assimilates, and projects
energy.

"*Cliches of great discoveries float in space.*" Nothing
in the world can be created if the prototype of that
object does not already exist in the subjective world.
That prototype is the idea, thoughtform, or vision of
that great Entity in which we are living.

The Hindus have a beautiful saying — that the
Great Life has a flute which He plays and all Creation
comes into existence. Each note of His music is a great
prototype. The objective side of the prototype is manifestation. One must be able to see both sides of Existence, developing *sight* and *psychic energy.*

The true meaning of sight is the Soul, the Inner
Dweller, the Inner Source of light, love, and power.
Psychic energy is true light, true love, and true willpower. Psychic energy comes from a center within you
which is the center of Light, Love, and Willpower. There
is also psychic energy in the universe and in Cosmos.
This means that our universe also has its own Soul
from which energy pours.

The key to peace, understanding, and harmony is
the process of sublimation, transmutation, and transformation. As you raise your level of consciousness,
you become a channel of Love, Understanding, and
Harmony. The reaction of people to incoming energies

creates what we call the history of humanity, through both individual and world events. One must use insight to see this and act accordingly. Psychic energy operates in those who respond to the demands of the new age.

1. Agni Yoga Society, *Infinity,* Volume I, para. 22.
2. *Ibid.,* para. 25.

CHAPTER 31

OUR PLANET

There are three ways of looking at the world and at the events going on around us. These three outlooks are optimism, pessimism, and carelessness.

Optimism means to see darkness in the world but still know that light can come, to know that a person is sick but also know that a remedy can be found; to see the burning building but be able to extinguish the fire.

Pessimism means to see all these conditions without being able to see solutions; to give up in the face of problems and difficulties.

Carelessness means to have apathy and non-concern toward the obstacles created by optimism and pessimism.

The Teaching challenges us to see the conditions of our planet and not to be trapped by any of these outlooks.

> *The conditions of the world have not improved. Not without reason are you full of expectancy. The abscess is coming to a head. We are on vigil, and he who is with Us is saved. But to be with Us means to know the Teaching; to know, means to apply.*[1]

This is the condition of the planet at this time. What should be our reaction to this condition?

> *...Precisely in the days of grave sickness of the planet it is important to be filled with courage.*

*By groping one does not pass, but the sword can
cleave the harmful veils. Very grave is the moment,
and it is necessary to intensify all courage.*[2]

Courage means to stand against the obstacles and
find ways and means to annihilate them. The "sword"
is your truth, your spiritual values, your faith. If you
have that sword, you can destroy the veils that are
forming between you and reality.

People see the moral and spiritual degeneration in
the world today and become very pessimistic about the
future of the planet. The challenge of discipleship is to
see the condition of the planet as it really is, but
inspire courage in oneself and in others to stand up and
try to improve the world situation.

*Earthquakes, volcanic eruptions, storms, fogs,
shoaling, changes of climate, epidemics, poverty,
wars, revolts, heresy, treason — what other signs
does humanity expect of the threatening time?
Prophets are not needed, the most insignificant
scribe may testify that never as yet have so many
dreadful forerunners of the Earth's disintegration
been gathered. But deaf is the ear and obscured the
vision. There has never been such an hour of disintegration as this planetary year! It is as if a path
were being laid for the waves of fire and the obsolete monsters of other days creep away unwilling
to realize the value of what takes place. Verily the
World is sustained by Magnets as imperceptible as
the air and the flame of space, and just as indis-
pensable as Light. The Magnets sent by Us for
Our manifestation are like the anchors of a ship
tossed in the storm.*[3]

This verse is advising the disciple to know the
world situation and gather courage in himself to face
it. The disciple must have faith in the victory of Christ;
he must have faith that the human soul is going to
conquer, that the Forces of Light are going to change
this Earth. But he must not be blind to the crime that is
going on in the world. It is only one's selfish urges and

desires that make him deaf and blind to the conditions of the world.

"There has never been such an hour of disintegration...." This sentence does not necessarily refer to the world or to humanity. We must apply this sentence to ourselves as individuals. People as individuals are going through disintegration of their morals and values. Selfishness and egotism are taking over their lives. The national and world outlook that "I don't care about you; I only care about myself" is coming from the growing attitude of selfishness in individual human beings. We must not forget that the condition of the individual human being is the replica of the condition of the Earth.

"Verily the world is sustained by magnets...." Who are these magnets? They are the men and women of goodwill in the world, the people who have the standard of right human relations in their hearts. They are those people who are trying to do something good for their nation and for humanity. They are those people who are trying to bring illumination, love, and harmony wherever they can in the world, through their speech, writings, work, and lives as a whole.

The more anyone renounces, the more he receives. But nations have forgotten how to renounce; even the smallest thinks only how to receive. Meanwhile, the planet is ill and all is sinking in this sickness. And someone wishes to evade the final battle through infection of the whole planet. And some hope to be setting sail in broken fragments, forgetting that the ocean is also departing. It is easy to picture that the planetary body can be just as sick as any other organism, and the spirit of the planet is affected by the condition of its body. How to name the illness of the planet? Best of all as a fever from poisoning. Suffocating gases, from the accumulations of the lower strata of the Subtle World, cut the planet off from the worlds which could send assistance. The Earth's destiny can be ended by a gigantic explosion if the thickness of the cover be not pierced. A stupendous acceleration is forcing all lines to shake. It could have been expected that acceleration was urgent for a certain country, but it is needed for the whole planet.[4]

The philosophy behind this verse is that people must create beautiful karma; they must sow beautiful things now so that they reap beautiful things later. As a whole, the world has forgotten this advice. For example, nations have forgotten the purpose of the United Nations and are trying to use it for their individual welfare. Who is going to renew the world vision?

First of all forget all nationalities, and apprehend the fact that the consciousness is developed by perfecting the invisible centers. Some await a Messiah for a single nation, but this is ignorant; for evolution of the planet can be only on a planetary scale. Precisely, the manifestation of universality must be assimilated. Only one blood flows, and the external world will no more be divided into races of primitive formation.[5]

To forget all nationalities means to start thinking in terms of one humanity. Once your consciousness overcomes separatism and cleavages, you are ready for unfoldment and progress. Once you start *loving,* your consciousness will be illuminated and transformed.

People have a very wrong idea that knowledge gives enlightenment. Knowledge never brings enlightenment or leads you to survival unless it is passed through the fire of love and inclusiveness.

If you look at the problems of the world, you will see that most of them are caused by intelligent, "knowledgeable" people who misuse their knowledge. Knowledge is never bad, unless you misuse it. Your knowledge must always be controlled by the qualities of Beauty and Goodness. Otherwise knowledge will be like a bomb in the hands of a child.

Once one of my Teachers was offered the position of chief of twenty monasteries. He was very well-qualified, and he was especially skilled in his organizational abilities; but he refused the position.

Later I asked him why he had refused. He told me, "My heart is not ready yet. Immediately when they offered me the position of being chief of twenty monasteries, I felt a pride in my heart... and I don't want that snake to grow there."

There are many such examples in history and mythology of Great Ones who resign from power and knowledge when They see that Their love-nature and heart are not yet ready to handle the responsibility.

How can we balance this grave condition on the planet? Only with the fire of the heart, using that fire to destroy all the poisonous gases suffocating the planet. The greatest weapon we have is our thoughts of beauty, love, and goodness. Such thoughts are like fires which will balance the destructive fires on the planet.

> *The word that issues from the heart saturates the space. Hence the thoughts which flow in an impetuous torrent form a sphere which is like a defense against the poisonous gases of the planet. Thoughts form a defensive net for humanity. Only these bright emanations give the strength to withstand the darkness. Hence it is so important to stratify the space with words of the heart. They contain light. Thus humanity is uplifted upon the wings of thoughts. Thus evolution is being built.*[6]

1. Agni Yoga Society, *Fiery World,* Volume I, para. 481.
2. Agni Yoga Society, *Community,* para. 48.
3. Agni Yoga Society, *Hierarchy,* para. 117.
4. Agni Yoga Society, *Community,* para. 49.
5. *Ibid.,* para. 71.
6. Agni Yoga Society, *Hierarchy,* para. 105.

CHAPTER 32

ENTHUSIASM — THE RAJ-AGNI

Raj-Agni — thus was called the Fire which you call enthusiasm. Truly this is a beautiful and powerful Fire, which purifies all surrounding space. The constructive thought is nurtured upon this Fire. The thought of magnanimity grows in the silvery light of the Fire of Raj-Agni. Help to the near ones flows from the same source. There is no boundary line, no limitations for the wings radiant with Raj-Agni. Do not think that this Fire can be kindled in an evil heart. One must develop in oneself the ability to call forth the source of such transport. At first one must prepare in oneself the assurance that the heart is offered to the Great Service. Then one should reflect that the glory of the works is not one's own, but belongs to the Hierarchy of Light. Then it is possible to become uplifted by the infinitude of Hierarchy and affirm oneself in the heroic attainment needed for all worlds. Thus not for oneself, but in the Great Service is kindled Raj-Agni. Understand that the Fiery World cannot stand without this Fire.[1]

Enthusiasm is a flow of energy, an electrical fire, which comes from higher realms and makes people energized and divinely kindled.

You see people around you full of inertia, people who are emotionally stagnant and mentally dull and sterile, just like a machine whose energy source has been cut off. When the current of enthusiasm is released into such people's systems, you see a great change in them. Their machine begins to work. They become physically active, emotionally responsive, and mentally creative.

What is the nature of this fire? This fire has not yet been detected by our contemporary instruments, but it exists, and the proof of it is its results, its effects.

This electric fire has five sources. The first source is from the Inner Guide, Who watches your development throughout ages. The Inner Guide slowly releases the current of enthusiasm as your threefold mechanism develops, integrates, and aligns. Premature release of the flow of enthusiasm is like turning on the electricity of a motor whose mechanism is not yet properly assembled. It is like turning on the water in a hose which is cracked in many places, or burning a fire in a wooden container.

The Inner Guardian knows how to regulate the flow of the divine fire. Premature release of energy can create physical, emotional, mental, psychological, and social problems. You can see people caught by certain ideas and visions: like fiery balls they run here and there, to warn people, to rouse them into certain actions, or to stop things, all without having the proper means, proper intellect, and proper mechanisms.

Such people may have a certain body of knowledge or vision, but because they dress it up with a ridiculous presentation, they make their ideas and visions appear worthless in the eyes of the public. If the mechanism is ready, however, the current of enthusiasm performs miracles. The enthusiasm coming from the Inner Guide is mostly related to the personal life of the individual.

The second source of enthusiasm is your Teacher. When you are ready to receive the current of energy coming from your Teacher, you start doing things that you might have considered an impossibility before. The enthusiasm inspired by your Teacher leads you to a field of service for which you are equipped. In that field of service, you act like a dynamo; you put many mechanisms into *motion,* into *action.* The greatest lesson in this field will be to learn how much current should be released, in order not to create an overflow of energy, cracks, or panic, but rather an increasing group cooperation and an advancing momentum of creativity.

When you begin to receive the enthusiasm from your Teacher, you use the energy very intelligently. Sometimes you shut off the current to let the machines repair themselves. Sometimes you decrease the current to make the cooperation between them more smooth. Sometimes you open the current fully to test the machines, to create shocking results, or to surmount an obstacle.

In this stage, you realize that things which were previously impossible for you become possible. Your mastery over your body, emotions, and mind increases. Your influence over the area of your group service creates more results.

Your enthusiasm makes you not only energetic and active, but also alert and awake, especially to those people and forces which bring in cleavages and slow down the machinery of the group using various destructive techniques.

Enthusiasm is not only a current of energy, but also a source of vision. At this stage, enthusiasm brings to you the vision of your Teacher, about you, about your service, and about the future possibilities and achievements of your labor.

The third source of enthusiasm is the Higher Worlds. What are the Higher Worlds? We may say that they are spheres in which greater amounts of energy and vision are concentrated. These spheres are found not in physical, emotional, and mental matter, but in the ethereal electrical fields, as centers which accumulate the energy of enthusiasm from still greater sources, beyond our solar system.

These centers are called by various names, such as Ashrams, Hierarchy, Shamballa, the Hall of Wisdom, Global Executives, the Tower. These names scare certain crystallized people, but one can change the names and enjoy the essence. For example, Ashrams can be called electrified fields of new knowledge, or rain clouds of wisdom. Hierarchy can be called the planning commission of the world construction. Shamballa can be called the house of the administration of solar energies. Or these centers can all be called X, Y, and Z centers of enthusiasm.

Thus, enthusiasm coming from the Higher Worlds is not for individuals, but for groups. This is why, as a person prepares himself to be able to receive electrical energy from his Teacher, so a group prepares and equips itself to receive energy from Higher Worlds and to use it to render service for humanity.

Enthusiasm coming from Higher Sources makes the group members world disciples, whose influence spreads into all corners of the world, creating Beauty, Goodness, Righteousness, Joy, and Freedom. The members of a group who are enthused by Higher Worlds are individuals whose egos have evaporated, whose mouths are clean, whose minds are highly creative and free of crystallization, and whose hearts are full of compassion.

The members of such a group have unlimited horizons in front of them. They know that only through expanding their horizons can they transcend themselves and become an instrument for a greater service in a greater field.

The path of perfection is trodden by individuals and groups who transcend themselves, who break limitation after limitation, cage after cage. A prison is good for a thief, but not for one who wants to serve as a free soul. Freedom is not a physical condition, but a state which evokes the confidence of Higher Worlds to inspire you with greater wisdom and allow you to serve in greater fields.

A prison is good for a thief, and a thief is one who wastes his time, energy, and life making his pitiful self happy....

The fourth source of enthusiasm is your Inner Core. All agents of light and all centers of wisdom have one supreme goal: to lead you, as a Self, to your Core, which is called in the Ancient Wisdom, the antechamber of the Most High. The core is the Divinity living within you, as your true Self.

The electricity of enthusiasm coming from this source releases you from the fetters of global activities and makes you an interplanetary servant. Such a servant works 24 hours straight, in the labor given to him to relate the global centers. In the Ancient Wisdom, such servers are called the servants of the glory of the One.

The enthusiasm coming from your Inner Core reveals for a second the face of the Most High. The bliss of the Most High is fused with the current of enthusiasm, and no one can take such a bliss away from you.

The fifth source of the energy of enthusiasm is called the Central Spiritual Sun — "from Whom all things proceed; to Whom all things return." This is the energy which makes you a server in solar fields or in the galactic field. It is from this source that come the Avatars, Who are condensed sources and embodiments of the energy of enthusiasm. Avatars are fiery, electrical currents, symbolized by a human figure.

It will be interesting to know that the dark forces also have their particular energy, by which they inspire their agents, lead them into destructive action, malice, slander, and treason, and encourage them to use techniques of slavery, exploitation, and totalitarianism. This energy is the same energy of enthusiasm, but it is perverted through the motives of the dark forces.

You can see their agents working day and night with a dark zeal to prepare a greater amount of destructive tools, to hinder the path of true servers, to discredit the names of great heroes, to spread confusion, forgery, and fabrication, and to prepare the field for crimes, terrorism, and war.

What does the electrified current of Raj-Agni really do?

1. It tunes an individual to the center of inner direction, where he becomes aware of the source of enthusiasm. Each source has its own direction. For example, the direction given from your Inner Guide is

to make you bloom all your flowers in your field of beingness. If you follow the direction or the guidance of the Inner Guide, you will bloom with beauty and fragrance.

The Inner Guide communicates with you through the voice of your conscience. If you listen to that voice you advance on the path of Raj-Agni and radiate the beauty of joy. All true service is charged with joy, and you do not let personality currents of mud be mixed with that joy. Labor with joy is a technique to accumulate energy in your system.

Try to put the joy of enthusiasm into all your activities at home, into your relationships, into all your emotional responses, into all your thoughts, and into all your creative activities. It is also necessary to put enthusiasm into your gratitude. People are so blind to the gifts they receive. Sometimes even if they feel grateful, their gratefulness lacks enthusiasm. There is a great difference between gratitude that has enthusiasm and one that does not.

2. Enthusiasm charges your actions, feelings, and thoughts with its electrifying energy. You can see this in the speeches of great leaders, in the actions of great executives, and in the thoughts and feelings of great artists. Enthusiasm is an energy which travels with all that you create or do in enthusiasm.

A deed done without enthusiasm turns into a burden on you and on others. Someone brings you a flower and you cry with joy. Someone else brings you a bouquet and you feel indifferent. Someone writes you an intimate letter, and you feel cold. Someone else writes you a few words, and you feel great. Someone shakes your hand and you feel exhausted. Someone else shakes your hand and gives you a supply of energy for a week.

Enthusiasm electrifies you. Lack of enthusiasm makes you barren.

3. Enthusiasm makes you proceed on the path of your daily labor with joy, love, and freedom. I had a teacher of engineering once who was full of joy, love, and freedom. It was a great opportunity for me to be in

his presence. I never had any difficulty learning from him because his knowledge and teaching techniques were charged with enthusiasm. He had joy, which made the students love him and understand him. He had a love by which he evoked from us a deep trust in him. He had a freedom in his experiences that made our consciousness open and released.

All of his expressions were fearless. Gradually I understood that freedom is absence of fear. He used to express his ideas in such a way that you felt liberated from the prisons of prejudices, superstitions and fabrications of the mind.

People build prisons for us. Such people have many fears. That is why they are not free to cooperate, unite, or synthesize. Observe leaders or teachers who build prisons for you. Observe those who bring you freedom. One day history will expose those who brought slavery to mankind and those who brought freedom to the souls of mankind. Enthusiasm radiates out as Joy, Love, and Freedom.

Christ once said, "Seek the truth and the truth will make you free." How can one search for truth, the most dangerous thing in the world, if he is not fearless? Those who have fear also search for truth, but their truth is the product of their own standards, as once a thief told me: "The truth is that I came to take your money and your clothing."

I answered him, "The truth is that you could not steal anything from me if you knew what the truth was."

Years later, when I was traveling in the mountains, I visited a monastery. The man who greeted me at the door was that thief. He had become a student and then a teacher, to learn the truth and to teach it.

A few months later, after my visit that day, he whispered in my ear, "You could not steal anything from me if you knew what the truth was." And he added, "The truth is fearlessness in the search for light...." And he gave me a great hug.

Joy, Love, and Freedom are three friends, electrified by the energy of enthusiasm. All great achievements are built on this foundation of Joy, Love, and Freedom —

Enthusiasm. Success in all its positive forms is the result of enthusiasm.

All five of these sources of enthusiasm stand as symbols of great success. God is success; that is His most modern name. Because of His success, we have flowers, trees, birds, animals, geniuses, planets, solar systems, galaxies....Those who walk on the path leading to God are successful people. Their success is not a form of exploitation. Their success is not achieved at the expense of others. Their success is a process of flowering. Their success is manifestation of their inner wealth and glory.

Enthusiasm expands your consciousness and makes you successful. Expansion of consciousness cannot be achieved through accumulation of knowledge. One can become an encyclopedia of knowledge without being able to expand his consciousness. Expansion of consciousness comes through self-mastery.

4. Enthusiasm creates magnetism, by which you attract your co-workers and all that you need to accomplish your plan. Magnetism exists on four levels. You become magnetic physically, emotionally, mentally, and spiritually. Enthusiasm creates a kind of magnetism which draws only things that have great value, and it repulses things that will cause trouble or hindrances on the path of your service. The thieves of life cannot stand in the fire of enthusiasm, and they drop away.

Your magnetism is dispersed by belittling criticism, slander, complaints, and negativity. Your magnetism increases when you follow the path of Beauty, Goodness, Justice, Joy, and Freedom. Of course, because of your magnetism and enthusiasm people will feel jealous of you. Even then, smile at them, because jealousy is their way of keeping your beautiful image in their minds and possibly trying to be like you.

Enthused people feel that what all other people have is theirs. Once when I was a little boy walking my mother on a riverbank, I saw another little boy with a beautiful bicycle. "Mother," I said, "I wish I had a bicycle like that."

After keeping silent for a while, she said, "You will have one at the right time, but until then think that it is yours and you are enjoying it." When we were on the hill, she showed me all the beautiful fields full of red and yellow poppies and said, "Do you realize that all these fields are also yours?"

"Mine?"

"Yes. They belong to your great, great, great Heavenly Father, so they are yours also."

I remember the smile I put on and said, "Of course, you are not joking?"

"No," she said, "they are all yours, if you *accept them.*"

This conversation became a formula in my life later, and I was able to conquer any attack of jealousy. My mother's words were so deep that even now I cannot find the bottom of them.

5. When you are charged with enthusiasm, you attract the attention of the supervisors of the path of service and perfection. Unless you are radioactive, you do not attract the attention of Great Ones. When you are enthused, people *hear* you, *see* you, and *feel* you. They sense your striving and labor to remove obstacles from the road of life. People say, "He is fiery; let's help him."

An electrified group is a mechanism of an immense labor, because it is overshadowed by Higher Forces.

Enthusiasm makes you able to live with your consciousness in the spheres of those who are heroes and builders of a higher culture and civilization. You stand by those who gave their lives to uplift and make humanity free. You stand by those who dare to walk the path of beauty and sacrificial service. Enthusiasm helps you to find your level, where you can radiate your talents.

One day, while we were talking about the inner meaning of having a level, my father took a piece of wood and strongly pushed it underwater in a lake and said, "Watch now. Look what will happen." The wood came right back to the surface. "That is its level," he said. "Everyone and everything has its level. A great law helps each one to be at his or its level. The only thing you cannot hide is your level."

Invisible supervisors try to place you in such a location where you can do the most.

6. Enthusiasm carries your ideas, visions, and thoughts into Space and makes them sources of inspiration to those who can attract them. It is through the fire of enthusiasm that your thoughts, visions, and ideas survive in the stormy ocean of Space. Space is full of electromagnetic storms, typhoons, and waves of destructive forces. Only through the fire of enthusiasm can you hold your beam of light toward the stars. Because of enthusiasm your beam never flickers; it is never interfered with; and you broadcast your message of Beauty, Love, and Joy into Space, in spite of storms of darkness.

What are the enemies of the fire of enthusiasm?
1. Drugs, alcohol, marijuana, excessive sex.
2. Sexually transmissible diseases.
3. Hatred, fear, anger, jealousy, revenge, and greed.
4. Vanity, ego, pride, and separatism.
5. Exhaustion.
6. Irritation.
7. Gossip, slander, malice, and treason.
These are the chief enemies of enthusiasm.

Those who cannot develop the fire of enthusiasm or put it out become charcoal; they become touchy, lazy, and self-centered; they always think in terms of their self-interest. They feel that everybody is against them, that everyone intends to steal their wives or husbands, etc....

Enthusiasm makes you loving, caring, free, beautiful, and strong. Enthusiasm heals depression and inertia.

How to increase your enthusiasm?
1. Develop a conscious communication line between you and your Inner Guide by:
  a. following the conscience of your heart.
  b. demonstrating a life of Beauty, Goodness, Righteousness, Joy, and Freedom.
  c. doing regular meditation and study.

      d. attending regularly and punctually all group meetings and taking part in group labors.

These are four steps by which you bring an increasing amount of the energy of enthusiasm from your Inner Guide.

  2. You can further increase your enthusiasm by:

      a. building a conscious communication line between you and your Teacher.

      b. spreading his teaching.

      c. living according to his instructions.

      d. serving humanity as a whole, "with self-forgetfulness, harmlessness, and right speech."

  3. You can further increase the voltage and volume of enthusiasm by:

      a. building a communication line between you and Higher Worlds, thinking about the Higher Worlds and living your life as a preparation to be fit for the Higher Worlds and actualizing higher virtues.

      b. being inclusive and universal.

      c. developing sensitivity to the presence of Higher Beings around you.

      d. trying to penetrate into Higher Worlds through joy, admiration, ecstasy, and deep sleep.

  4. You can further increase your enthusiasm by coming in contact with your Inner Core. Your Inner Core is the door into Infinity. You can build such a contact by:

      a. learning how to sacrifice yourself for the Common Good.

      b. demonstrating heroic achievements.

      c. trying to pass into the Fourth Initiation.

      d. being sensitive to the directions of the Tower.

A person of enthusiasm is like a fiery ray on the way to the Father's Home, like a gardener who leaves behind him the beauty of the flowers of his deeds.

---

1. Agni Yoga Society, *Fiery World,* Volume II, para. 22.

CHAPTER 33

THE COSMIC MAGNET
AND SHIFTINGS

*The great purpose in Our actions is to aid
humanity in the shiftings of consciousness. Our
disciples are appointed as such helpers. Each
shifting of thought produces its effect. Therefore,
Our mission is to lead human consciousness into a
shifting, and the mission of Our disciples is to set
the pace with the Cosmic Magnet. Our Stronghold
contains the essence of the shifting of the consciousness and the directing of it toward the center
of evolution. Hence, the shifting of thought is the
paramount healer of mankind.*[1]

The Cosmic Magnet is a center in the universe
which draws all particles of light toward itself. This
Magnet is the Source and Home of all living Sparks
scattered in the universe. Sparks are found on different levels and they are engaged in different labors.
Some of them are in line with the Purpose of the Cosmic Magnet. Some of them are not in harmony with it.

The Central Magnet or the Cosmic Magnet has for
humanity a definite purpose to be accomplished within
a definite period of time. The direction of the Cosmic
Magnet is sensed only by the consciousnesses of
human beings. The more conscious one is, the more
sensitive he is to the directions of the Cosmic Magnet.
But due to many reasons, the consciousness of a certain number of human beings is not sensitive to the

directions of the Cosmic Magnet.

The consciousnesses of such people must change and expand so that humanity registers the currents of the Cosmic Magnet and finds the path toward the Home. This change and expansion of consciousness is called "the shifting of consciousness," as we shift the gears of our consciousness from first, to second, to third, and so on.

This shifting is done by the labor of the Hierarchy, which presents to humanity new energies, new Teaching, and new ideas, and tries to shift the consciousness of humanity from material values to spiritual values, from personality to soul, to spiritual, to universal values. The disciples of the world help the Hierarchy in this process of shifting. What does this shifting do?

1. It makes the human mind reevaluate its standards and measures.

2. It makes the human mind break limitations and remove obstacles to shifting.

3. It makes the mind reorient itself toward more inclusive and more universal values.

4. It makes the human mind synchronize physical, emotional, and mental actions toward spiritual goals.

5. It creates harmonious cooperation in and between the seven fields of human endeavor.

6. It makes the human mechanism sensitive to the currents of the Cosmic Magnet.

7. It creates a new culture and a new civilization.

Shifting produces many kinds of conflict and even wars in man and in humanity. Those who are attached to old ways of living do not easily abandon their corners of interests. Those who are attracted to new currents do not allow the attached ones to retard their progress. Such a conflict starts and the progressive part of humanity generally loses the battle for a time; but eventually it receives in its consciousness energy and advice from Higher Sources, and it gradually makes its position firm and strong. Thus during a shifting process, the dark and the light stand face to face in equal force.

Of course, *shifting* is a law, and when the time comes shifting takes place; but it is possible to shift without bloodshed and destruction. Shifting can be done through negotiation and sincerely facing the issues. Here we are referring to a battle not between the forces of light and darkness, but between those human beings who stand in their old consciousness and those who are enlightened with new visions.

The disciples of the world help the Great Ones to increase Their help in the shifting process through peaceful means and with as little destruction as possible. Disciples in all walks of life try to expand human consciousness, show people a vision of the future, and convince them that shifting is beneficial for all and that with each shifting, a greater glory descends upon humanity. They also teach humanity that shifting is unavoidable.

1. The disciples of the world try to help humanity to reevaluate its standards and measures. Standards and measures cannot stay the same as our consciousness expands. Our boundaries must be broken, and our measures must be adapted to our level of consciousness. Old standards do not help for our survival and happiness. When the fish grows, it needs bigger pools in order to survive. The pool of our consciousness is getting smaller and smaller and our vision greater and greater. Either the pool must be changed, or the fish must search for a larger body of water; otherwise it will die.

There are people who, in order to feel free, lower their standards. Others use old standards. But disciples raise the standards and make it more difficult to achieve so that they create more striving and more efforts.

Disciples change the measures and make them group measures, national measures, global measures, or even solar and galactic measures. *"The mission of our disciples is to set the pace with the Cosmic Magnet."*

2. Disciples of the world help humanity to break limitations and remove obstacles to shifting. Shifting

requires a heavy labor to break limitations and remove obstacles to shifting. Limitations are found in the crystallized thoughts of the human mind. It is a stupendous job to break these limitations and expand the horizon of humanity. It is very interesting to note that often humanity is more advanced in consciousness than its leaders, who are often the guardians of limitations. Leaders who are limited by their self-interest or national interest cannot understand the global interest. Average humanity understands it, but unfortunately it cannot make its voice heard in "high" places.

Disciples try to help the masses and make them ready for shifting. They teach humanity that money, possessions, and positions are not measures of their greatness; but that self-sacrificial service, cooperation and sharing are greater measures, by which a new humanity will be measured.

3. Disciples of the world try to reorient humanity toward more universal and more inclusive values. People look for greater values to get greater benefit. Greater values help a greater number of people. To have a greater value, one must leave behind smaller values. As one strives to the Cosmic Magnet, his values become more universal and more inclusive. The children of the world must be educated to see better values and strive to achieve them.

The measure of the effect of an object on your progress is the *value* of that object. Objects have value; thoughts have value; ideas have value. The value of objects, thoughts, and ideas is the measure of the contribution that they make for your success, progress, and expansion of consciousness. For example, the value of a dollar is equal to ten pencils.

You have value because people can benefit from your wisdom, position, and money. You have value because you have insight, foresight, and a greater power of creativity.

4. Disciples of the world help humanity to synchronize physical, emotional, and mental actions toward spiritual goals. Spiritual goals are ever-advancing and ever-inclusive goals; goals that bring abundance,

health, joy and freedom to a greater number of people and open the possibility of including more people in the future. Shifting of consciousness is not possible unless the personality vehicles are integrated and their actions are not contradictory to each other.

5. Disciples of the world help humanity to create harmonious cooperation in and among all fields of human endeavor. The disciples of the world are those who are going to become the heads of all fields of human endeavor, as they are climbing by different routes to the Cosmic Magnet. All of these are the executives who will eventually come together to guarantee the survival and progress of humanity and lead it toward the Cosmic Magnet.

6. The disciples of the world make the human mechanism sensitive to the currents of the Cosmic Magnet. The disciples of the world in every field are seeking perfection. Such a demand is putting a heavy pressure upon the mechanism of humanity, to meet the challenge for perfection and to make them able to use the fruits on the path of perfection.

The disciples of the world are presenting those new visions and disciplines by which the physical, emotional, mental, and intuitional natures of humanity will go through a new process of development and unfoldment. As this process of development and unfoldment is going on in the vehicles of people, the pull of the Cosmic Magnet will increase in them and will create among them closer cooperation and a better response to the pull of the Cosmic Magnet.

7. The disciples of the world will create a new culture and a new civilization. Disciples in the world are helping to prepare a new shift and bring to humanity universal and inclusive visions. As human beings are becoming more sensitive to these ideas and visions, they are formulating a new culture in all departments of life. It is this culture that is gradually changing the form of the civilization.

Thus, every time the Cosmic Magnet increases Its magnetic pull upon all living beings, there will be only one safe way to respond to that pull: to create a shift in consciousness. Unless such a shift is carefully managed, the whole of mankind will be in danger of self-destruction. To prevent self-destruction, we must expand our consciousness and shift it to higher gears.

> *Only when the consciousness adopts the course of the Cosmic Magnet will it be possible to affirm the predestined. Only when man understands the direction of the Magnet will it be possible to affirm a new step. Thus, when We direct to a new step the course of the nations is drawn taut by the Cosmic Magnet. Verily, the epoch of purification approaches! The Cosmic Magnet creates the future. Therefore, the shifting is inevitable and only a broadened consciousness can keep in pace with it, having assimilated all creative perturbations. Thus, all tensified currents create a new step. Thus, a manifestation of urgency grips the countries. The strivings toward construction and toward destruction balance the planet. Thus, the impelling force of Our actions proceeds with the Cosmic Magnet.[2]*

---

1. Agni Yoga Society, *Infinity*, Volume II, para. 118.
2. *Ibid., para. 175.*

CHAPTER 34

INFINITY

In olden ages, the great Teachers of humanity, knowing the healing power and the uplifting, expanding, and transforming nature of the concept of Infinity, created myths, mysteries, and religions in which omnipresent and omniscient Gods were related to man and to Infinity. Thus they paved the way of the human being toward steady unfoldment, improvement, daring, and perfection.

The greatest incentive for a human being is the vision of Infinity, given with enough encouragement or inspiration to create striving in him toward that vision. When we say Infinity, we refer to:

limitlessness
continuity
duration
endlessness on the path of expansion
Cosmic powers
cycles of creation, destruction, and recreation
the possibility of ever-progressing unfoldment
omnipresence
omniscience
ever-renewing opportunity
the Great Spirit
the Almighty Source of manifestation
Space

Infinity means continuity. Life is continual. It changes forms, but it continues endlessly. Nothing is lost in the universe. Existence means continuity. To be continuous means that you and Infinity are in relationship. It is also the meaning of immortality.

When Christ said, "Be perfect as your Father in heaven is perfect," He was talking about Infinity. The concept of Infinity is related to the urge for perfection, not to knowledge, because knowledge is always fallible and will turn into a grave if the urge for perfection does not exist.

People may think, "If I am not able to cope with my finite affairs and my daily routine, and meet the desires of my heart, then what is the use of talking about Infinity?" The answer is simple: only in expanding our minds to a higher dimension can we handle the problems we meet on the lower planes.

Man is controlled by his reactions to the influences coming from higher realms. Infinity is the next plane, the next dimension, the more subjective dimension, about which you have some information but no control yet. Because you do not have control on the next plane, you cannot control this plane; the subjective causes of this plane exist on the next higher plane.

Any limit on any level is a crime and a failure; the separative way of thinking is the grave of the soul. We must step on our achievements and strive beyond, thus opening ourselves to Cosmic impressions and creativity.

The greatest quality or characteristic of the human soul is his ability to expand toward Infinite domains.

Our daily routine work at home or in business creates crystallized thoughtforms in our minds. This crystallization slowly weighs heavily on our nervous system and creates many psychological problems. To get rid of this pressure, you need to take a *vacation* from routine work. The best way to do this is to turn your mind to new and abstract subjects, which will open new doors and windows in you and make you able to see things in their true proportion, thus giving you a release from routine problems. An expanded mind can better solve your problems.

Those who suffer from crystallization usually spend long hours in small, crowded rooms, narrow streets, prisons, etc. These conditions cause many emotional and mental contractions, and later sickness of the nerves. The same is true for the inner space. When people are living within a narrow thought life and emotional life, they eventually crystallize and become mentally sick. The remedy is Space and Infinity.

There was a kind of sickness that my Teachers used to heal by telling the patient to widen the space of his view. They would tell the patient to go and sit in the high mountains or at the seashore and watch the unobstructed space toward the horizon. They would also tell him to lie on his back and look at the sky. I do not know what the name of this sickness was, but it was connected with the nervous system, heart, and liver.

Infinity means an ever-expanding consciousness, awareness, and realization, without losing the focus of your experiencing unit. Infinity is limitless striving to surpass your former achievements and enter new fields of realization. There is Infinity within man and Infinity within the Cosmos.

> ...*How beautiful is the vast horizon! How powerful is the thought penetrating Space! What new ways are disclosed by communion with Infinity! Seek these treasures; in them is the guarantee of your advancement. Of what use is knowledge which brings one to closed gates marked by the sign "we know no more?" Limitation of knowledge is a grave. Therefore, fathom Infinity! The limitation of consciousness is the death of spirit....*[1]

For the average person, everything is an end in itself. For a selfish person, everything exists for himself. But for an advanced person, everything is a step leading to something else; everything exists to form a part of an ever-expanding whole. Infinity challenges limitless, endless striving.

> ...*Eternally moving, eternally striving, eternally aspiring to the heights, eternally manifesting vigilance, affirming Truth, manifesting the radiant thread of the Mother of the World by the*

armor of infinite beauty, assailing the darkness of
ignorance, promising to the abode of humanity
the glory of the stars — thus walk, saying, "World,
I wish to accept all thy gifts; I wish to fill to the
brim the chalice of attainment; I wish, O Lord, to
drain the chalice of the Wisdom of Thy Coven-
ants!"...[2]

Most of our suffering and difficulties in life are the result of the prisons in which we live. These prisons start from the mental plane and descend into the emotional plane. Then we often find ourselves in physical limitations or even physical prisons. Thinking and studying about Infinity can break our limitations and cause a tremendous expansion in our consciousness. Through this expansion three things will happen:

1. More light will pour into our system.
2. We will have more energy.
3. We will have better health.

Limitation is a state in which you cannot grow and expand; limitation creates prisons. Psychologically, a prison is an aura in which the lines of light turn back toward the body instead of projecting into Space. This creates a shell around the brain and mind, causing various sicknesses which come from tensions between the expanding essence and the shell. These sicknesses are also the result of the burning of the network of the etheric body. This accumulating pressure eventually expands, causing great psychological damage.

All vices are the result of limitation. For example, ignorance is limitation, and out of ignorance comes every kind of crime. Fear is limitation; guilt is limitation. We may even say that Satan is nothing else but limitation.

You must ask yourself, "For what am I working — finite things or Infinity? Am I serving limitation, or am I serving Infinity? Am I serving my physical nature, or am I serving my spiritual nature?"

The breaking of limitations must be gradual, and the concept of Infinity can be introduced gradually into people's lives. The finite mind and the finite heart must be opened to Infinity on a gradient scale. When the mind is occupied with immediate objects such as the stomach and sex, it must turn toward visible objects in the immediate environment; then toward the family, national, and international environment; then beyond the planet, to the solar system, the Milky Way, other galaxies... and into Infinity.

Similarly, if the heart is working only for its own love, it must be expanded toward children, relatives ...its race and nation...humanity, other kingdoms... the solar system...the Self...beyond the galaxies.... This is how Life tries to pave the way toward Infinity.

All creativity is a result of expansion. As one expands, the level of his creativity increases. All culture is the witness of the expansion of heart and mind.[3] The ability to reproduce as much Infinity as possible is creativity in all branches of human endeavor. For example:

Politics must reflect the order and harmony of the Cosmos with Its laws and principles.

Education must reveal the knowledge of how the Cosmos operates and how to harmonize human life to greater Infinity.

Philosophy and communication must reflect the beauty of relationship witnessed in Infinity within human life.

Art must reflect the beauty and creative function of the Cosmos.

Science must reveal how one can function as a part of Cosmos.

Religion must reflect the possibility of the conscious relationship between Infinity and man.

Ceremony must reflect the orderly functions of Infinity and thus create a rapport between the forces operating in Infinity and in man.

Advancement toward Infinity creates co-measurement.

The concept of the Hierarchy is closely related to the concept of Infinity. Hierarchy is a group of personnel who have graduated from this school of life. They

are a mysterious group of Teachers who have graduated from one level of life and are entering a higher
level of understanding and actualization. We read in
esoteric books that there are many Hierarchies. For
example, those who have finished the planetary school
form a Hierarchy. Those who have finished the solar
school graduate to another level and form another
Hierarchy.[4] Actually, Hierarchy stands for progressive advancement into greater states of awareness,
consciousness, and relationship, and Infinity means
there is no end to your progress.

The Ancient Wisdom teaches that your consciousness will expand forever if you strive for it and if you
pay the needed price for it. You are going to go forward
into Infinity. Every graduation is a station on the path
which you must eventually transcend in order to enter
the next degree of development and expansion.

A great Sage says that in order to understand this
mystery of unending progress we should go outside
and watch the stars at night. In watching the stars we
can see the concept of Infinity....Man's destiny is
nothing else but the unfoldment and blooming of his
spiritual nature. We are not mortal bodies, earth-
bound, money-bound, hatred-bound, pride-bound....
We are travelers on the path of Infinity.

> *...As passengers on a short journey are men their
> earthly life, facing Infinity.[5]*

> *The Teaching of Life must first of all affirm
> the concept of life beyond the limits of the earthly
> envelope. Otherwise, why the concept of Brother-
> hood if that which is most precious must be devel-
> oped for only a few decades? Not for tomorrow
> must consciousness be amassed, but for eternal
> paths into Infinity. It is useful to repeat this truth
> in the light of day and at night.[6]*

The "most precious" refers to your consciousness
or your awareness of the future. The only thing that
gives joy and hope is the concept of the future, the hope
of the future.

> *...let us place on the balance the most urgent concepts of the great approaching Age — Infinity and Hierarchy.*[7]

> *The superiority of the spirit will not come if we do not strive towards it. One must assimilate the thought about the transitoriness of the earthly hour and of the immutability of the Infinite. Thus inseparably are linked Agni Yoga and Infinity and Hierarchy....*[8]

---

1. Agni Yoga Society, *Infinity*, Volume I, para. 9.
2. *Ibid.*, para 7.
3. See *The Flame of Beauty, Culture, Love, and Joy,* by Torkom Saraydarian.
4. See Chapter 8, "The Twelve Creative Hierarchies" in *The Psyche and Psychism,* by Torkom Saraydarian.
5. Agni Yoga Society, *Leaves of Morya's Garden,* Volume I, para. 129.
6. Agni Yoga Society, *Brotherhood,* para. 266.
7. Agni Yoga Society, *Hierarchy,* para. 345.
8. *Ibid.,* para. 401.

INDEX

M

Magi(c), 221
Magnet, Cosmic, 73, 338-343
Magnetism, 334
Magnets, 324
Maitreya, 71, 72, 201, 206-207
Man
    becoming himself, 35
    def., 12, 34, 35
Man-God, 77
Manas, 217
Marijuana, 94, 175
    and stopping smoking, 39
Master(s), 176, 198
    and karma, 166
    def., 40, 66
    messages of, 167
Matter, disidentification with, 70
Meditation, 238-239, 319, 320
    def., 22
    right, def., 137
Messages, 87-88
Messenger(s), 252-259
Method(s), new, of solving
    problems, 23
    artificial, 82
Mind, 115, 172-173
    controlling, 30
    lazy, 127
    push buttons in, 137
Miseries, 107
Mission, 253-254, 311-312
Mistakes, 193-194
Monad, 35
Mother of the World, 212
Motives, 31
    right, developing, 138
Music, disco, rock, 17, 175

N

Nature, 220, 221
    beauty of, 144
    contact with, 143-144
    joy of, 144
    link with, 146
Need, def., 61
Negativity, 149
New, the, 21, 42
New Era, 210
"New ones", 21
"New ways", 21

O

Observation, 78, 79, 196-197, 279
    of motivating forces, 31
Obsession, 15
Obstacles, 110, 208
"Old ways", def., 21
Optimism, 322
Overstimulation, 318

P

Parables, 279-286
Past, 13, 16, 119
    being caught in, 23
    def., 12, 23
Path
    of probation, 170-171
    qualities needed, 88
Patience, 247
    def., 22, 138
Peace, 43
    key to, 320
Peacemaking, def., 43
Perfection, 125-126, 128, 345
    path of, 243-250, 330
    weapons against
        human soul on,
        168
Persistence, def., 22, 138
Pessimism, 322, 323
Petty concerns, 110
Philosophy, 348
Plan, 84-85, 129-130, 132, 219
    adjustment of, 140
    Divine, and labor, 134
    the, 130, 135, 289
        and action, 138
        and meditation, 137
        sensitivity to, 134
    three measures of, 134
Planet, 251-252
    and path of evolution, 71
    our, 322-326
Planetary Life, 13, 245
Politics, 348
    and past, and future, 18
Pollutants, 166-167
Pollution, 18, 94
Possession, 182
Prayer
    rela. to hope, 98-99
    source of, 98